INTEGRATING THE BALKANS

Conflict Resolution and the Impact of EU Expansion

MÁIRE BRANIFF

I.B. TAURIS

LONDON · NEW YORK

Published in 2011 by I.B.Tauris & Co Ltd.
6 Salem Road, London W2 4BU
175 Fifth Avenue, New York NY 10010
www.ibtauris.com

Distributed in the United States and Canada
exclusively by Palgrave Macmillan
175 Fifth Avenue, New York NY 10010

Library of European Studies 17

ISBN 978 1 84885 669 1

A full CIP record for this book is available from the British Library
A full CIP record for this book is available from the Library of Congress

Library of Congress catalog card: available

Printed and bound in the UK by CPI Antony Rowe, Chippenham and Eastbourne
Camera-ready copy edited and supplied by the author

Máire Braniff is Lecturer in Politics at the University of Ulster, Northern Ireland, and also holds a research assistantship at Dublin City University, Ireland. She was awarded a PhD in Politics by Queen's University Belfast.

For my husband Stephen,
my children Emilie and Daniel,
and my parents.

CONTENTS

LIST OF TABLES

GLOSSARY AND ABBREVIATIONS

Acquis	*Acquis communautaire:* entire body of laws passed by the European Union. Includes all directives, treaties and regulations, as well as judgements by European Court of Justice
AKP	Justice and Development Party (Turkey)
Avis	Statement issued by the European Commission on the acceptability of a formal application by a state for EC membership
BP	Bosniak Party
CARDS	Community Assistance for Reconstruction, Development and Stabilisation
CEEC	Central and Eastern Europe countries
CEPS	Centre for European Policy Studies
CFSP	Common Foreign and Security Policy
DG Enlargement	Directorate-General for Enlargement (EU)
DOS	Democratic Opposition of Serbia
DPS	Party of Democratic Socialists
DSCG	Democratic League of Montenegro
DSS	Democratic Serbian Party
DUA	Democratic Union of Albanians
EEC	European Economic Community
EC	European Community
EP(s)	European partnership(s)
EPC	European Political Cooperation; the forerunner of the CFSP
EU	European Union

FRY	Federal Republic of Yugoslavia
GS	Civic Party (Montenegro)
HDZ	Croatian Democratic Union
ICTY	International Criminal Tribunal for the former Yugoslavia
IRA	Irish Republican Army
ISPA	Pre-Accession Structural Instrument
JNA	Yugoslav National Army
LPD	Liberal Democratic Party (Serbia)
MEP	Member of the European Parliament
NATO	North Atlantic Treaty Organisation
NS	People's Party (Montenegro)
OBNOVA	EU programme providing financial assistance for war-torn SEE states instituted in mid-1990s
PHARE	Poland and Hungary: Assistance for Restructuring the Economies programme (has subsequently expanded to other countries in Central and Eastern Europe)
Sabor	Serbian church assembly
SAPARD	Special Accession Programme for Agriculture and Rural Development (EU)
SEE	South Eastern Europe
SFRY	Socialist Federal Republic of Yugoslavia
SDP	Social Democratic Party
SDSS	Independent Democratic Serbian Party
SNP	Socialist People's Party
SNS	Serbian People's Party
SPS	Socialist Party of Serbia
SRS	Serbian Radical Party
TEMPUS	Special Programme for the modernisation of higher education in neighbouring countries (EU)
TRNC	Turkish Republic of Northern Cyprus
UCR	United Cyprus Republic

ACKNOWLEDGEMENTS

I am greatly obliged to my colleagues and friends at the School of Politics, International Studies and Philosophy at Queen's University Belfast for their insights and assistance for the duration of this project. To my doctoral supervisors: Professor Adrian Guelke, for his continuous encouragement, insights and for prompting my interest in conflict research since my time as an undergraduate. My research benefited from many discussions on ethnic conflict with Professor Guelke and I am grateful for his encouragement to think critically and for his confidence in me. And to Dr David Phinnemore for his valuable comments on the many draft chapters and for his constant availability, responsiveness, advice, support and inspiration during my time at Queen's University Belfast, and not least for generating my interest in the Balkans and European integration and for nurturing my academic abilities. My gratitude goes to Dr Othon Anastakaskis and Dr Roberto Belloni, for their insightful and timely comments. To Dr Joanne McEvoy many thanks for her comments on earlier drafts. My thanks go also to Maria Marsh at I.B. Tauris, Matthew Brown and Allison McKechnie for their indispensable help.

The research project was generously funded by the Department of Education and Learning (Northern Ireland) and the William and Betty MacQuitty Travel Scholarship, to which I am indebted as it made travel and interviews possible. I am grateful to the generous and candid cooperation from all interviewees, which made the field research so interesting. I am grateful to the many who generously gave their time and insights. In particular, I am indebted to Mr Antun Babić for his kindness, hospitality and sincerity.

My deep gratitude goes to my parents and family for the constant and unending support they have provided. Without their complete support, encouragement and continued certainty in me, this project would have been much more difficult to accomplish. A special thank you to my mother Anna, for her meticulous proofreading of earlier drafts. To my brothers for their continued support. To my husband Stephen, for his constant patience, faith, support and love during this endeavour. For the joy and peace found in Emilie and Daniel, my eternal thanks.

INTRODUCTION

The European Union (EU) is one of a number of major international actors which affect the context of contemporary conflicts, especially on its immediate borders. The EU's relationship with the countries of the Western Balkans, including Croatia and Serbia, evolved as a result of the EU's development as an actor in conflict resolution. The conflict in the countries of the former Yugoslavia involved war between states (Croatia, Serbia and Bosnia-Hercegovina) which resulted from manifest and manipulated ethnic conflict as well as conflict among the political elites. Collectively, EU institutional actors have proposed that, by offering the conditional carrot of EU membership, the EU can motivate a transformation of the structures and relationships of conflict in Croatia and Serbia. The interpretation of the conflict and the post-war experiences in Croatia and Serbia have been transformed and impacted by Croatia and Serbia's respective bids to become members of the EU.

The aim of this book is to investigate the common belief that the EU has viewed the EU enlargement project as potentially having the capacity to transform the legacies of conflict in the countries of the Western Balkans. It has been a widely held expectation within the EU member states and institutional actors, as well as within the political elites and societies in countries of the Western Balkans, that integration with and the prospect of joining the EU provides the EU with a transformative capacity concerning conflict. In this book, 'integration' with the EU refers to the processes which involve both candidate and potential candidate states, whereas the term 'accession' is used to denote the processes of integration with the EU which result in formal membership.

The book examines and analyses the recent historical relationship between the EU and Croatia and Serbia respectively, in the context of the violent dissolution of Yugoslavia and the EU's embryonic foreign and enlargement policies. It seeks to add to the existing narrative and empirical material on EU foreign policies and enlargement approaches and chronicles the development of relations from the emerging crisis in the former Yugoslavia to Croatia and Serbia's preparation for membership. The key findings of the book are that the processes of integration and the very prospect of joining the EU had a discernable but often contradictory impact on the conflict in the two cases. Specifically, this book shows that the EU contributed to the transformation of conflict in Croatia and Serbia through the incentive of EU membership, yet the enlargement instrument often impaired the EU's actual results. The overarching aims of the integration process were democratisation, stabilisation, member state building and conflict transformation. However, I point out that these aims are fundamentally at odds with one another. For example, an inherent inconsistency was manifested in the EU's attempts to prepare Croatia and Serbia for membership while at the same time pushing them to cooperate fully with the International Criminal Tribunal for the former Yugoslavia (ICTY). The Croatian case encapsulates the challenges faced by the EU when engaging in a post-war situation. Indeed, the example of Croatia highlights the EU's strategic and often clashing interests. Thus, while the EU prioritised ICTY cooperation and refugee returns, this triggered a politicisation of Croatian EU membership and linked that membership directly and explicitly with the structures and relationships of conflict. The slow process of socialisation and the difficult, mistimed and inconsistent application of EU conditionality have produced inherent ambiguities in the EU's attempts to embed a more stable political dispensation in Croatia and Serbia. I address this issue in the book's conclusion.

Europeanisation literatures and conflict resolution literatures have previously merged to explore the EU's practice of intervention in conflicts. However, the combined study of Europeanisation and conflict transformation has not been addressed adequately by the existing literatures, which do not provide a detailed critical analysis of how conflicts change, and of the role that the EU plays in dynamic conflicts. The conflict transformation approach departs from traditional conflict approaches because it emphasises the need for systemic change to alter the structures and relationships within which conflicts are embedded. As an increasingly significant and visible actor on the international stage, the EU affects the structures and relationships of conflicts within and outside its borders. This book proposes that a conflict transformation approach can be used to investigate and evaluate the EU's role in intervening in conflicts on its immediate borders (in Croatia and Serbia). Additionally, the book expands existing conflict transformation approaches to include the impact of external actors such as the EU.

The European Union in conflict transformation

The European Union (EU), or, as it was until 1992, the European Community (EC), has been involved in preventing, managing and transforming conflicts. Historically, the peace that has existed between the EU member states has produced a belief that the EU has managed to internalise and institutionalise a peaceful method of conflict resolution. Initially, the European integration project was economic in nature (the European Coal and Steel Community, the European Economic Community and the European Atomic Energy Community). Hence, there emerged a belief that financial assistance and economic funding could bring peace and stability to a conflictual situation. In its recent history the EU has played an intervening role in significant conflicts both within and outside its borders. The cases of Northern Ireland, Cyprus and the countries of Central and Eastern Europe are of particular interest because they have all experienced conflict and also experienced the potential of the processes of integrating into and joining the EU. These cases introduce this book and clarify the basis for the EU's decision to utilise a membership perspective to impact conflict in Croatia and Serbia.

As a longstanding, violent and protracted intra-state and inter-state conflict, Northern Ireland represented an opportunity for the EU membership dynamics to have an impact on conflict transformation. At various stages in the history of the conflict in Northern Ireland the EC/EU engagement was significant. Salmon (2002) contends that ahead of British and Irish accession to the EC in 1973 hopes were high that EU membership could catalyse a solution to the conflict in Northern Ireland. Salmon points out that in Dublin former Taoiseach Garret Fitzgerald argued that common EC membership could lead to the removal of psychological and economic obstacles to Irish unity. However, the timing of British and Irish membership of the EU coincided with the violent escalation of the conflict in Northern Ireland and the EU was marginalised. Nonetheless, despite the limited influence of the membership perspective ahead of accession in 1973, confidence in the conflict resolution capacity of EU membership prevailed after membership. The Social Democratic and Labour Party (SDLP) leader John Hume consistently contended that the EC/EU could catalyse an opportunity for conflict resolution in Northern Ireland. More recently, O'Donnell (1999: 70) stressed the significance of the EU for the Northern Ireland conflict and contended after the 1998 Good Friday Agreement that 'one of the striking things about the Belfast Agreement is that, to anyone who knows the EU, one immediately recognises that [the agreement] was written by people who also know the EU and have worked its systems quite extensively'.

Salmon concludes that, ultimately, the EU had not 'completely fulfilled its own ambitions ... in terms of external and internal conflict resolution. It still has some way to go, to both operationalise concepts of conflict resolution and find the right instruments' (2002: 357). Salmon's compelling analysis disarms the proponents who would assert that the EU membership perspective acted as a means of conflict resolution. In Northern Ireland, the EU underachieved when it failed to transform the context of conflict and did not make a substantial contribution to ending the violence. However, the other side of the argument must be considered. While the EC/EU failed to have a significant impact during the mainly violent period of the conflict in Northern Ireland from 1969 until the Irish Republican Army (IRA) ceasefires in 1994 and 1997, its impact became more important when the conflict matured in the period following the IRA ceasefires. The Good Friday Agreement (1998) provided the EU with an opportunity to act more constructively in Northern Ireland, especially through cross-border cooperation, peace funding and British–Irish cooperation. As Tannam (2006) has pointed out, attitudinal change within political parties in Northern Ireland, especially within the Democratic Unionist Party (DUP), provided an opportunity for a more involved EU. Therefore, while Salmon's contentions accurately reflect the unfulfilled promise of a transformative EU membership perspective, it becomes clear that since 1998 the EU has had a greater impact on conflict resolution in Northern Ireland. This shift supports a growing belief in the conflict transformation capacity of the EU's integration and membership approach when the circumstances of the conflict are more conducive.

In the early 1990s, the EU began to recognise that it was equally important to play a role in managing, resolving and transforming conflict outside as well as within its borders. In the case of its borders in Central and Eastern Europe and with the three Baltic countries, the EU employed a strategy of stabilising conflict situations by linking them to closer integration with and the prospect of joining the EU through the Balladur Pact. In a different approach to that in Northern Ireland, the EU began to employ the incentive of EU membership to encourage the transformation of conflict sources in aspiring member states. The EU's foreign policy concern with ethnic politics in its periphery became increasingly salient after the end of the Cold War. With the emergence in 1990 of a queue of aspirants from Central and Eastern European states, the EU was challenged with tackling potentially violent conflicts between ethnic minorities within and across the aspirant member states. Kelley (2004) demonstrated that the incentive of EU membership, along with conditionality and socialisation, had an impact on ethnic and minority issues in Latvia, Estonia, Slovakia and Romania. In Latvia, strong

EU conditionality on citizenship law had the effect of altering party perceptions and attitudes on this issue, resulting in Latvia adopting a law that
was harmonious with EU citizenship law (Morris 2003). In Estonia, the
EU demanded that the Estonian political elites be more generous in their
treatment of the Russophone minority, which in 1993–94 helped prevent
an escalation of conflict. The Estonian government stepped back from its
threat to act against the towns in North-East Estonia and the Russophone
minority stepped back from its threat to secede. The Estonian government
then made concessions by giving Russophones the right to participate in
local government (Kelley 2004; Smith 2003). Kelley (2004) argues that in
Slovakia (under Meciar) the incentive of EU membership had some limited
success when Meciar recognised the potential damage to his international
reputation if he failed to comply with the EU in reaching agreement on
a treaty with Hungary. Recognising that the EU's influence was least successful where membership was most distant, Kelley argues that the EU's
potential for impacting minority and ethnic politics in Romania was limited mainly because the EU put questions of ethnic minorities 'on the back
burner'.

Other studies concur with Kelley that the EU membership perspective
and the instruments of conditionality and socialisation resulted in policy
and attitudinal change within a potentially violent conflict situation.
Hughes and Sasse (2003) have shown that the rights of minorities were
given high rhetorical dominance during the EU enlargement process and
this affected the resolution of potential conflict between minorities ahead of
accession. Moreover, Brusis (2003) demonstrates that the EU 'supported the
emergence of consociational/power-sharing arrangements between political
actors that accommodate ethnic cleavages in accession countries' with a special focus on Bulgaria, Romania and Slovakia. Vermeersch (2003) argues
that EU conditionality on ethnic minority issues in the Czech Republic,
Poland and Hungary prevented a violent escalation because of the incentives
of association with and membership of the EU. This evidence demonstrates
that the EU can have a role to play in the initial phases of conflict and thus
can prevent the violent escalation towards conflict.

However, as we know, the EC/EU ultimately failed to prevent the violent
escalation of conflict in the former Yugoslavia in the early 1990s. What
Kelley's (2004) study does not illuminate is the role that the EC/EU's membership perspective plays in countries where violent conflict has occurred
and the conflict may appear to be at a 'ripening' stage, as was experienced
long after membership had been achieved in Northern Ireland. Zartman
(1989) argued that resolution attempts are most likely to be successful if a

conflict is 'ripe', in that it has reached a 'hurting stalemate' which the parties cannot maintain without huge cost, and where neither party sees itself as likely to achieve victory. Although it failed to prevent the outbreak of conflict in Yugoslavia, the EU integration framework has the potential to be successful when the parties in the conflict are seeking an alternative; when the conflict is ripe for intervention.

The case of Cyprus provides the most appropriate example of how the EU membership perspective and integration processes can impact upon a previously violent and protracted conflict. Cyprus represents a recent significant test of the assumption of the transformative capacity of EU enlargement and integration processes on aspirant member states. Ahead of Cypriot accession in 2004, EU engagement had the potential for conflict resolution in the divided island. Before the 2004 accession date, it was commonly assumed by academics and practitioners alike that the EU, through the incentive of memberships, could transform the border conflict (Diez 2004; Christou 2002). At the same time as the EU was hoping that the offer of membership and the integration framework could catalyse a solution to the Cyprus conflict, the EU offered a similar carrot to the countries of the former Yugoslavia.

The EU most visibly intensified its strategy in the Western Balkans at the Santa Maria de Feira European Council in 2000 – four years before the 'partial failure' in Cyprus in 2004. However, the EU's foreign policy in Cyprus, and also in the case of Yugoslavia, as will be shown in Chapter 2, had not been able to respond efficiently to the challenges of these conflicts. Eralp and Beriker (2005: 118) argue that the EU's assumption of the transformative capacity of the enlargement approach in Cyprus was inefficient since on 1 May 2004 the EU imported a protracted ethnic conflict into its political domain. The outcome achieved in 2004 can be described as only a 'partial failure' because of the circumstances in the immediate run-up to the May 2004 deadline. On February 2003 Papadopoulos won the presidential elections in the Republic of Cyprus and in April 2003 the Turkish Republic of Northern Cyprus (TRNC) eased border restrictions for communal visits, a move that the EU supported financially with a 15 million euro investment. Furthermore, the Justice and Development Party (AKP) won the Turkish parliamentary elections in November 2003 and in the TRNC a pro-change coalition government was formed under the leadership of Talat. In 2004 the EU introduced a 35 million euro package to support Greek–Turkish cross-border cooperation (Rumelili 2007: 121). As with Northern Ireland, the EU utilised economic incentives to encourage transformation of the parties regarding the contentious border issue. The EU engagement in Cyprus had further similarities with EU engagement in the Northern Ireland conflict, namely the intervention and diplomatic pressure at the state level. For example, the EU has encouraged diplomatic initiatives between the Greek and Turkish parties in the way that it previously encouraged a diplomatic relationship between Britain and Ireland. These changing circumstances came against a background of considerable pressure by the EU and the UN for the populations on both sides of the border to vote positively in a referendum for a solution on the island, as set out in the Annan Plan.[1] This referendum took place on 24 April 2004 and 65 per cent of voters in the TRNC demonstrated support for the Annan Plan while only 24 per cent of voters in the Republic of Cyprus voted in favour. This signalled that the efforts of the international community had achieved partial success and partial failure, which created mixed feelings about the transformative capacity of the EU's enlargement approach.

This comprehensive overview has demonstrated that the EU's favoured integration and enlargement approach to dealing with conflict in its member and candidate states has produced a series of mixed results. Therefore, questions must be raised about the transformative capacity of integration with and membership of the EU on conflict. Nonetheless, since the EU adopted a more intensified strategy in 2000 it has identified the processes of integration with the EU, as well as the membership perspective, as the most appropriate mechanisms to transform conflict in Croatia and Serbia. This book investigates whether the integration and membership perspective mechanisms have been the most suitable way of dealing with the challenges posed by the post-war situation in Croatia and Serbia, and it examines the ways in which these mechanisms have impacted on the structures and relationships of conflict.

Undeniably, the integration process and the EU membership perspective have been the primary instruments for encouraging conflict transformation in Croatia and Serbia since 2000.[2] Despite the mixed results from the EU's recent engagements in conflict, confidence in the transformative capacity of the EU enlargement process has been widespread (Ashdown 2005; European Commission 2006a; Vachudova 2003: 141). According to Common Foreign and Security Policy (CFSP) High Representative Solana (2000) the EU enlargement strategy

> offers a model as well as the instruments for peace through regional integration, for the reconciliation of former enemies and for the effective guarantee of human and minority rights … no other solution could offer such hope for the Balkans.

More recently, Solana (2007) proposed that enlargement had been a 'historic success' in that the EU has reunified Europe 'without imposing anything on anyone, simply through the enormous power of attraction'. Likewise, academic literature has espoused the transformative capacity of integration with the EU (Grabbe 2006). According to Everts (2004), the ability of the EU to 'exert influence in countries wishing to join the EU has been nothing short of revolutionary ... This form of regime change EU-style is cheap, voluntary and hence, long-lasting'. However, Everts' contention is questionable in the case of the Western Balkans, where the issues associated with the decade-long conflict are more challenging for the EU enlargement policy. This book investigates the significance of this new testing ground as a catalyst for conflict transformation in the aspiring member states Croatia and Serbia, and considers the ways in which the EU can transform conflict in these cases, in the context of integration and enlargement.

Yugoslavia was dissolved by a series of wars that involved, at one time or another, all six republics. In 1991 Slovenia went to war for independence. In the same year Croatia engaged in a successful struggle against Serbia for Croat independence and territorial sovereignty. The Slovenian war lasted ten days. The Croatian war endured for four years. The Croatian experience was complicated by the presence of a sizable minority of Croatian Serbs within Croatia. War then spread to Bosnia-Hercegovina in 1992. This lasted until 1995 and saw Serbia, Bosnia-Hercegovina and Croatia engage in armed conflict for territorial supremacy and authority. In 1995, the Dayton Peace Agreement stabilised the conflict and ended the wars that had consumed Croatia, the Socialist Federal Republic of Yugoslavia (SFRY) and Bosnia-Hercegovina throughout the previous four years. The Dayton Peace Agreement was insufficient to quell the growing crisis in the territory of Kosovo-Metohja (hereafter referred to as Kosovo).[3] War broke out in Kosovo in 1999, which became a major humanitarian and military crisis for Europe. As we shall see in the following discussion, the EC/EU was one of a number of agencies of European security that were engaged in attempts to stabilise and manage the violent conflict in Yugoslavia. The legacies of this violent warfare in Croatia and Serbia continue to dominate the political agendas and discourses to this day. Croatia and Serbia are significant and valuable cases as they contribute critically to an understanding of how the 'power of attraction' of integration with and membership of the EU can contribute to conflict transformation. Therefore, not only does this book help us understand Croatia and Serbia but the cases also help us to understand the utility of the conflict transformation approach and the role of the EU in conflict transformation.

Before commencing a literature review on Europeanisation and conflict transformation in Chapter 1 it is helpful and necessary to clarify what kind of conflicts this book is dealing with. The violent conflict that led to the dissolution of Yugoslavia was largely focused on territorial and sovereignty claims in Bosnia-Hercegovina but also involved ethnic groups within Croatian or Serbian territory. According to Bianchini (1995: 15) the main feature of the inter-Yugoslav war was the refusal to accept difference and the focus on ethnic homogeneity. Alternatively, for Papić (1995: 45) the main cause of war in Yugoslavia in the 1990s was the nature of the regimes in Croatia and Serbia, which were 'totalitarian and dictatorial' and used aggressive nationalism to create war. Agreeing with Bianchini and Papić, Janjić (1995: 66) stresses that the conflict between political organisations such as parties, political blocks and institutions of power on the issues of control of the state and the rights of individuals and groups within the state represented the main cause of violent conflict in Yugoslavia at the outset of the 1990s. This discussion serves to elucidate and introduce a more detailed discussion in Chapter 2 regarding the nature of conflict in Croatia and Serbia. However, for now it is appropriate to reassert that the escalation of conflict in the 1990s was brought about by ethnic aggression fuelled by political and interstate hostilities. Moreover, academic literature espoused an established, but not dominant, view that ancient hatreds between the people in Yugoslavia meant that Yugoslavia as a construct was doomed from the beginning and conflict was preordained. This discourse featured in the debates among the political elites at the time. According to Uvalic (1997: 19), the prevalent view in discourse in the early 1990s was that people from the Balkans were 'uncivilised, inward looking and primitive'. In hindsight and from a critical standpoint this view has largely been discredited. Yet it is important to mention this debate, as it clearly informed policymaking regarding Yugoslavia in the early 1990s. Aside from the implications of externally held views on the Yugoslav crisis, the internally held perceptions about the crises mattered immensely. According to Schopflin (1997: 173) 'the principal communities in Yugoslavia never sought genuinely to understand the other's perspectives, interests or aspirations'. Such perceptions fuelled the violent dissolution of Yugoslavia. Moreover, the intellectual, political and civil society leaders manipulated perceptions.

Existing literature reveals that the dissolution of Yugoslavia can be explained by long- and short-term political and economic factors. These factors included Tito's legacy and the 1974 constitution;[4] the economic crisis, which impacted parts of Yugoslavia differently; the emergence of political entrepreneurs such as Tuđman and Milošević; and international intervention.[5] According to Silber and Little (1994), Yugoslavia did not die a natural death; it was 'deliberately and systematically killed off by men who had nothing to gain and everything to lose from a peaceful transition from state socialism and one party rule to free market democracy'.

Each of these impressions of the reasons for conflict helped determine EU policy and attitudes in the former Yugoslavia.

Croatia and Serbia capture the features and dynamics of the phenomenon of post-war states that are engaged in the integration and EU enlargement process. On the EU periphery there exist a number of conflicts and post-war situations in which the EU plays a role: Bosnia, the Former Yugoslav Republic of Macedonia (hereafter FYR Macedonia) and Kosovo, as well as the Moldova–Transnistria, Israel–Palestine and Georgia–Abkhaz disputes. As with these conflicts, the root causes of conflict in Croatia and Serbia were many and were manifested violently and destructively. The conflicts experienced in Croatia and in Serbia were diverse in nature, with hostilities ranging from local to national, from ethnic to political and from intra-state to inter-state. These conflicts continue to have significant legacies, which frame those countries' transition towards EU membership.

At the core of the EU's transformative capacity on conflict in Croatia and Serbia is what Munuera (1994) has defined as the 'power of attraction'. Munuera asserts that 'the lure of membership can help to prevent conflicts outside the EU's borders by suggesting the advantages of good behaviour to eager candidates and by giving the EU leverage where they do not take the hint'.

This is an important point, because the case studies under investigation have different levels of attraction toward the EU, which can be judged from the electoral success of the pro- and anti-EU political parties in the respective territories. In Croatia, EU membership is overwhelmingly attractive for all political parties across the political spectrum. This is not the case in Serbia, where a substantial percentage of the vote traditionally goes to an anti-EU party, the Serbian Radical Party (SRS). This is significant for this book, as it permits a comparative analysis of the attractiveness of the membership perspective and the outcomes of the transformative capacity of integration with the EU and EU membership perspective in two case studies where they are perceived differently. At the core of this book is the research question of whether and how the mechanisms of integration with the EU and the prospect of becoming a member of the EU influence conflict transformation in Croatia and Serbia.

The structure of this book

Chapter 1 explores how the EU has approached the issue of conflict transformation through the promise of a widened membership. This incentive – what is known as the 'enlargement approach' – has had ambiguous and problematic outcomes in the Western Balkans. This has been the case in Serbia in particular, where EU enlargement became (and remains) an intensely politicised issue and one that has seriously undermined the stated goals of conflict transformation and democratic stabilisation. The chapter outlines the qualitative methodology used in the research and engages with the existing and relevant literature on EU enlargement and post-conflict Serbia. Furthermore, it briefly outlines the main aspects of this book's new and original contribution to the study of the EU and conflict transformation: the deconstruction of the under-appreciated effects of EU enlargement in Serbia; the importance of this relatively under-researched area to wider debates on conflict transformation and EU self-development; and a critical analysis of the opportunities and limitations offered by the EU's enlargement-conflict transformation approach.

Chapter 2 focuses on the relationship between the EU and Croatia, examining the development of relations between Croatia and the EU during the period under investigation (1990–2000). The year 1990 marked the onset of violence in the Balkans. This chapter establishes an understanding of the types of intervention and the rationale behind the episodic interventions. For much of the 1990s the EU was constrained because of limited capacities and contradictory member state interests, yet it consistently attempted to engage more proactively with the escalating conflict. The failure to impose its goals on the conflict is important as it highlights the policy and power limitations of the EU during the period when it first began to present itself as an actor in the area of conflict transformation.

Chapter 3 takes up the theme of the evolution of the EU's strategy and looks at how it attempted to develop a more coherent conflict transformation policy through its 'enlargement approach' after 2000. The year 2000 is taken as a year of change in EU policy in the Balkans and this argument is sustained in the chapter with empirical and qualitative discussion. Therefore, the primary focus of this chapter is to discuss the qualitative shift in the EU's approach and examine the institutional, operational and political implications for the EU that were played out in the decade that followed. The chapter focuses on how the nature, design and timing of conditionality and social learning changed over the past decade as a result of institutional lesson learning within the EU. The chapter shows how the EU's enlargement approach has evolved and what the implications are for its transformative power in Croatia.

Chapter 4 focuses on the specific effects that EU intervention had on the conflict relationships and structures in Croatia, with a detailed focus on the transformation of political parties in Croatia. This chapter builds on the insight that the past conflicts continue to affect the present and points out that the issue is still debated among the political elites and continues to be open to political contestation. In other words, this chapter engages directly with the debate over the meaning of the recent past for the political parties and draws the lesson that unless the historical and institutional legacies of conflict are explored by the political parties in Croatia, the tendency will be to further marginalise experiences of conflict in Croatia. Following on from the conflict transformation narrative, this chapter considers the EU's intervention in the post-2000 period, framed around the prospect of EU membership, and examines its impact on the political parties and their preparedness to deal with the legacies of wars, represent evolving structures of conflict and confront the ongoing political contestations in Croatia and the Balkan region. This chapter examines the key transitions of political parties through investigations of electioneering, electoral results, policymaking, primary sources and interview material. Certainly, the main issue of conflict – full cooperation with the International Criminal Tribunal for the Former Yugoslavia – has been a crucial condition for Croatian membership, and this issue has served to divide and shape the response of Croatia to EU membership. This chapter conducts a detailed analysis of the impact of the EU on this issue, as well as the issues of refugees and displaced persons.

Building on the previous chapter's discussion of the political elites, the chapter examines the impact of the EU's intervention on the changing *relationships* of conflict. Attention here is focused on relationship transformation; that is, how the parties to the conflict perceive the conflict and how political parties interact with one another on central issues. 'Relationship transformation' refers to how each party to the conflict perceives the other parties to the conflict, and how they perceive the way in which power is distributed between the parties. Relationship transformation in Croatia is examined by investigating two linked micro-studies: the influence of Croatia on Bosnian Croats, and the return of refugees and displaced persons. In this chapter, these two empirical examples illuminate how conflict is being transformed in Croatia and what role EU conditionality and socialisation is playing in this transformation.

Chapter 5 charts the evolution of relations between the EU and Serbia and explores the impact that the prospect of becoming a member of the EU has had on the transformation of conflict in Serbia. As we know from the previous discussion, since 2000 Serbia has experienced the same set of EU instruments, policies and initiatives as Croatia. However, Serbia's progress towards closer integration and eventual candidacy has lagged behind Croatia's. This chapter examines the conditions which have prevented Serbia's advancement towards integration into and institutional membership of the EU, given the similar pre-accession pressures and opportunities. As in the previous chapter, this chapter focuses on the relationships and structures of conflict that have been affected by the EU membership perspective. Drawing on electoral results and electioneering, policymaking and primary sources including interview material, this chapter charts the transition undergone by political parties in their handling of central issues relating to the recent conflict, such as full cooperation with the ICTY and refugees and displaced persons. The chapter also examines intra- and inter-state relations.

Chapter 6 assesses the EU's intervention in the cases in terms of short-comings and successes. This chapter focuses on the EU. It provides an opportunity for a detailed discussion about the policy shortcomings and successes, and evaluates the reasons for these outcomes. The chapter evaluates the EU's approach under the following five subheadings: the EU's management of the process; institutional lesson learning within the EU; the pathways of EU influence; timing and nature of socialisation and political conditionality; and the role of domestic factors. Consequently, the chapter focuses on addressing the question: is integration into the EU a panacea for conflict in Croatia?

The Conclusion explores the policy implications of this book's discussion of EU–Croatia and EU–Serbia relationships. For example, it asks under what circumstances the EU can be more effective as a transformative power. It argues that the Croatian case demonstrates the importance of examining the relevant actors, issues and relationships and identifying their capacity to influence change. I point out that the [specific] political conditions in Croatia have been instrumental in shaping the EU's policymaking and policy implementation.

Taking the Croatian and Serbian cases as an illustrative example, this chapter recommends a series of policymaking principles regarding the EU's effectiveness as an actor in conflict transformation. For example, the EU can be most effective as a transformative power on conflict when dealing with conflict parties and issues when political conditionality is rigorously and consistently applied. The conclusion points out that while these observations draw on the specificities of the Croatian and Serbian cases they have relevance for other post-conflict situations; an importance that will develop and evolve as the EU positions itself as a major strategic and military power on the global stage. Furthermore, this chapter widens the application of this study to consider implications for the broader study of European enlargement, security, foreign policy, conflict transformation and regional studies.

1

THE EU ENLARGEMENT APPROACH AND CONFLICT TRANSFORMATION

This chapter explores how the EU has approached the issue of conflict transformation through the promise of a widened membership. This incentive – what is known as the 'enlargement approach' – has had ambiguous and problematic outcomes in the Western Balkans. This has been the case particularly in Croatia and Serbia, where EU enlargement became (and remains) an intensely politicised issue and one that has seriously undermined the stated goals of conflict transformation and democratic stabilisation.

This chapter outlines the qualitative methodology used in the research and engages with the relevant existing literature on conflict transformation, EU enlargement and post-conflict Croatia and Serbia. It also outlines briefly this book's new and, it is hoped, original contribution to the study of the EU and of conflict transformation; the deconstruction of the insufficiently appreciated effects of EU enlargement in Croatia and Serbia; the importance of this relatively under-researched area to wider debates on conflict transformation and EU self-development; and a critical analysis of the opportunities and limitations offered by the EU's enlargement and conflict transformation approach.

Transforming conflict the EU way

Historically, the process of integration with the EU and the EU enlargement approach was connected with issues of peace and conflict (Eilstrup-Sangiovanni and Verdier 2005; Giamouridis 2007: 184). First, the Franco-German integration secured peace and reconciliation on a continent long characterised by ethnic, national and power rivalries. Successive enlargements have, however, been marked by specific and notable ethnic and border conflicts, as with the accession of the United Kingdom (UK) and the Republic of Ireland over Northern Ireland, Greece, with Turkey, Cyprus and other disputes and, with the 2004 enlargement, Cyprus and Kaliningrad.[1] Democratic peace theory proposed that a community of democratic states that share liberal and democratic norms will not enter into violent conflict with each other (Doyle 1983a, 1983b; Ray 1998; Mansfield and Snyder 2002).[2] This relates to Kant's (1795) concept of *foedus pacificum*, which is based on the precept that communities of states share and communicate norms, practices and laws, and that these interlinkages prevent them from entering into such conflict. The EU embodies this premise as, according to Eilstrup-Sangiovanni and Verdier (2005), an EU member state is unlikely to enter into violent conflict with another such state.

In the light of the extensive expansion of the EU – from 15 to 25 members in 2004, and to 27 in 2007 – academic inquiry has emphasised the notion of the EU's normative power (Manners 2002) and the 'Europeanising' power of the EU enlargement project (Ágh 1998; Linden 2002; Schimmelfennig and Sedelmeier 2005; Grabbe 2006). Moreover, contemporary academic discussions have focused on how the processes of integration with the EU and then of EU membership have transformed the politics and economies of candidate states, especially in Central and Eastern European countries (CEEC) (Grabbe 2006; Pridham and Ágh 2001; Grabbe and Hughes 1998; Schimmelfennig and Sedelmeier 2005).[3] However, the extant literature does not deal adequately with the issues raised by enlargement in the Western Balkans, particularly with regard to additional coverage of the 1990s conflicts and their legacies. Nonetheless, it is on this existing debate about the 2004 and 2007 enlargement processes that the premise rests for the assumption that EU membership can transform conflict in Croatia and Serbia – or, in other words, 'if the recipe worked once … it would work a second time' (Noutcheva 2004: 3). According to Batt (2006: 171), if the EU is to repeat this success in the more 'precarious circumstances of post-war Balkans', it will represent a 'major test of the proposal that integration with the EU is key to solving ethnic conflict'.

The EU's transformative capacity is defined as its ability to implement change in states which are candidates or potential candidates for EU membership. The nature of this ability is summed up by Giddens (1979), who argues that transformative capacity is defined as 'actors' attempts to get others to comply with their wants'. Put simply, it is the ability to persuade a party to do something it would otherwise not have done, and to do it willingly (Rummel 1976). This is central to this discussion. Have the processes of integration with the EU, and the prospect of becoming a member state, persuaded actors to do things willingly that they would arguably not have done in the absence of the EU's relational power? (Power, in this relational sense, concerns the capability of actors to secure outcomes where the realisation of these outcomes depends upon the agency of others.) The EU's power here is most accurately described as 'soft' power (Nye 2004), and therefore the EU's transformative capacity relates to its ability to secure its desired outcomes in candidate and potential-candidate states. This capacity is explicitly linked to the notion of normative power in Europe; according to Anastasakis (2007: 12), the EU

> contributes to cooperation among European countries and endorses a common approach based on agreed rules and procedures, criteria, and conditions. It changes the way administrations operate and officials think, contributing to the modernization of state apparatuses, the consolidation of democracies, and the strengthening of national economies.

The EU's role in candidate and potential candidate states has been subject to study by Ágh (1995; 1999). In his 1995 study he describes societies then on the periphery as 'penetrated societies', whose politicians are impacted by the external environment, including the processes of integration with the EU. In his 1999 study Ágh notes that 'linkages exist between interrelationships and interdependencies between external and internal developments in the EU and the Balkan countries' (1999: 264). Therefore, the EU's transformative capacity is impacted by the nature of the relationship that the EU has with the third country; and in the cases of Croatia and Serbia, this relationship is based around the processes of integrating into the EU.

Vachudova (2005: 65) introduces the terms 'passive leverage' and 'active leverage' to assess how the asymmetric interdependence on EU membership criteria influenced economic and political reform in Central and Eastern Europe. For her, passive leverage is the 'traction that the EU has on the domestic politics of credible candidate states by virtue of its existence and its usual conduct'. This traction exists because of the political and economic benefits EU membership can bring. The mechanisms of the accession and pre-accession processes potentially equip the EU with substantial active leverage over the aspirants. For Grabbe (2006), EU candidacy and potential candidacy is a significant means of motivating and consolidating the necessary reforms in the country concerned, as the perceived gains of EU membership are sufficiently attractive to overcome resistance to reform. She has shown that at certain times, in certain policy areas and for certain elites, the prospect of becoming an EU member and of involvement in the processes of integration with the EU has stimulated change within the candidate country.

Further significant insights emerge from a variety of sources in the literature which empirically examines the impact of the EU on conflict. Ultimately, for Emerson (2005), Maull (2005) and Munuera (1994), the EU's ability to transform candidate and potential-candidate states lies in its power of attraction. Emerson (2005) contends that it relies on the gravitational pull exercised by the prospect of joining the EU. The basis of this gravitational pull lies in the desire of the candidate to join (Maull 2005: 782) and in the EU's ability to maintain the credibility of the membership perspective. The appeal of becoming a member of the EU can transform economic, political and social conflict in aspiring members, and gives the EU an influential position over the behaviour of potential candidates (Munuera 1994: 91). Based on this, it is possible to ascertain that for the EU to have an impact on conflict structures and relationships a credible, attractive and tangible membership perspective must be presented. Therefore, it is particularly significant to raise the question of whether it will be possible, if an EU membership perspective (no matter how tangible) is seen as unattractive by the political elite, for the EU to have an impact on the political parties concerned.

Manners (2002) argues that the EU is a normative power in international politics,[4] as a norm-maker and norm-sharer. Given the asymmetrical and conditional nature of its enlargement processes, the EU is in a strong position to persuade non-member states to adopt, implement and harmonise with EU norms, legislation and practices – and persuasion is a key EU method. Zimbardo *et al.* (1977: 57) identify four processes that determine the extent to which a person will be persuaded by a communication, using the 'Yale approach': attention, comprehension, acceptance and retention. To clarify, first the EU must gain the *attention* of Croatia and Serbia for it to have any prospect of impacting on conflict transformation. Then, *comprehension* of the mechanisms, expectations and capabilities on both sides of the process (the EU on one side and Croatia/Serbia on the other) is necessary. Following Zimbardo's framework, for the EU to persuade Croatia and Serbia to transform it is then necessary for them to *accept* the demands of the EU, and furthermore to *retain* and implement these changes. Axelrod argues that 'a norm exists in a given social setting to the extent that individuals usually act in a certain way and are often punished when seen not to be acting in this way' (1986: 1097). Alderson points out that the institutionalisation of norms take place through legal harmonisation, the creation of bureaucratic actors mandated to enforce norms, and at a deeper, more pervasive level.[5] The institutionalisation of norms reflects the capacity of both the receivers (in this case Croatia and Serbia) and the giver (the EU) to make it stick (Alderson 2001: 418). Crucially, it is the capacity of Croatia and Serbia to institutionalise the EU's norms and effect conflict transformation which, in conjunction with the EU's efforts, ultimately determines the outcomes of Europeanisation in conflict transformation.

While the existing academic literature has failed to discuss adequately the additional challenge(s) posed by an enlargement to the Western Balkans, it is not appropriate to ignore or neglect this literature since it has much to tell us about the EU's transformative power. For example, the literature suggests that the prospect of membership gives the EU powerful leverage to influence the outcome of reform efforts in aspiring members (Anastasakis and Bechev 2003: 5; Grabbe 2006). In what ways can this leverage impact candidate and potential-candidate states? The straightforward and compelling explanation offered by Emerson and Noutcheva (2005) is that the processes of integration with the EU and Europeanisation can be understood in terms of the legal obligations generated by EU and/or Council of Europe requirements; the economic and institutional changes contingent on closer relations with the EU; and changes in discourse, identity and group politics. Potentially, therefore, through harmonisation with and implementation of EU conditions, the EU can transform economics, politics and the legacies of the past in Croatia and Serbia. Furthermore, the existing literature focuses on how member states create, share and institutionalise EU ways of doing things.[6] Consequently, Europeanisation involves legal adaptation, approximation and harmonisation, together with the adaptation and adjustment of policies, as well as of institutions. This helps us to understand the adaptational pressures that Grabbe (2006) mentions in her appraisal of the EU's transformative power in Central and Eastern Europe, but it fails to convey fully the ways in which the EU's influence can be put into practice. For that reason, it is necessary to consider the mechanisms at play in EU conditionality and social learning.

Mechanisms for change: EU conditionality and social learning

According to Checkel (2000), Europe is a particularly 'rich laboratory' for examining the role of political conditionality and cooperation, as well as exploring its normative influence in non-member state domestic politics, because of the recent expansion of the Union. Since the enlargement process of the 2004 enlargement the EU appears to have learned that neither strict conditionality nor stand-alone dialogue works and is implementing this lesson in the Western Balkan countries. The EU institutions, in particular the Commission, recognise that strict conditionality cannot produce incremental change in the Western Balkans and any conditionality must be accompanied by progressive dialogue.[7]

According to Smith (2001: 37), political conditionality entails 'the linking, by a state or international organization, of perceived benefits to another state ... to the fulfilment of conditions relating to the protection of human rights and the advancement of democratic principles'. Schimmelfennig and Sedelmeier (2005: 672) argue that the effectiveness of political conditionality relies on the size and speed of rewards, determinacy of conditions, the extent of adoption costs and the credibility of threats and promises. Political conditionality enables the EU to have an impact through a compulsory pathway since, through political conditionality, the EU targets political elites by supporting and strengthening pro-reform actors or by making the cost of non-compliance much too high. In his analysis of the Czech Republic and Slovakia and regionalisation, Brusis (2003: 11–12) points out that 'EU conditionality existed and functioned, but was essentially complementary and instrumental in a process driven by domestic needs and interests. Rule adoption occurred because the ideas underlying these rules resonated with national political discourses.'

In an ideal world, the EU member states would hope to see all aspirants implement reform in the manner that the EU would specify. However, there are problems with this: the lucidity of EU conditionality and rewards and the nature of the receptor government and society. First, it is arguable that EU conditionality can be vague and open to various interpretations. This relates to the intergovernmentalism within EU policymaking, which means that there are many traditions and practices within various policy fields, making any single EU template impossible to import. Then, the situation within a recipient country can diminish adaptation of EU norms and practices. Sadurski (2004: 378) points out that

> the degree of specificity of EU political conditionality varied from one domain to another, and so it might have been much more effective where there was a determinate set of rules that the candidate states were expected to observe, rather than in cases in which the criteria laid down could be at best characterised as a vague template.

Checkel (2000) criticises the hard conditionality applied by the EU as being less successful or not working in cases where it will have detrimental consequences for the future success or survival of political parties. For example, when domestic costs of compliance with EU conditionality are too high for the political parties, the political parties could cooperate only partially or reluctantly, or refuse to cooperate with the conditionality altogether. This relates to the above point that, in some instances, this condition is just too difficult for the aspirant to accept. However, domestic factors also relate to the role of society. If the condition being applied is perceived negatively by society and public opinion, given the governing elite's desire to retain power, it makes adoption of the condition awkward at best and impossible at worst.

Nonetheless, despite these limitations to the use of political conditionality the fact remains that conditionality can be a successful method of impacting change in non-member states. So, why do aspirants comply with EU conditions? Schimmelfennig and Sedelmeier (2005: 3) use their 'external incentive model' to capture the dynamics of political conditionality. In contrast to the 'logic of appropriateness', the external incentive model is premised upon the 'logic of consequences'. The logic of appropriateness is a perspective that sees human action as driven by the acceptance of rules or behaviour that is deemed to be appropriate, legitimate and expected. The logic of consequences approach supposes that the elites make a cost-benefit appraisal of the rewards of membership in contrast to the costs of non-membership in order to decide if compliance with the EU's conditions is worthwhile. According to Brusis (2005: 293), conditionality is assumed to effect a policy change by influencing the cost-benefit calculations of domestic actors, but it may be combined with processes of learning and socialisation through which domestic actors adopt shared belief systems. Indeed, the EU's leverage relies on its role as doorkeeper when it can threaten exclusion or reward with membership. The EU can threaten to and/or reduce assistance, suspend association and delay the prospect of EU membership should the aspirant fail to comply with any of the conditions set by the EU. It is this gatekeeping mechanism that can provide the EU with a more significant transformative power. To expound, Haughton (2007: 223) argued that the EU's 'transformative power is at its greatest when deciding to open accession negotiations'. Access to the EU, to negotiations and to further stages in the EU integration process is a key instrument of the EU to influence reform in aspiring countries. Grabbe (2006: 75–6) notes a paradox with this instrument: the EU's efforts to promote democratic development are at odds with the incentives created by the accession process, where the EU gives priority to efficiency over legitimacy.

Schimmelfennig and Sedelmeier (2005) help to explain the achievement of different results of conditionality across case studies; when conditions of the same design, nature and timing are applied to more than one country it is possible that the intended outcome will be different. This suggests that the EU's transformative capacity on an aspirant member state relies heavily on the adoption capacity and domestic equilibrium in the aspirant member state. Schimmelfennig and Sedelmeier suggest that the following variables impact the transformative power of EU conditionality: the size and speed of rewards; the credibility of conditionality; veto players and adoption costs; legitimacy of rules and processes; identity and resonance which fit with the external incentive model. Moreover, in cases where society and elites support the case for EU membership, such as Croatia, the EU can maximise its transformative impact. However, in the case of Serbia, cross-party and societal support for EU membership is not evident. Therefore, out of the two cases, it is more likely that Schimmelfennig and Sedelmeier's (2005) appraisal will not be applicable to Serbia. This leads us to question, then, whether compliance with EU conditions takes place because of this cost-benefit analysis or whether the logic of appropriateness helps to explain why Croatia and Serbia are willing to accept EU conditionality.

Aside from the explicit conditions specified in the accession criteria, as part of the accession process[8] the candidates can experience a degree of social learning. This premise emanates from the work of March and Olsen (1989), who suggest that through engagement in a process the aspirant will adapt its behaviour and practices to become more similar to the normal practices and behaviours of the agencies within the club they wish to join. The logic of appropriateness as defined by March and Olsen (1989) suggests that the aspirants behave according to what is accepted or perceived as normal; therefore, it is more about persuasion than coercion; about complex learning rather than behavioural adaptation. International socialisation literature and democratic peace theories make significant contributions to conflict transformation literature. International socialisation is important when considering how the EU, as an international organisation, exports its norms, acting almost as a 'nanny' to non-member states which are undergoing transition (Linden 2002). This social learning that comes from being a member of a social community, sharing norms, laws and practices, has been interpreted as a form of colonialisation imposed from above (Chandler 2007). Therefore, the morality of the EU's approach to the countries of the former Yugoslavia is questionable (Vaknin 1998; Detrez 2001). This will be examined further in the research findings.

Since the 1990s the rationalist and reflectivist paradigms of international relations have been increasingly challenged by a 'middle ground' constructivism. At its core, constructivism argues that through interaction and communication, people and states come to form ideas of what constituted their interest, reality and behaviour; hence, for constructivists, rationality is socially constructed and context-bound (DiMaggio 1998: 700; Nee and Strang 1998: 706–7). Constructivist approaches help to explain why actors alter their behaviours by suggesting that actors follow either a logic of appropriateness or a logic of consequentiality.

An understanding of the relationship between the EU and the two cases here requires an understanding of the theoretical contribution of constructivism. As Schimmelfennig (1999: 6) argues, international organisations like the EU not only 'regulate state behaviour but also contribute to shaping actors' identities and interests'. The main contribution of constructivist approaches to this book is that we can expect the EU to admit countries that share its norms and practices; therefore, socialisation is inbuilt into the integration and pre-accession process. As stated above, integrating with and preparing to become a member of the EU is not purely about harmonising with the acquis; social learning is an integral part of the integration and accession process.[9]

In the absence of explicit coercion, the EU changes attitudes and behaviours through persuasion and social learning. Persuasion is defined as:

> An activity or process in which a communicator attempts to induce a change in the belief, attitude or behaviour of another person … through the transmission of a message in a context in which the persuadee has some degree of free choice (Perloff 1993: 14).

This definition refers to the negotiation and argument that a person, state or entity such as the EU can employ to convince a third party, namely aspirant states. In his appraisal of conditionality and compliance, Checkel (2000) discovered that compliance with international institutions occurs through social learning involving knowledge and norm diffusion through learning and persuasion. Checkel identifies three 'modalities' of conditionality: pre-conditions, trigger actions and policy provisions. Pre-conditions involve the realisation of governments' actions which have been agreed upon during negotiations before the EU or an international institution approves assistance, association or accession. Trigger actions, in the case of the EU's association, assistance, or accession involve adoption and harmonisation with the acquis communautaire. Finally, Checkel argues that policy provisions are the least likely to induce compliance yet involve socialisation of the aspirant. Checkel points out that while this can be the least binding aspect of EU conditionality it is often most effective in states that suffer from poor policy environments, where strict conditionality can often fail. This is crucial to understanding the impact of the EU's conditionality in Croatia and Serbia, yet the impact of the EU's tough line on certain conditions (such as ICTY cooperation) must not be ignored. The adoption of both stringent and persuasive means of encouraging compliance shows flexibility in the EU's strategy. Successful socialisation and social learning processes ultimately result in the internalisation of norms and behaviours by an aspirant. This internalisation is demonstrated by the aspirants' demonstrative commitments to accepting and practising EU norms and behaviours (Parsons 1969: 440–56).

This reasonably representative overview shows that existing literature places an emphasis on the transformative power on states which are aspiring to become EU members and which have a visible framework for realising this ambition. Moreover, this existing literature does not deal adequately with the post-war situation in Croatia and Serbia. The Europeanisation literature appraised in this section has shown that the EU can wield significant influence on the politics and economies of candidate and potential candidate states. Therefore, as candidate and potential candidate states, the EU's potential influence on Croatia and Serbia would be substantial; nonetheless, it is still necessary to illuminate the potential for exerting an influence on conflict.

While existing conflict transformation literatures and Europeanisation literatures do not interact, the conceptual gap between conflict studies and European studies has been bridged somewhat by approaches which bring together the EU's roles in conflict prevention, crisis management and conflict resolution. The following discussion is limited to a review of Europeanisation in conflict resolution since it is most apt for this book. Dovetailing conflict transformation and Europeanisation literatures necessitates a critique of the existing literature which has focused on the EU's role in resolving conflict.

EU engagement in conflict resolution

There is a small but compelling body of literature emerging on the EU's role in conflict resolution. Existing literature that examines the EU's role in conflict resolution includes Salmon (2005), Coppetiers *et al.* (2004), Tocci (2004; 2007), Diez *et al.* (2004) and Bendiek (2004). This existing literature has made substantial advancements in the field of examining the EU in conflict and each offers novel approaches of how to examine and understand the EU's capacity in conflict transformation. Diez *et al.* (2004) propose that the EU is a 'perturbator', which implies that the EU can influence and change the conflict.

In their examination of the EU's role in border conflicts Coppetiers *et al.* (2004: 2) found that the EU can resolve border conflicts through multi-level governance. This comprehensive study showed how and why processes of integration with the EU and multi-tier governance can support sustainable solutions to secessionist conflicts at the periphery of the EU by resolving antagonisms between opposing sides to the conflict. Coppetiers *et al.* note that the 'EU generates a new type of multi-level governance which leads to the transformation of the notion of sovereignty', thus allowing for the resolution of a conflict through regional integration, transformation of sovereignty and a federalisation of foreign policy. Yet the limits of the EU as an actor in conflict transformation are noted: 'the EU has a long way to go before becoming a master in the art of conflict resolution' (Coppetiers *et al.* 2004: 253). This study provides insights which are useful in the theoretical framework of this book. It acknowledges the difficulties of Europeanisation as an independent or intervening variable. It considers the framework and role as a player that the EU contributes to the conflict. It underlines the significance of conditionality and social learning and it highlights the challenges for conducting research on the EU in conflict transformation.

Significantly, Coppetiers *et al.* assert that the EU's transformative capacity in conflict transformation is reliant on linkage of the outcome of a conflict to a degree of integration into European structures. The processes of integration and the prospect of becoming a member of the EU comprise social learning and conditionality mechanisms. It is these mechanisms which explain the effectiveness of the EU's transformative capacity at different points in time. Kavalski (2003) notes that through conditionality and socialisation the EU can facilitate a gradual absorption of externally acceptable behaviour, regional cooperation and the emergence of an EU-promoted framework of order. This book investigates these assumptions that processes of integration and the project of joining the EU are the pivotal instruments for transforming the legacies of the past conflict and consolidating peace in the Western Balkans.

Tocci (2004, 2007) followed Kavalski's study with an intensive study of the EU's role in resolving conflict. Tocci's research analyses 'the interrelationship between the evolution of the conflict and the development of relations between the conflict parties and the EU in the context of (EU) enlargement' (2004: vii). Tocci's (2004) study provides insights into the reasons behind actions or inaction by the EU in the case of Cyprus and makes an assessment of the EU's capacity in conflict resolution. However, Tocci's key achievement for the purposes of this book lies in the finding that it was the wider context of EU enlargement that provided a motivating force to the parties of conflict in Cyprus. In her 2007 publication, Tocci found that there are several factors that determine the extent and manner in which EU conditionality, social learning and passive enforcement can positively influence ethno-political conflicts: the value of the benefit and the credibility of obligations (2007: 9–26). For Tocci (2007: 18) the 'value of the benefit' is determined by the objective and subjective value of the benefits offered by the EU which outweigh the costs of compliance. The 'value of the benefit' is affected by the timing of rewards, which is particularly significant for this study in that EU membership is particularly distant for Serbia (less so for Croatia). This indicates that the EU's transformative influence could be limited because the reward appears further from reach. Tocci highlights that for the EU to be effective in conflict transformation its obligations must be credible (2007: 23). In sum, the existing literature has found that the EU's credibility relies on its track record of delivering on promises it has made; on its consistency in deploying rewards and punishments; and on the recipients' perception of how likely the EU will be to follow through on its commitments (Tocci 2007).

In an investigation that is particularly useful for this study, Diez *et al.* (2004: 3) consider how, through integration and association, EU involvement in border conflicts succeeded in transforming conflict into less violent and more cooperative forms of cross-border relations. Their study distinguishes different levels of conflict and identifies four pathways through which the EU can scale down the intensity of any given conflict. In their study there exist two potential mechanisms of EU influence (2004: 22):

(a) whether EU policies directly or indirectly aim to transform basic communicative patterns relating to border conflicts; and
(b) whether these policies are directed towards the political leadership of conflict parties or to a wider network of societal actors.

This helps to identify four different paths through which an actor can help de-escalate a conflict. These are summarised in Table 1.1.

It is imperative to remember at this point the multi-faceted nature of the EU; it consists of Commission, Parliament, Council and member states among other agencies. This is crucial as it provides an insight into the channels of EU influence.[10] Diez *et al.* (2004) propose that EU influence is both direct and indirect and is directed at both societal and elite level. In the first pathway, the EU can have a compulsory impact on the conflict by

Table 1.1 Pathways of EU impact

		Approach adopted by the EU	
		Direct	**Structural**
Direction of incentive vis-à-vis conflict parties	**Primarily political leadership**	(1) compulsory impact	(2) enabling impact
	Principally wider societal level	(3) connective impact	(4) constructive impact

Source: adapted from Diez *et al.* (2004: 15).

compelling actors to change their policies and it relies on the parties wanting to become a member of the EU. Therefore, it should be expected that when the desire to join the EU is absent, the potential for a compulsory impact would be diminished. In the second pathway, the EU can have an enabling impact on specific actors within conflict parties because the actor can justify desecuritising moves that were previously illegitimate. To clarify, the concept of peace and integration represents a diffuse incentive for local parties to give up exclusionary discourses and promote cooperation with former enemies. In simple terms, because of the presence of the EU, adversaries can relegate destructive discourses and behaviour using the EU integration process as a scapegoat yet at the same time willingly transform. This relates to the socialisation of political parties and is important for the relationship transformation investigated in this book. In the third pathway, the EU can have a connective impact through supporting and facilitating contact between conflict parties, for example by providing financial support for common activities. Finally, in the fourth pathway, the EU can have a constructive impact on conflict transformation by reconstructing identities and thus permanently sustaining peaceful relations between conflict parties.

While these theoretical and empirical contributions to investigating the EU in conflict zones highlight the potential for effectiveness, they also highlight the constraints and the unintended negative impacts of EU intervention. This is significant because, as the book shows, conflict transformation can be both positive and negative and the EU can have both intended and unintended impacts on conflict. This overview suggests that examining the EU in conflict zones is a valid research area.

Perspectives from conflict transformation literature

Azar (1990: 5) provides a functional and encompassing definition of conflict: 'Conflict is an inseparable part of social interactions involving two or more parties ... Mutually incompatible goals among parties amidst a lack of coordinating or mediating mechanisms give birth to conflict.'

The incompatibility of goals suggested in this definition speaks to a broader understanding of conflict which demonstrates that conflict does not simply end once a peace agreement has been signed. Therefore, in order to understand the progress toward peace it is imperative to consider how the conflict which had previously escalated into violence has been transformed. This definition is particularly applicable to the conflict experienced in Croatia as it indicates that a conflict should be understood as not only a manifestation of actors' incompatible goals but also in the wider context of the 'lack of coordinating or mediating mechanisms' which give rise to conflict. This also suggests that an external agency such as the EU can have a role to play in establishing such mechanisms to transform conflict.

The dynamism of conflict is characterised by phases of initiation, escalation and management, and this can lead to transformation (Sandole 1993: 6). According to Mitchell (2002: 7), the initiation phase of a conflict is when 'incompatible interests emerge into parties' consciousness, through mobilisation of support for the achievement of shared goals', while the escalation phase of a conflict is characterised by intensified coercive and violent behaviour. This can lead to the management phase where third parties, such as international institutions, regional actors or neighbouring states, become involved. Finally, the fourth phase is the transformation phase in which the structures and relationships of the conflict are changed. In the transformation phase, one would anticipate profound change in aspects of the conflict or the socio-political system in which the conflict is embedded (Mitchell 2002: 6).

The management and transformation phases of conflict are predicated on a 'ripening' of the conflict (Zartman 1989: 4). According to Zartman, when the conflict parties 'find themselves locked in a conflict from which they cannot escalate to victory and this deadlock is painful to both of them, they seek a way out'. This concept is useful for this book as it suggests a way in which parties seek to transform. The concept of ripeness is most useful because it is commonly accessible for both analysts and practitioners in conflict, yet parsimony dictates that it must be clarified in order to apply it justifiably to the case study analysed in the book. In Croatia, it is not possible to follow Zartman's terminology faithfully, owing to the nature of international and domestic contextual change. In terms of the experience of Croatia, it is more useful to think more clearly about why parties to the conflict sought an escape route. At the time when we see a ripening of the conflict in Croatia, the parties involved were mainly those that had been in opposition to the dominant parties of the 1990s. Zartman includes in his analysis of ripeness a 'perception of a way out'; the parties do not need an identifiable solution, only a possibility for a solution. This is particularly straightforward to apply in the case of Croatia, where it is possible to show that various parties to the conflict indicated that they felt a solution could be reached. The removal of the Tudman regime provided an opportunity for other parties to realise the costs of continued struggle and recognise that it would be more beneficial to pursue different strategies for a negotiated future.

Dealing with, transforming and resolving the causes and effects of conflict lie at the core of contemporary efforts to theorise and practise conflict transformation (Väyrynen 1991; Rupensighe 1995a, 1995b; Burton 1996; Miall 2001; Richmond 2002; Miall *et al.* 1999; Albin 2005; Tocci 2007). The basic tenet of the conflict transformation approaches is that the sources of conflict can be transformed to provide a more peaceful way of dealing with the conflict. Hence, the approaches espoused in conflict transformation literature contribute to how conflict and post-war transition can be understood and analysed. Existing conflict transformation literature explains that conflicts can be transformed but fails to actually agree on what is transformed and who transforms it. According to Dukes (1999: 48), conflict transformation is a relatively new term which has 'accrued a number of meanings, including transformation of individuals, transformation of relationships, and transformation of social systems large and small'. Owing to the relative newness of this term, which has become current in the last two decades, it is imperative to emphasise that conflict transformation is not merely a debate on semantics; it represents a shift from resolution approaches. *Conflict resolution* intimates that it is possible for actually, or potentially, violent conflict to be transformed into peaceful (non-violent) processes of socio-political change, which means that the structure and the nature of a conflict has been resolved (Miall *et al.* 1999). The resolution of a conflict indicates that the needs and desires of all adversaries are satisfied. *Conflict settlement* approaches are concerned with ending violence and are less concerned with satisfying the long-term basic needs of all parties to conflict. *Conflict prevention* indicates that operational and structural measures can be enacted to prevent the immediate escalation of violent conflict. *Conflict management* theorists debate the consequences of conflict. On one hand, some conflict management theorists see 'violent conflict as an ineradicable consequence of differences of values and interests within and between communities', where the aim is to end the violence and replace it with 'normal' politics (Miall 2001: 3). On the other hand, conflict management theorists such as McGarry and O'Leary (1993) argue that the outcome of ethnic conflict can be regulated, managed and terminated.

The contemporary approaches in conflict and peace studies are valuable, but for this study it is important to develop a similar clarity on the approaches found within conflict transformation literature. According to Väyrynen (1999: 151), conflict transformation 'aims to redefine and rearrange key parties and their coalitions, issues, rules and interests in a manner that the conflict becomes less violent and destructive'. According to Miall the conflict transformation approach is 'a re-conceptualisation of the field in order to make it more relevant to contemporary conflicts' (2001: 3). Tidwell (1998) notes that conflict transformation approaches contend that conflicts are not resolvable and conflicts are constantly in a state of flux and dynamic in nature. Conflict transformation theories inform approaches and methods that can be employed by practitioners involved in reconciliation and mediation (Bercovitch 1996; Fisher 1997; Bloomfield *et al.* 2003; Keating and Knight 2004; Miall 2001). The bulk of conflict transformation theory concerns the issues, parties and relationships between the parties as the basis for mitigating incompatibilities between them. However, the issues, parties, and relationships between the parties will change over time as an outcome of the shifting social, economic, political and international dynamics of a country. According to a principal proponent of conflict transformation, Lederach (1995: 201), the approach of conflict transformation is 'descriptively rich in regard to conflict dynamics and prescriptively embedded in a framework that underscores a more holistic view of conflict'. Ultimately, at its core transformation theory involves a profound and qualitative change.

One approach within the conflict transformation literature suggests that the deep-rooted sources that instigated the conflict cannot be addressed sufficiently for the conflict to be seen as resolved (Kriesberg *et al.* 1989; Väyrynen 1991). Therefore, the tensions, deep-rooted sources and symptoms of a conflict are transformed, rather than resolved, through peaceful negotiation and progression. This relates to a structural understanding of conflict which is commonly found within approaches in conflict transformation literature. For Burton (1996) and Azar (1990) a structural analysis incorporated in a transformation approach provides a more comprehensive picture of the causes of a conflict and therefore offers an understanding of how these causes can be transformed. Burton (1996) maintained that the resolution of conflict involves the satisfaction of basic human needs of all people impacted by conflict. According to Burton (1996: 2), conflict emerges from the deep-seated needs and emotions of the conflictual parties, 'in respect of which there can be no compromise'. The satisfaction of basic needs is compelling as it pushes for a comprehensive alteration of the structures and deep-rooted sources of the conflict in order to create peaceful processes of social change.

Adding to the diversity of the embryonic literatures on conflict transformation is another approach, set out by Galtung (1995). The transformation rather than the resolution of a conflict alludes to the transfer of energy. For Galtung (1995), the energy of the conflict does not disappear once the violence ends; rather it is channelled elsewhere. The transfer of energy denotes that energy cannot be dissipated but rather the energy is altered into something positive and proactive rather than negative and destructive. This book does not embrace this view. Rather, it is argued that such a qualitative judgement should not and cannot be made about the outcome of transformation. Instead, in any process of transformation, all sides will both 'win' and 'lose' to some extent so that they can 'sell' the transformation process to followers as something they will benefit from. A party may make gains on a certain issue only to suffer a loss on another issue. Furthermore, if we remember the chronology of conflict established above (initiation, escalation, management and ripening) it is difficult to argue that each of these phases does not 'transform' a society or a region in which the conflict is occurring.

In conflict transformation literature most theorists agree that the transformation of a conflict refers to the reversal of the negative forms of change. Surely, a *reversal* of the negative forms of change is not a sufficient aim or description of conflict transformation. A reversal indicates that the conflict will revert to the status quo before the violent conflict. This is not a desirable outcome as the causes of the conflict would remain untransformed. Therefore there is a need not only for major change in the parties, issues and relationships of conflict but also for a major change in the socio-political and economic situation in the society. A change in the social, political and economic situation can facilitate or create the conditions in which a profound transformation of the structures and relationships of conflict can take place. Clearly, conflict transformation should not seek to suppose that a conflict is 'transformed', but rather that conflict transformation is a process which must involve the parties, a concentration on the main issues of conflict and a focus on the relationships between parties or adversaries to the conflict. Sensibly, Mitchell (2002: 5) proposes that it is reasonable to conclude that conflict transformation can stand both for an end state (or at least a set of identifiable conditions) when the conflict can be viewed as 'transformed' and for a set of processes through which the end state is achieved.

This is pertinent for this book, which does not assume or expect to find that conflict structures and relationships have been profoundly changed in Croatia and Serbia as a result of EU engagement, but rather that the processes through which change can be achieved are being initiated, facilitated and socialised by the presence of EU engagement and an EU membership perspective.

Miall *et al.* (1999: 203) have set out the main tasks for transforming conflict and creating peace: transformation of cultures of violence; establishment of a tradition of good governance; healing psychosocial wounds and long-term reconciliation; integration into cooperative and equitable regional structures; and economic development. Likewise, Gadamer (1979) places an emphasis on the need to share an understanding of the key issues of the conflict. Conflict transformation practices engage the parties in conflict in an 'attempt to find a shared reality for the purposes at hand, and the process of searching for a shared reality involves the parties in interpreting meaning and values' (Väyrynen 2001: 8). Gadamer's approach is valuable in that it accounts for the desperate need to *face the past*, come to terms with the crimes and inhuman actions and proceed in a respectful and peaceful way (Gordy 2005). Gadamer's approach is particularly important for an assessment of how the EU contributes to the perception and re-conceptualisation of identity politics, and also what role the EU plays in facilitating the recognition of shared history of war crimes in Croatia. This has resonance in the EU's decision to condition the progression of relations with countries of the former Yugoslavia on their cooperation with the International Criminal Tribunal for war crimes in the former Yugoslavia (ICTY). This limitation makes it necessary to refine the existing approaches and look for commonly distinguishable features in the conflict transformation approach.

These various inputs augment the wealth of the conflict transformation approach but fail to provide a clear analytical framework which could be used in this book. What changes are fundamental to describing the conflicts as experiencing transformation? The diversity found in the literatures complicates any attempt to develop a coherent operational conceptual framework. One way of overcoming this inefficiency is to distinguish what is actually involved in the transformation process.

According to Väyrynen (1991), conflict transformation can happen in different ways: actors, issues, rules and structures of the conflict are transformed.

1   *Actor* transformation takes place through the emergence of new actors and/or parties and internal changes to existing parties/actors.
2   *Issue* transformation alters the political agenda of the conflict.
3   *Rule* alteration involves changing the rules by which the conflict was pursued. To clarify, the rules which parties/actors adhered to during the conflict undergo change as a consequence of which the way in which parties/actors behave is transformed when the rules which govern them change.
4   *Structure* transformation refers to the changes in the interests and positions of actors in a conflict (Väyrynen 1991: 4–7).

Miall (2001) added to Väyrynen's (1991) typology, pointing out that the international context of a conflict is significant. Kriesberg (1989) argues that conflict transformation comprises the conflict parties, conflict issues and the social system in which they are fixed, while Lederach (1995) maintains that it is the relationships between the parties and the change in the overall social system which is central to moving towards tractability. These resonate with the approach adopted by Väyrynen (1991), particularly with his emphasis on parties, issues and structures.

In the attempt to develop a more serviceable approach to conflict transformation it is helpful to acknowledge the overlaps between the indicators set out by Väyrynen (1991), Miall (2001), Gadamer (1979) and Miall *et al.* (1999). The dimensions set out by Väyrynen (1991) and Miall (2001) have some commonalities and overlap, making a transposition of the four dimensions for use in a conceptual framework difficult. It is necessary to be critical of the existing debates in order to develop a coherent framework for understanding conflict transformation and applying it as a lens in the book. The approaches discussed so far do not provide a well-designed analytical framework; thus, this discussion will focus on systematically evaluating the processes of transformation with the intention of establishing a valid and robust analytical framework. This will mean that some of the approaches appraised above will be dismissed while others will be defended and advocated as useful approaches. Ultimately, the book adds to the approaches defended here and the research findings contribute to the Europeanisation and conflict transformation approaches in particular ways.

In Väyrynen's (1991) typology there exist some similarities between the four dimensions which complicate any effort to utilise them in a robust theory of conflict transformation. For example, the actor change can only be understood in reference to the issue change since it is impossible to fully understand the transformation of political actors without examining their attitude towards issues of the conflict. Moreover, the rules of the conflict are an inherent dynamic of the conflict process as opposed to a discernible process of change initiated by EU engagement. Rather, the transformation of rules of conflict relates more to the progress of a conflict and fits more with the ways in which a conflict progresses through various phases of escalation and management. Under Väyrynen's approach, structure transformation explicitly overlaps with the applied definition of actor and issue transformations; in other words, Väyrynen's description of structures shares similar concerns with actor and issue descriptions. Therefore, it is useful to shelve Väyrynen's approach of four characteristics and instead utilise the most robust aspect, that is, structural transformation. This critical evaluation has shown that it is not useful to adopt the four dimensions established by Väyrynen but much more productive to refine his approach to consider purely structural transformation which is defined by change in parties as well as a change in issues.

Most conflict transformation theorists and practitioners concur that structural change is necessary (Albin 2005: 342). In Väyrynen's analysis the structural change consistently appears in the literature on conflict transformation. Miall (2007) points out that the other three types of change are akin to the normal dynamics of conflict. Rupesinghe (1995: 76–7) argues that structural transformation requires attitudinal changes within society and new institutions to address outstanding issues. Therefore, structural transformation can be defined and characterised as the transformation of political parties and agenda issues. In Croatia, the transformation of political parties is particularly important given the attitudes, policies and behaviour of the dominant ruling classes during the 1990s. Moreover, the transformation of principal agendas such as the issue of war crimes is a determinant of structural change. Structural change involves shifts in intra- and inter-party relations as well as agenda issues. It speaks to a wider profound change in which the actors involved in the conflict may be altered so that the conflict is wholly changed. To clarify, this book builds on the approach successfully applied by Albin (2005) by advocating that structure transformation should be understood and analysed in terms of party change (numbers, identities, interests, rhetoric) and issue change. This is an accepted method and is backed up in the literature. Väyrynen's (1991) structure transformation is reproduced and reiterated repetitively in the literature, as is the importance of the role of actors and issues.

Structural transformation alone does not help us to explain the transformation processes; it provides only a partial account of the transformation taking place. The role of relationships between adversaries on conflict issues is also prominent in existing literature. It is a prevalent theme in conflict transformation literature that there needs to be a change in the patterns of interaction between parties to the conflict. The adversaries' relationships with each other must be changed. Curle (1971: 1–20) argues that parties need to move from 'unpeaceful' to 'peaceful' relationships. For Curle, relationships which are mutually harming and demonstrate a limited awareness of the other's position may be transformed into a relationship which is built upon 'active association, planned cooperation and intelligent efforts to forestall or resolve potential conflicts' (1971: 15). Throughout the 1990s, relationship conflict was at the heart of the conflict in Croatia and Serbia. In these states the relationship with ethnic minorities within their territories formed a large part of the problem. Also, the relationship between states, their relationship with each other, as well as the relationship with Bosnia, represented additional dimensions to the conflict. However, as Mitchell (2002) contended, the conflict transformation approach is least clear on what characterises this transformed relationship. To assist in categorising a transformed or transforming relationship, it is helpful to define a changed relationship as a change in the content and nature of qualitative interactions and exchanges between adversaries.

To digress, from a review of the conflict transformation literature it is reasonable to conclude that the approach used to determine transformation is shaped by the overall understanding of conflict. This is why the earlier clarification on the definition of conflict and the understanding of phases of conflict is pertinent. While on a conceptual level the definition of conflict and conflict transformation is necessary for this investigation, it should also be noted that these terms and concepts are also part of the conflict. To make clear, efforts are made by the key parties of the conflicts to define what the conflict is about with a view to ultimately shaping how the conflict is perceived (internally and externally) and having an impact on how the conflict is managed and transformed. With proper caution, the contestation of issues, behaviours and perceptions of a conflict speaks particularly to the relational dimension under investigation. If it is assumed that conflict transformation is defined by profound change, surely transformation occurs, if not in each of the four phases set out above, most certainly in the escalation phase and the final phase: 'transformation'. In the escalation phase, the conflict is transformed from an articulation of incompatibilities to a violent outbreak of hostilities between incompatible parties and interests. Nonetheless, the existing debates on conflict transformation have chosen to focus on the positive aspects of transformation. While this may be the case, it is more important to view both conflict and its transformation in a more open-ended way. To reiterate, the conflict transformation process can involve successes and setbacks for all parties involved.

Existing conflict transformation debates share some common dimensions and agree that the transformation of a conflict entails changes in individuals, structures and relationships. Albin (2005) and Mitchell (2002) agree that dimensions commonly distinguished in the literature involve changes in people, structures and relationships.

For Albin and Mitchell relationships and structure represent the axiomatic, central, fundamental and most important aspects of transformation. Albin (2005: 343) proposes that it is 'often as a result of profound structural and/or relationship changes that other changes occur'. Without relationship changes, structural change may well be in vain. The two are interreliant. Albin places a strong emphasis on the transformation of structure and relationship as central to understanding how a conflict can be transformed (2005: 342). Therefore, emphasis on these two types of change best distinguishes the conflict transformation approach. Structure and relationship change are key to understanding how conflict in Croatia can be transformed. In this book, 'structure' refers to the structure of the conflict. It draws in part on the larger context of the conflict. At the core of a conflict structure and structure change are the parties (the actors) of conflict. Relationship change refers to how the conflict is perceived by each party to the conflict. Relationship change, therefore, examines how parties approach the political agendas of the conflict (issues). Ultimately, for Wallensteen (1991: 130) a transformed conflict 'is one where the parties, the issues and the expectations are changed so that there is no longer a fear of war arising from the relationship'.

At the core of structure transformation are *the parties*, which can be defined by the number of parties, their identities, representation and power, and *issues*, which can be defined as the number and nature of issues in dispute. Central to relationship transformation is how each party perceives the conflict in terms of its own interests and their situation in relation to the other, and then how it acts upon those perceptions and the behaviour of its adversaries.

Ultimately, this assessment has demonstrated that conflict transformation theories are relevant to and make significant contributions to international relations and socio-political sciences. Research into conflict transformation is an important part of the study of international conflicts.[11] Conflict is widespread and costly (Brown 1996: 3). Armed conflict creates genocide, ethnic cleansing, rape, displacement and other abhorrences that have immediate and long-term effects on the nature of conflict and the opportunities for peace. The extensive and invasive implications of violent conflict represent convincing arguments for the continued need for original scholarship on the impact of conflict and conflict transformation. By conducting further research into the sources and nature of conflict and its transformation it is possible to develop innovative and appropriate mechanisms for transforming conflict. The central achievement of conflict transformation approaches, and part of the reason why they are so appropriate for this book, is that they seek to enhance the understanding of conflicts while also deepening the understanding of how conflicts can be transformed. By identifying the symptoms of the conflict, it is possible to trace the causes of the conflict. Thus, clarifying the symptoms of a conflict makes it easier to attend to the deep-rooted sources of a conflict.

Qualitative methodology

Existing literatures on conflict transformation or on Europeanisation do not analyse adequately the situation and processes of change in Croatia and Serbia. Croatia and Serbia's integration into the EU not only requires the traditional 'member state building' associated with the pre-accession process but also necessitates dealing with the legacies of the conflicts of the 1990s. How the mechanisms of integration with the EU and the prospect of joining the EU provide the EU with an opportunity to transform the structures and relationships of conflict in aspiring member states must be clarified.

This leads to a key question: how can the processes of integration with the EU and the prospect of becoming a member of the EU transform the structures and relationships of conflict?

Since the structures and relationships of conflict centre on parties, issues and party perceptions of conflict, a direct link exists with the nature and design of EU intervention in the case studies. To clarify, the nature and design of the EU's conditionality and social learning strategies target the political (as well as technical) criteria associated with membership. Thus, EU conditions and socialisation are aimed at the structures and relationships of conflict, not just the technical preparations for membership. This is what makes the book valuable and interesting. It is not another analysis of the impact of the EU on a policy area or institutional development. Rather, it is focused on how the EU's mechanisms of integration and attraction directly cause the political parties to the conflict, the agenda issues and the party perceptions of the conflict to change.

There is no accepted paradigm for analysing and judging how a conflict is transformed, or even what a transformed conflict would look like. Moreover, there is no accepted framework for assessing the EU's impact on conflict transformation. This section establishes how we can recognise a process of transformation and what role the processes of integration with, and the prospect of joining, the EU play in achieving transformation.

The diversity and lack of agreement within conflict transformation literatures necessitate that the book limits the conceptual framework and focus on two areas. Albin (2005: 342) places a strong emphasis on the transformation of structure and relationship as central to understanding how a conflict can be transformed. Emphasis on these two types of change can best distinguish the transformation of conflict. No matter how different they appear, transformed conflicts will share some common dimensions, most significantly that people, structures and relationships will change. These dimensions of conflict are at the heart of the transformation of conflict. Therefore, structure and relationship are central to understanding how conflict and the legacies of conflict in Croatia and Serbia can be transformed.

In this book, 'structure' transformation is concerned with the transformation of the conflict parties (their interests, identities and representation), and conflict agenda issues which are disputed. In the cases of Croatia and Serbia this can be extensively explored by investigating the transformation of the key political *parties* and a key conflict *issue*, cooperation with the ICTY.

Here, 'relationship' change refers to how the parties to the conflict perceive the conflict and how political parties interact with one another on central issues. It is important to clarify that 'relationships' refers to how each party of the conflict perceives the other parties to the conflict and how they perceive the way in which power is distributed between the parties. Moreover, it is about how adversaries, who are already engaged in a relationship, change the relationship. To clarify, a relationship transformation may mean that the mutual relations between parties will experience a qualitative change. This has implications for how the parties interact with one another in terms of the balance of power between parties, whether they have effective relationships or whether their relationships are competitive, hostile or cooperative. In Croatia and Serbia, relationship transformation can be examined by analysing the political elites' and the governments' relationships with refugees, Bosnia and, more specifically, Bosnian Serbs and

Bosnian Croats, as well as their attitude to other issues of conflict. In the case of Serbia, the relationship with Montenegro will also be considered.

In both structures and relationships of conflict, credence is given to power. In conflict situations, such as in Croatia and Serbia, power is significant in the transformation of conflict specifically in relation to how the balance of power changes over time (Väyrynen 1991; Miall 2001; Curle 1971; Albin 2005). According to Albin (2005: 343), securing structural power over resources enables a party to 'pressurise or coerce another to do something against its will', whereas relational power refers to the 'ability to persuade a party to do something it otherwise would not have done'. The attainment of structural and/or relational power can produce effective results for the political parties. Therefore, it is important for the book to consider the impact of the structural and relational power of political parties in both Croatia and Serbia.

Much of the existing discourse on Europeanisation has focused on the EU's transformative capacity in aspiring member states. Europeanisation is important to studying the effects of the EU on conflict in Croatia and Serbia as the two cases have established contractual relations with the EU within the wider context of becoming a member of the EU. This study is confined to assessing the impacts of the processes of change driven by the pre-accession and accession requirements. As suggested by the literature review, the book assumes that the EU has an impact on the political systems and institutions in Croatia and Serbia because these countries are engaged in a pre-accession process. With this assumption, the book investigates the effects of the EU enlargement approach on conflict transformation.

As will be shown in Chapter 2, the nature of the EU's relations with Croatia and Serbia, which centred on trade, aid, sanctions, technical assistance and crisis management between 1990 and 1999, shifted towards a deeper integration with the EU after 2000. A determining factor of this transformative capacity relates to the degree of integration; the closeness or perceived closeness of EU membership affects the transformative power of integration with the EU. Central to this analysis is that degrees of integration with the EU can be traced. This is important for two reasons. First, it allows analysis of the degree of integration necessary for the transformative power of integration to be most effective. Second, it provides an analysis of how EU engagement evolves in response to conflict in states with an integration and membership perspective. Thus, it is possible to understand the impact of various stages of integration and the impact that each of these stages has had on the transformation of conflict. For example, we can trace EU engagement chronologically in terms of ongoing financial assistance, diplomatic endeavours, through to feasibility reports, opening of Stabilisation and Association Agreement negotiations and accession status. Essentially through EU integration, conditionality and social learning, the EU is seeking to make aspirants able to function as EU member states; in essence, making aspirants more like them. However, the response of Croatia and Serbia to this 'member-state building' should be taken into account (International Commission on the Balkans 2005).

Assessing the impact of integration with the EU on conflict in Croatia and Serbia requires an examination of the timing, design and impact of political conditionality and social learning at each stage of integration with the EU. The stages of integration are utilised because integration into the EU is an evolving process in two senses. First, the process of integration is evolutionary in terms of development and deepening. As an aspirant candidate achieves progress at one stage, it can move on to the next stage, where political and financial rewards and expectations grow. Second, integration with the EU is an evolutionary process; the integration process with the EU is reflexive and, as a result of the reflexivity, it evolves and changes. To clarify, the pre-accession processes experienced by the 2004 accession candidates were very different from those experienced by the 2007 accession states, not only because of the different countries involved but also because the technical processes of integration changed in response to earlier lessons learned.

This study measures the impact of EU influence on conflict in Croatia and Serbia. According to Grabbe (2006: 86), the EU's influence 'seems to defy measurement precisely because EU influence is interwoven with domestic politics and other external influences'. Despite the methodological limitations of studying EU influence, it is possible to identify adaptational pressures from the EU and judge the outcome of these pressures. How can such adaptational pressures be identified, and in what ways can their outcome be judged? Adaptational pressures from the EU can be defined as conditionality and socialisation mechanisms. It is possible to judge clearly the intended outcomes of political conditionality and social learning mechanisms from the ambitions stated by EU agencies and documents and then judge their successes based on how the outcome relates to their stated intentions. The literature on Europeanisation suggests that the domestic impact of EU adaptational pressures may be varied. This is when the framework of Albert *et al.* (2004) becomes important. Albert *et al.* have suggested that through compulsory and enabling impacts the EU can exert adaptational pressures on the domestic aspiring member states. In the compulsory impact, the EU can compel actors to change their policies. This relates to Grabbe's claims that Europeanisation pressures have the effect of empowering modernisers to change policies and create policy space for new initiatives (2006: 51). The enabling impact suggests that the EU can exert adaptational pressures to persuade political parties to change interests and behaviours in the new context brought about by the ripening of the conflict and the possibilities of EU integration.

This examination of the mechanisms of EU integration and accession dynamics reveals the conditions and circumstances under which the EU can have greatest impact. Building on Kelley's (2006) study, this book specifically investigates the processes of integration with the EU through the Stabilisation and Association process and the use of institutional membership as an incentive impact on conflict. In addition, it investigates how the benefits that accompany progress towards admission, with specific attention paid to the timing and design of conditionality and social learning strategies, have impacted the structures and relationships of conflict in Croatia and Serbia.

Case studies and time frame

Because this book seeks to understand the role of integration mechanisms with the EU on structures and relationships of conflict, it focuses its assessment mostly on the post-2000 period in Croatia and Serbia. These two countries provide a compelling analytical set: they have shared experiences of conflict, history and culture; they each have an EU membership perspective; and they have experienced ethnic conflict, vociferous and violent war between each other and with other states, as well as conflict between political elites. Thus, there are good grounds for a comparative analysis. The varied nature of conflict in Croatia and Serbia represented a challenge for this study. The conflicts experienced in Croatia and Serbia were ethnic in nature, wars between states and conflicts between political elites within the countries. While choosing countries that are former territories of Yugoslavia narrows the scope of the investigation, the case studies provide a rich comparative basis without compromising the validity of the research. Ultimately, the varied nature of the conflicts experienced in Croatia and Serbia has implications for the outcomes of the conflict transformation process. As the findings of the book show, these differences determined, in part, the impact that the EU's mechanisms could have on the transformation process in the cases.

Croatia and Serbia share similar features in terms of the structural and relationship dimensions of conflict. This adds to and is central to the case study selection in this book. The structural and relational aspects of conflict which were set out above facilitate an understanding of the initiation, escalation, management and transformation of conflict in Croatia and Serbia. In the initial and escalation stages, most fundamental to the war between Croatia and Serbia were the nature and number of issues involved. It was a conflict over ethnic identities and groups, political interests and territorial claims and power. In terms of the structures of conflict, Croatia and Serbia share similar experiences. During the *initial* stage of conflict and the *escalation* of conflict in Croatia and Serbia in 1991 the structures and relationships of conflict were intensified and politicised. In both case studies, throughout the 1990s a regime pursued violent and conflictual strategies. Chapter 2 analyses the nature and impact of EU engagement in Croatia and Serbia during the 1990s and argues that the EC/EU's engagement had very little success in stopping intercommunal ethnic violence from getting worse. As in Northern Ireland during the late 1960s and early 1970s when violent conflict was intensifying, there was little that outside intervention could achieve. There are opposing views on this. On the one hand, once violent conflict has commenced and escalates it is much more difficult to achieve successful mediation. On the other hand, there is also a view that escalation can either lead to negotiation or worsen conflict (Zartman and Faure 2005). In a situation where tit-for-tat violence builds on itself in perceived logical cycles it is arguable that mediation attempts will be ineffective. Therefore, it is argued in Chapter 2 that during the initiation and escalation periods of conflict in Croatia and Serbia it was unlikely that EU intervention could have had any impact.

Beginning with the structure, Croatia's aspiration and battle for independence was fought by many *parties* at many levels. Croatian independence was contested at local and national level by political parties. In the late 1980s and early 1990s, before the advent of Serbian hegemonism with the arrival of Milošević on the political landscape, the incompatibilities over Croatian independence among political parties in Croatia were increasingly relevant. As Cviić (1991) points out, in 1987 Serbs comprised 11.6 per cent of Croatia's population yet made up 19.4 per cent of all party members. This was compounded by Serbs holding key managerial, administrative and security posts in Croatia. Therefore, in the face of mounting calls for Croatian independence, Serb authorities branded these claims as a threat to 'brotherhood and unity' (Cviić 1991: 72). According to Soberg (2007: 33), a key player involved in Croatia's 'journey from a republic in socialist Yugoslavia to an independent, democratic state' was the Croatian Democratic Union (HDZ) under the leadership of Franjo Tuđman.[12]

Tuđman was elected president of Croatia's *Sabor* (Parliament) on 30 May 1990 after an election in which the HDZ, with 41.5 per cent of the vote, won 58 per cent of seats in parliament.[13] Following his election Tudman focused on achieving a successful transition from communism and realising Croatian independence from Yugoslavia (Cohen 1997: 76). However, as Cviić points out, Tudman and the HDZ were reluctant to pursue Croatian independence until declaring it on 25 June 1991, because of the recognised vulnerability to Serb army pressure. According to Soberg (2007: 37), the focus of the HDZ and Tudman on independence and statehood lessened the priority of democratisation in Croatia and Serbia. As the dominant party in Croatia, the HDZ's pursuit of Croatian independence was its primary interest during the initial and escalation period of conflict.

Fundamental to explaining the element of structure in the formation and violent expression of conflict in Croatia and Serbia during the early 1990s is the nature of the *issues* involved. The conflict in Croatia and Serbia between 1991 and 1995 was a conflict over many issues: political interests, territorial sovereignty and ethnic identities and symbolism. At the centre of the conflict in Croatia was the presence of a sizable minority of Croatian Serbs in Croatia which complicated the aspiration for territorial sovereignty and ethnic homogeneity. The Croatian Serbs rejected any option of Croatian independence because of fears of how they would be treated under an independent Croatia; fears based on the recent memory of Serb persecution under Pavelic's Croatia. According to Bideleux and Jeffries (2007: 197), upon his election, Tudman refused minority rights to the 600,000 Croatian Serbs, and rejected any demands for territorial autonomy, which alienated the Croatian Serb minority. Then the Tudman regime utilised and promoted the revival of Ustaše symbolism, which compounded the political alienation of Croatian Serbs and further polarised Croatian society along ethnic lines (Soberg 2007: 38).[14] This negatively impacted intercommunal relations between Serbs and Croats, especially in the Knin and Krajina regions. Serbs in Krajina proclaimed themselves part of Serbia in March 1991. The political alienation of the Croatian Serb community was further aggravated by the successful re-election of the HDZ and Tudman in 1992 which demonstrated, according to Cohen, that Croatian nationalism was 'respectful and popular' (Cohen 1997: 92). The domestic policies pursued by Tudman and the HDZ during the initial and escalation period of the conflict, which attracted most criticism and attention from the international community, were those directed at the Serb minority living in Croatia. Tudman recognised that the Serb minority, which comprised approximately 13 per cent of the population, presented the most significant challenge to his authority and to Croatia (Meier 1999: 146).[15] In 1995 the incompatibility of the structure of conflict was manifested in violence in Krajina. On 4 August

1995 Tudman launched Operation Storm in which Croatia retook the Krajina region, leading ethnic Serbs to flee. Bideleux and Jeffries (2007: 523) contends that this exodus was encouraged by 'ruthless Croatian attacks on fleeing Croatian Serb civilians, as well as by the looting and destruction of Croatian Serb homes and offices'.

In the initial and escalation stages of conflict in Serbia, the structure of conflict is fundamental. In Serbia, as with Croatia, the interests of political *parties* added to the manifestation and development of violent conflict. The key political party to dominate Serbian politics in the 1990s was the Socialist Party under the presidency of Milošević. Milošević was elected President of Serbia in 1990.[16] Cviić (1991: 69) lays blame on Milošević for inspiring spoiler violence among Serbs in Croatia, and Slovenia, which led to the escalation of the conflict.

The situation in Bosnia is pivotal to understanding the escalation of conflict in Croatia and Serbia. Indeed, at this point, relational and structural elements of conflict help explain clearly the escalation of conflict. The main *parties* to the escalation of conflict between Serbia and Croatia over the *issue* of territory in Bosnia were Croatia and Serbia and their proxies in Bosnia. Two months after Cyrus Vance negotiated a ceasefire in Croatia and Serbia, Bosnia-Hercegovina proclaimed its independence (29 February 1992). Indeed, the actions of the EC were a major factor in Bosnia's declaration of independence. In the aftermath, Bosnian Serbs under the leadership of Karadžić created their own independent state, Republika Srpska, which was heavily supported, politically, militarily and financially, by the Milošević regime in Belgrade. A conference convened by Carrington and Cutiliero proposed to divide Bosnia into three ethnically based cantons which had the support of the parties to the conflict: Croatia and Serbia, and the Bosnian Serbs. However, the lack of financial, military or political support for Bosnia left much of Bosnia vulnerable to violent attack by Milošević and Karadžić (Sharp 1997: 107). This vulnerability was further intensified by the outbreak of hostilities between Bosnian Muslims and Bosnian Croats. The Vance-Owen peace plan in 1993 moved away from the Carrington-Cutiliero plan and sought to maintain the multi-ethnic nature of Bosnia. By 1994 international support focused on strengthening Muslim Croat capabilities in the face of a strong Serbian force. By summer 1995 the fall of Srebrenica and the attacks on Sarajevo prompted the USA, France and Britain under the aegis of NATO to launch a bombing campaign on Serbia and Bosnian Serbs. Also, in the summer of 1995 the Croatia Serbian conflict escalated in the West Slavonia and Krajina areas when the Croatian army regained the areas which had been held by Croatian Serbs.

In the efforts to negotiate an end to war in the countries of the former Yugoslavia, an agreement was compelled by the USA in Dayton, Ohio in November 1995. It was later signed in Paris (14 December 1995) by the Bosnian president Alija Izetbegović, the Serbian president Slobodan Milošević and the Croatian president Franjo Tuđman. It was during this *management* stage of the conflict that the opportunity for structural and relational change was possible. The management of the structures of conflict was particularly difficult to achieve agreement on because of the number of *parties* involved: Serbia, Croatia, Bosnian Serbs, Croatian Serbs, Bosnian Muslims, as well as the EU, the USA, the UN and Russia. The primary *issues* for management at Dayton were the borders of Bosnia, a federation between Muslim and Croatian parties and the future of eastern Slavonia. Ultimately, the *relationship* element of conflict managed at Dayton was the relationships between the parties and their perceptions not only of the conflict but of the agreement reached.

The conflict in Serbia was not wholly *managed* at Dayton. Rather, the Kosovo issue had been deliberately left off the agenda at Dayton. By 1998 the structure of conflict between Kosovo and Serbia was initiated and escalated. This is not to imply that Kosovo was a source of instant conflict, since Kosovo had not been a source of conflict for much of the 1990s. The murder of a Kosovo Albanian by Serb forces at a demonstration in March 1998 heightened the expression of incompatibilities between the Kosovo and Serbian *parties*. The EU sought to intervene in the escalating conflict in Kosovo and Serbia by using sanctions against the Milošević regime in Serbia. The emergence of an ultra-nationalist party in Serbia, the Serbian Radical Party, represented a further complication for the *parties* of the conflict in Serbia. For example, the EU decided to freeze funds, launch an oil embargo and impose flight bans on the Milošević regime.

The relational aspects also explain the conflict in Croatia and Serbia since the 1990s. In the initial and escalation stages of the conflict Croatia's and Serbia's perceptions of the conflict became increasingly clear and salient. During these phases of the Croatian war for independence, the country's perceptions of the conflict focused on its own aspirations for territorial sovereignty, which it perceived to be incompatible with those of the Serbian political elites. Furthermore, the presence of a large minority of Croatian Serbs within Croatian territory presented a problem for the Croatian political elites who aspired to achieve Croatian independence from the Federal Republic of Yugoslavia (FRY).

At the same time, the case studies in this book provide a compelling testing ground for the assumption that attraction of EU membership can transform conflict in aspiring member states. Another major reason for choosing these cases is the nature of their contractual relations with the EU. The different rates of progress make the cases interesting for comparison. After all, Croatia and Serbia are both exposed to similar consistent elements: a single set of instruments coordinated by similar institutions and personnel. Yet the two states are progressing very differently on the journey towards EU membership. Croatia is more advanced, having commenced accession negotiations, while Serbia only initialled its Stabilisation and Association Agreement in 2007. The case studies of Croatia and Serbia utilised in the book assist the investigation of the evolving capacity of the EU's mechanisms to transform structures and relationships of conflict. Specific attention is paid to the development of new forms of contractual agreements and relationships between the EU and Croatia and Serbia, namely the Stabilisation and Association Agreements, which were specifically tailored to the structures and relationships of conflict from the 1990s.

Another reason why these case studies were chosen is because they remain, at the time of investigation, outside the EU. The chosen case studies are not members, regardless of the existence of 'fuzzy' borders. Therefore, this permits an investigation of the power of attraction of membership. The countries of the former Yugoslavia border are part of the EU's periphery. Examination of how the EU deals with transformation of conflict outside its own member states and therefore outside its immediate zone of (arguably) direct influence provides insights into two areas: core–periphery relations and member–non-member relations. Incorporating a study of core–periphery relations is important as it reflects not only on the periphery's identities, strategies and policies but also on those at the core. Buzan (1991: 433) points out that a major question for states in the periphery is how their own security agenda will be affected by the new patterns of security among the major powers.

The case studies of Croatia and Serbia are exceptionally useful for examining the transformative capacity of EU integration on conflict. As will be shown in Chapter 2, the EU's relationships with Croatia and Serbia have been closely linked to the crises in Yugoslavia and the EU's evolving capacity to deal with these crises. Croatia and Serbia constitute valuable case studies of the uncertainty of Europeanisation in post-war societies. Country comparison is a useful way of looking at a political phenomenon (such as Europeanisation) in one or more countries. Furthermore, comparative case studies enable countries to be classified and therefore more easily understood. In the case of Croatia and Serbia we can classify them in three ways: transition states, states recovering from conflict, and in terms of their

relationship to the EU (Croatia is a candidate state, while Serbia is a 'potential' candidate state, at time of submission).

Investigation of these cases highlights how the transformative influence
of the integration with the EU varies at different levels of pre-accession and
accession process. The stability of Croatia and Serbia is important for the
stability of the entire region. Arguably there is a definite need for stability in
Croatia and Serbia – if not, everything else falls apart (Glenny 2005). Furthermore, these case studies are important for understanding how the EU is
perceived in the region. Croatia and Serbia represent comparable cases for
the focused comparison of strategy. Choosing these countries of the former
Yugoslavia allows this research to be 'more intensive and less extensive',
thereby examining the nuances of each country study (Landman 2003: 28).
This research draws on the similarities between Croatia and Serbia and then
points to differences between them to examine if and why their experience
of conflict transformation and engagement with the EU has been similar or
different.

In sum, Croatia and Serbia share key features which are crucial to
the book: they were both countries of the former Yugoslavia, they both
endured violent conflicts during the 1990s and they were both exposed to
engagement with the EU. However, differences exist and will be examined
during this research: the degree of integration into the EU, socio-economic
advancement, political stability and capacity to harmonise and implement
EU laws and norms. Investigation of these factors enables an understanding
of how the EU can impact conflict transformation in Croatia and Serbia.
However, to analyse and assess the EU's capacity to impact the transformation of conflict in the former Yugoslavia it is imperative to assess the
circumstances that brought about the end of Yugoslavia. An overview of the
events which dissolved Yugoslavia places the EU's engagement in the wider
context and provides for a more complete, less disjointed appraisal of the
EU in Yugoslavia.

To understand the key issues involved in this research it is necessary to
place the book in the wider historical context. Therefore, analysis will draw
on EU engagement with the chosen cases since the outbreak of conflict in
1990. Owing to the precedent of EC enlargement and the emerging like-
lihood of EU enlargement to Central and Eastern Europe, the prospect
of becoming a member of the EU would have emerged for Croatia and
Serbia in early 1990. However, internal dynamics took over in Yugoslavia
that pushed the idea of achieving an EU membership perspective far into
the background. As the key question of the book relates to the transformative power of EU integration, it is necessary to examine the relationships

thematically, in terms of the events of integration. Therefore, the book is concerned with the qualitatively different nature of relations between 1990 and 1999, and after 2000, when the EU strategy began to intensify. The book takes 1999/2000 as a turning point when the EU membership perspective became much more visible following the launch of the Stability Pact in 1999 and the Santa Maria de Feira European Council decision in 2000.

This book is particularly interested in the post-2000 era, when varying degrees of integration in Croatia and Serbia reveal much about the EU's transformative capacity on conflict transformation. With the inauguration of reformist governments in Croatia and Serbia and across the Western Balkans in 2000, it was time to launch a more intensified strategy. The first sign of this intensified strategy came in June 2000, when the European Council confirmed:

> that its objective remains the fullest possible integration of the countries of the region into the political and economic mainstream of Europe through the Stabilisation and Association process, political dialogue, liberalisation of trade and cooperation in Justice and Home Affairs. All the countries concerned are potential candidates for EU membership.[17]

However, with Milošević's leadership in Belgrade looking increasingly untenable, the European Council confirmed that 'a democratic, cooperative FRY living in peace with its neighbours will be a welcome member of the European family of democratic nations'.[18] After the removal of Milošević on 24 September 2000, the EU held a further summit to commence this more intense strategy. At the Zagreb summit in November 2000, post-Milošević, the EU reaffirmed 'the European perspective of the countries participating in the stabilisation and association process and their status as potential candidates for membership in accordance with the Feira conclusions'.[19] These were concrete signals that integration with the EU and membership of the EU was increasingly visible for the countries of the Western Balkans. Therefore, it is in this post-2000 period that the book is primarily interested.

2

THE EU, CROATIA AND
SERBIA, 1990–99

This chapter details the case studies dealt with in this book, namely, the relationship between the EU and Croatia and Serbia. I examine the development of relations between Croatia, Serbia and the EU during the period under investigation (1990–2000). The year 1990 marks the onset of violence in the Balkans. This chapter explains the types of intervention and the rationale behind the episodic interventions. For much of the 1990s the EU was constrained because of limited capacities and contradictory member state interests, yet it consistently attempted to engage more proactively with the escalating conflict. The failure to impose its goals on the conflict is important as it highlights the policy and power limitations of the EU during a period when it first began to present itself as an actor in the area of conflict transformation.

While the EU acted according to its strengths by providing economic incentives, the inconsistent diplomatic initiatives were insufficient. The ends to which diplomatic initiatives were used will be discussed below. At the time of an embryonic Common Foreign and Security Policy (CFSP), the EU was not prepared or equipped to act militarily in Croatia and Serbia during the 1990s, which meant that targeted sanctions and diplomatic endeavours were diluted by the absence of a threat of physical force. At the same time, and quite appropriately, some EU member states and institutions were willing to negotiate with but not to offer any incentives such as closer integration or membership to Serbia and Croatia because of ethnic cleansing and the violent wars. The EU member states deemed this an inappropriate background to offer the traditional instruments of external engagement such as economic assistance, prospects of association and membership. Clearly, during the initiation and escalation of violent conflict in

Croatia, Serbia and Bosnia, the integration and enlargement instruments were wholly inappropriate. Therefore, pursuance of the *civilian* power approach, which eschewed a military approach, along with the emerging presence of other international actors such as the USA, NATO and the UN, progressively marginalised the EU in the 1990s.

A marginalised actor?

Relations between the EU and Yugoslavia date back to a non-preferential Agreement (1970) which was succeeded in 1973 by an Agreement that included an EC–Yugoslavia Joint Committee. The Joint Committee facilitated negotiations that led to the signing of a Cooperation Agreement on 25 February 1980. These agreements were primarily economic in nature and the institutional relationship between the EC and Yugoslavia was fortified in 1980 with the establishment of the Commission Delegation in Belgrade (European Commission 1988). Writing in 1990, Karadzole pointed out that Yugoslavia was a European country in that it was 'firmly planted in the European continent and an integral part of its common cultural and historical heritage', and that Europe was Yugoslavia's 'common home, our common heritage and our common destiny' (1990: 93). A rapprochement in relations between what was then the European Economic Community (EEC) and Yugoslavia occurred in January 1988 when several Members of the European Parliament (MEPs) argued that Yugoslavia should join the EEC (Agence Europe 21 January 1988). Later, in 1988, the EEC held the first 'political dialogue' meeting with Yugoslavia, with Greek foreign affairs minister Mr Papoulias chairing the meeting. At this 'political dialogue' the issue of closer integration between the EEC and Yugoslavia was raised in the wider context of the future nature of the EEC, be it 'fortress Europe' or a more open grouping (Agence Europe 21 December 1988). This revealed an early aspiration in Yugoslavia for closer links between Yugoslavia and the EEC and vice versa. Throughout 1988, Yugoslavia often featured on the agenda of MEP discussions, which casts significant doubt on claims that Yugoslavia was *terra incognita* for the EC to excuse EEC failure. Undoubtedly, the EEC was informed of the looming crisis in Yugoslavia. A report by MEP Rossetti in January 1988 stated that 'serious differences among the various republics have appeared ... which could affect the country's political stability' (Agence Europe 14 January 1988). This provided evidence that the prospect of joining the EEC did feature in political discourse within the former Yugoslavia in the early period of the unfolding crisis. Still, the ensuing crisis and war of dissolution in Yugoslavia interrupted any development of relations between the EEC and Yugoslavia.

Existing debates rightly point out that the crisis in Yugoslavia exposed the limits of the EU in terms of its capacity for external relations (Gow 1994). In these debates the EU's ineffectiveness was characterised as 'a period of disorientation and hesitation' (Grabar-Kitarović 2007). The consensus in academic literature on the Balkans is that throughout much of the 1990s the EU 'was not an effective international actor in terms both of its capacity to produce collective decisions and its impact on events' (Hill 1993). Cameron (2006: 100) argues that the EU lacked 'cohesion, determination and instruments' to bring the evolving crisis under control. Nuttall (1994: 22) argues that the EU was neither willing nor able to send a military force to deal with the crisis in the former Yugoslavia. Moreover, criticism of the EU is also found in elite discourse: speaking in his annual address King Baudouin of Belgium launched a scathing attack on the 'excessively timid response' which was 'deplorable' and jeopardised European collective security (Agence Europe 28/29 December 1992). The EU lacked political cohesion, momentum and confidence, as well as the instruments to realise its political ambitions, which ultimately relegated the EU to a marginal role alongside the United States and the North Atlantic Treaty Organisation (NATO) and limited the EU's capacity to transform conflict in Yugoslavia; it is correct to say that the EU was 'present but not operational'.[1]

The division and reluctance that permeated the EU's handling of the dissolution of Yugoslavia caused it to play a subsidiary role to the United States and NATO during the early 1990s. The institutional incompatibility of an infant CFSP and the salience of member state national foreign policy interests explained why the EU's effectiveness was constrained. For Hill and Wallace the crisis in Yugoslavia demonstrated the 'contradiction between the ambitions of EU member governments to play a larger international role and their reluctance to move beyond an intergovernmental framework in doing so' (1996: 5). For Papadimitriou, the dissolution of Yugoslavia and the escalating war in Bosnia highlighted 'the difficulties of subordinating national agendas under an EU-led foreign policy' (2001: 81). Plainly, the Yugoslav crisis revealed the EU for what it was, regardless of any alternative ambitions: an economic actor with the capacity for financial sanctions or the reward of financial aid as the only weapons in its arsenal in the case of the Western Balkans. While some debates reveal a more sympathetic approach to explaining the EU's failures (Lendvai 1991: 260), it is important to examine critically the nature, timing and design of the EU's intervention in the initiation, escalation and management of conflict in Croatia and Serbia throughout the 1990s.[2]

From the outset, the initiation of conflict had been framed as a European problem. Jacques Poos stated: 'This is the hour of Europe. It is not the hour of the Americans', and the Italian foreign minister confirmed, 'Washington is being kept informed but is not being consulted' (*New York Times* 1991b). According to Santer, 'Yugoslavia is on our doorstep and it is not in our interest to see it destabilised' (*New York Times* 1991a). Yugoslav President Markovic reasserted the framing of the dissolution as a European one when he argued that the EC had a significant role to play in Yugoslavia in the 1990s (Agence Europe 16 November 1990). MEPs played an important role in framing the dissolution of Yugoslavia as a European conflict: 'a solution to the problem of Yugoslavia will only be possible with a European commitment and international mediation' (Agence Europe 13 February 1991). Therefore, a great expectation emerged within the EC, the Yugoslav republics and the wider international community that the EC could engage proactively to quell the emerging violent crisis during the initiation of conflict. Moreover, arguably, despite the murmurings in the late 1980s of Slovenian and Croatian independence, at the outset the international community avoided ethnic and nationalist framing of the conflict in favour of encouraging democratisation and liberalisation within the status quo, which was Yugoslavia (Edwards 1997: 174).

Maintaining the territorial integrity of Yugoslavia was the central approach of the EC and the international community during the initiation period of conflict. Therefore, attempts by Croatia to legitimise its territorial claims internationally were ineffective during this initiation period. By summer 1991 the emergence of violence and Serb autonomy declarations in Krajina meant that the patterns of exchanges between Serbia and Croatia added to the intractability of the conflict between the two states. Earlier, in 1990, the EC offered a conditional carrot for closer economic and political links between the EC and Yugoslavia. The April 1990 European Council meeting confirmed that an Association Agreement could be established if 'certain political and economic conditions are reunited in Yugoslavia' (Agence Europe 31 May 1990). This was a significant incentive by the EC to stabilise and maintain territorial integrity in Yugoslavia, but it was not embraced by Yugoslavia as it had been more concerned with Community aid than with deepening institutional links (Agence Europe 9 March 1990). Furthermore, the mistimed offer of an Association Agreement failed to impact on the increasing intractability of interests between parties of the conflict. The EC was not blatantly at fault here since it was only starting to recognise and formulate an external role in Eastern Europe and the Balkans. Nonetheless, it is possible to deduce that the carrot offered by the EC to the parties to help deal with the embryonic conflict was insufficient and badly timed.

The additional offer of an economic carrot to the countries of the former Yugoslavia by the President of the European Community Commission, Jaques Delors, in 1991 likewise proved futile. Delors offered an Association Agreement and aid (US$4 billion) if a peaceful solution of Yugoslavia's internal conflicts could be reached, and 'assert[ed] that the community would refuse to recognize breakaway republics or offer them benefits' (Hoffmann 1994: 98). On 2 December 1991 the EC restored trade relations and financial aid to the republics of Yugoslavia (excluding Serbia and Montenegro). This demonstration of support by the EC for the EC peace initiative persuaded Serbs that the EC was not neutral. Hodge contends that Milošević 'wasted no time in exploiting the EC disarray' and dispatched military forces to the Croatian border, affecting Dubrovnik, Vuckovar and the Croatian ports (2006: 12). Early humanitarian assistance was available through OBNOVA and, latterly, the PHARE Community programmes.[3] Overall, the EC's approach to Yugoslavia during the initiation period centred on economic assistance and political incentives rather than accession, and these incentives were poorly timed, were inconsistent and did not provide sufficient reason for the regimes in both cases to change tack.

Contradictions between member state attitudes and favoured strategies continued as the war in Yugoslavia escalated. Framing Yugoslavia as a European problem with a European solution was ineffective because of indecision and infighting between EC institutions and between EC member states. Mainly the EC produced numerous declarations of concern. EC reluctance and incapacity to have an impact on the dissolution of Yugoslavia was clear at the meeting of EC foreign ministers on 23 October 1990 when the message from the Twelve was one of 'concern about the attacks against the integrity of the Yugoslav state' (Agence Europe 23 October 1990). On 4 February 1991 the Twelve pleaded against the resort to force and advocated the maintenance of Yugoslavia's territorial integrity (Agence Europe 6 February 1991). Arguably, the manner in which the EC dealt with the dissolution of Yugoslavia was seen as likely to act as a precedent in other cases, and showed the EC's 'muddle' when EC member states were reluctant to state their aims and the means of pursuing them (Edwards 1997). Failure was compounded by the fear of precedent-setting behaviour and by an equally significant fear of not learning from lessons in the past. This was most evident in the British attitude on intervention in Yugoslavia in 1992:

Peacemaking would be a rather dramatic step. We have often reminded our partners of our own experience in Northern Ireland – it is much easier to get in than to get out (*New York Times* 1992).[4]

The claims for Slovenian, Bosnian and Croatian independence represented an opportunity for the EC to influence the structures and relationships of conflict during this initiation period. Instead, member states failed to adhere to and proffer common EC policy on recognising secession and the independence of Yugoslavia. Constantly aware of their domestic considerations, the EC Twelve were reluctant to recognise independence or the redrawing of borders as the MEPs were ever-fearful that the dissolution of Yugoslavia would be 'contagious' and followed by demands for autonomy within the Twelve (Agence Europe 14 May 1992). Challenged by the escalating violence in Croatia, Serbia and Bosnia, the EC insisted that the internal borders of the former Yugoslavia remain unchanged (Agence Europe 28 March 1992). A fear existed that the dissolution of Yugoslavia could trigger instability across Europe and beyond; national frontiers had to remain sacrosanct (Lewis 1993: 123). The immediate response of the EC to the dissolution of Yugoslavia was twofold: first, to maintain unity, supporting the federation of Yugoslavia, and, second, not to intervene militarily. Therefore, during this initiation period the EC's strategies targeted the structures and relationships of conflict.

The ambition to maintain unity focused on the political parties involved in the conflict and their patterns of exchange. The Brioni Accords of July 1991 urged diplomacy, dialogue and negotiations, not military response, and promoted the unity of Yugoslavia. To maintain unity the international community embarked upon a series of negotiations and mediations with all parties involved. Favouring mediation rather than military intervention presupposed dialogue with all parties involved and a refusal to designate an aggressor. Success was fleeting. The persistence of war between Serbia and Croatia from 1991 through to 1995 rendered futile the EC/EU hopes that their policies of preventative diplomacy and economic incentives would be sufficient to induce cooperation and peaceful mechanisms of conflict settlement between Serbia and Croatia. The EC hoped that the economic sanctions agreed on 11 May 1992 by the EC would 'give authorities in Belgrade cause to reflect' (Agence Europe 13 May 2006). This was in reference to Belgrade ordering Yugoslav National Army (JNA) incursions into Bosnia-Hercegovina in 1992. However, the strategy of sanctioning Serbia did not have the desired impact and there was no apparent 'reflection' by the Milošević regime.

The second approach, that is, not to intervene militarily, reflected an inability – a lack of will, appropriate measures and cohesion in the Community. Arguably, by ruling out military intervention, the international organisations involved in peacemaking and stabilisation efforts in Yugoslavia rendered their own threats, sticks and sanctions barely credible. The EC's reluctance and prevarication are criticised by Hodge (2006: 12): on the eve of the launch of a Peace Conference in September 1991 Lord Carrington stated that each republic's point of view must be listened to, which in Hodge's analysis was 'music to Milošević's ears'. Therefore the EC's attempts to affect the structures and relationships of the initial conflict between Croatia and Serbia failed to be effective.

A clear example of the disagreement over strategy among EC member states emerged in response to the demands for independence by Croatia and Slovenia. Previously the EC's strategy had been to maintain Yugoslavia, but this strategy became increasingly elastic and then superfluous. In May 1991 Croatia held a referendum on independence, which returned a 93 per cent vote in favour of independence with an 86 per cent turnout. Croatian Serbs boycotted the election because they were not able to have the same vote for self-determination. At this point, an ephemeral success of EC diplomacy was the three-month moratorium on declarations of independence (Bideleux and Jeffries 2007: 201). Challenged with Slovenian and Croatian demands for independence, the EC initially stressed its desire for territorial integrity and did not acquiesce to their demands for independence. The EC launched a conference under the chairmanship of Lord Carrington. This was in response to growing pressure from Germany to meet the mounting Croatian and Slovenian independence demands. Ultimately, German pressure to recognise Croatia and Slovenia undermined Carrington's conference. Member state consistency was impossible to achieve since Germany was firmly and vocally supportive of Croatian independence. On 16 December, just five days after the Maastricht Treaty on the EU was signed, the twelve member states admitted the shortcoming of the approach of linking recognition of new republics to an agreement and, therefore, decided to recognise all the republics that sought recognition and met a long list of conditions drawn from Lord Carrington's plan (15 January 1992). In early 1992 the European Parliament recognised that 'the federal republic of Yugoslavia no longer exists in its old form' (Agence Europe 17 January 1992).

Ultimately, inconsistency between member state agendas undermined any accomplishments in EC/EU foreign policy. Continued disagreement between EC member states mitigated the success achieved at Brioni. Disunity between the twelve member states regarding the deployment of peacekeeping forces into the conflict between Croats and Serbs on 7 August 1991 diminished EC success (Kintis 1997: 150). In December 1991, Germany recognised Croatia and Slovenia as independent successor states from the former Yugoslavia while the remaining eleven EC member states recognised Croatia and Slovenia on 15 January 1992. More importantly, these decisions were widely portrayed as a costly error by the EC as they led to the escalation of violence and outbreak of war in Bosnia-Hercegovina (Owen 1996; Holbrooke 1998: 31). EC mediation in Yugoslavia continued under the Vance-Owen negotiations, which established a peace plan in January 1992.[5] In July 1992 internal division within the EC on what attitude to adopt on Croatia, specifically regarding the extension of the PHARE programme to Croatia and Slovenia, limited the EC's capacity to transform conflict. At this stage, there was an opportunity to make no distinction between the two in terms of the EC's policy towards them, but given the EC's 'grave element of suspicion relating to an agreement to share Bosnia between Croatia and Serbia' the EC was divided on how Croatia should be treated (Agence Europe 8 July 1992).

Throughout this period, some successes of EC engagement are notable. Nuttall highlights the success of the EC's foreign policy in Yugoslavia when the EPC sent a troika of foreign ministers to Yugoslavia on 28 June 1991 to help broker an agreement on three issues: a ceasefire, a standstill on declarations of independence, and lifting Milošević's blocking of Mesić (1999: 14–15). Additionally, Cviić (1991: 96) argued 'the head-in-the-sand policy of sticking to Yugoslavia come what may had clearly become inadequate to cope with the new reality', and that the deployment of EC troikas and monitors represented a welcome and overdue change in EC policy. The EC dispatched troikas to the Balkans from 1991, which ultimately helped secure an Agreement at Brioni in July 1991. Crnobrnja (1996: 189) contends that the federal government of Marković and governments of Bosnia-Hercegovina and Macedonia all 'pinned great hope' on the visits by the EC troikas. Edwards confirmed that the success of this agreement showed that the EC intervention was greeted as 'proof of the EC's ability to act' (1997: 176). This EC-brokered ceasefire was very temporary and broke down shortly after signing, which suggests that the EC had the ability to act to secure a mediated agreement but did not have the capacity to ensure the maintenance of the agreement.

During the escalation of the war in Bosnia, in June 1992, the division between the attitudes of the Twelve on the response to the unfolding war in Yugoslavia was most apparent. The European Parliament failed to decide on a proposal to intervene militarily in Bosnia, raising concerns that the EC 'risked playing the role of judge', and thus decided simply to continue with sanctions against Serbia and Montenegro (Agence Europe 9–10 June 1999). For the Twelve, the underlying aim of applying sanctions on Serbia was to 'change the attitudes' and 'give authorities in Belgrade cause to reflect'

(Agence Europe 25–26 May 1992, 14 May 1992). Evidence suggests that the EC hoped the Belgrade authorities would be persuaded to cooperate with their aims, suggesting a lack of understanding about the conflict or even that the path-dependent mentality informing their approach to Yugoslavia was inherently flawed and inefficient.

The path-dependent mentality of the EC's approach during the escalation of conflict was evident in 1992, when the EC proposed that it should engage with the Yugoslav republics in a way similar to how it was engaging with the countries of Central and Eastern Europe. During a European council meeting in March 1992 German minister Genscher proposed that the Yugoslav republics should have Association Agreements analogous to those with Czechoslovakia, Poland and Hungary (Agence Europe 4 March 1992). It was therefore apparent in this escalation period that the EC was willing to engage constructively with the aggressive nationalism strategies of the Tuđman regime. However, this carrot was evidently ill-timed and insufficient to entice interest and relationship change among the political parties in Croatia.

To expound on this point, was it appropriate or suitable for the EC to employ the integration mechanism to target the ethno-nationalist mobilisation strategies deployed by the Tuđman regime? Arguably, making a moral judgement about the EC's strategy is inappropriate but it is imperative to consider the implications of the EC's tentative offers of more substantial political and economic carrots during the early escalation of conflict. The EC's offer to Croatia stood in stark contrast to its policy of continued sanctions against the Milošević regime. This raises a question about what was motivating the EC to become involved in Croatian politics in such a manner, since it suggested an inbuilt sympathy and understanding among some EC member states for Tuđman and Croatia. Undoubtedly, the EC was conditioning receipt of EC aid or development of political relations on Croatian cooperation on a variety of issues such as human rights and free and fair media, but it remains doubtful if the EC's preferred strategy of incentives was appropriate, especially given its limited impact. The implication is that a perceived preferential treatment of Croatia resulted in an assessment by Serbs that the EC member states were not impartial and thus undermined any impact and future impact of EC initiatives in Serbia.

Similar carrots were repeatedly offered by the EC/EU to Croatia, but not to Serbia, through the escalation period of conflict. In 1994 it looked increasingly possible that Croatia would join with Slovenia and the other countries of Central and Eastern Europe on the PHARE programme, after Commissioner Hans Van de Broek declared that Croatia could intensify its relations with the EU by negotiating a cooperation agreement and becoming part of the PHARE and TEMPUS (cooperation in education) programmes (Agence Europe 7 October 1994). Yet again the promise of deepening relations was conditional on satisfactory progress on human rights and free and fair media in Croatia. Throughout 1993 and until the end of 1994 the EC/EU's ambitions in Croatia focused on the decision to bring Croatia closer to the EC through association and assistance. The instrument of PHARE was primarily tendered by the EU to encourage compliance in Croatia. The war situation in Croatia, especially over Krajina, meant that from February 1993 through to October 1994 the decision to open PHARE to Croatia remained open. However, throughout 1993, the EC refused to make any progress in relations with Croatia due to the ongoing threat of a Greater Croatia, especially in Bosnian territory.

EC/EU policy was focused on maintaining territorial unity in Bosnia and was firmly against Serbia and Croatia carving Bosnia up between them. While the EC was keen to bring about a cessation of violence, it remained adamant that it would not support the expansion of Croatian or Serbian territory (Agence Europe 28 April 1993). In 1993 the EU threatened Croatia and Serbia with political and economic sanctions should they refuse to cooperate and participate in the Vance-Owen peace plan. Such measures were typical of the EC/EU's approach to Croatia and Serbia throughout the escalation of conflict: threats and promises without concrete physical action or at least the threat of it (Agence Europe 6 April 1993).

During 1993 the EU's policy toward Serbia created tensions in the relationships between Serbia and the EU insofar as the EU was perceived to have committed 'fatal errors' in its policy towards the crisis in Yugoslavia (Agence Europe 31 March 1993). This was significant in that there was a vast gulf between what Serbia expected from the EU and the EU's actual approach towards Serbia. In April 1993 the EC decided to impose stronger sanctions against Serbia should it fail to cooperate with the Vance-Owen plan, and threatened isolation for many years to come in the hope that this would persuade Serbia to accept the plan. This only isolated Serbia further (Agence Europe 6 and 26 April 1993). The President of the Yugoslav Federal Republic, Ćosić, stated that the EU should switch from 'balkanisation' to 'Europeanisation of the region' and that the Vance-Owen plan was not acceptable to the Serb population in Serbia and in Bosnia (Agence Europe 31 March 1993). This statement by Ćosić revealed the difference in attitudes towards how the conflict should be dealt with in comparison to the EC/EU's endeavours thus far. In response to this significant speech by Ćosić, MEPs questioned the content and logic of his speech. For example, the Chair of the European Parliament Delegation for relations with the Republics of former Yugoslavia Mr Avgerinos stated that the 'Vance-Owen plan offers a chance of peace, even if 20 per cent of the plan is not acceptable to Serbs'. This highlights the challenge faced in 1993, in terms of relations not only between Serbia and the rest of the region, but also between Serbia and the EU.

The structures and relationships of war in Croatia did not end or become transformed with the dawn of the Dayton Agreement in 1995. Following Dayton, authoritarianism and conflict prevailed in Croatia. This discussion has argued that the consistent path-dependent nature of the EC/EU's strategy of offering political and economic incentives did not alter the structures and relationships of conflict in Croatia. The electoral success of the HDZ in 1995 (45.2 per cent of the vote) ensured that the anti-Serb policies of the Tudman government would continue. Nonetheless, the EU sought to establish productive links with Croatia in 1995 with the offer to reward Croatia for its behaviour at Dayton by opening negotiations on a cooperation agreement – although this included the firm gatekeeping provision of stalling any negotiations or negotiated agreement on account of Croatia's continued observance of UN conditions (Agence Europe 10 April 1995). The EU continued as scheduled with negotiations on a trade and cooperation agreement in May 1995, despite escalating tensions, continuing intransigence and claims of 'ethnic cleansing' in early May (Agence Europe 5 May 1995). In a statement issued at its Cannes Summit of 26–27 June, the European Council of Ministers confirmed the authorisation to open negotiations for a trade and cooperation agreement with Croatia but reiterated its warning against recapturing Krajina through military means. Evidently, these carrots were insufficient to persuade Croatia not to intervene militarily in Krajina in 1995.

It remained clear that the EU and the international community acquiesced to this behaviour, seeing it as a necessary stage in the continued dissolution of Yugoslavia. US Secretary of State Warren Christopher stated that the Croatian offensive against rebel Serbs could be an advantage in solving the crisis, and argued that Croatia may have launched the offensive but it was purely in response to the Serb attacks on the Bihać enclave (*Croatian Radio News* 1995). Despite reports from EU monitors which stated that the Croatian army had a 'deliberate hostile policy which included killings, burning of houses, looting of property (*Guardian* 30 September 1995), the EU did not deploy a suitable conflict-prevention strategy. Ultimately the EU's response to Operation Storm was to exclude Croatia from participating in the PHARE programme. In response to the Croatian Army offensive in the

Krajina region, on 4 August the EU suspended negotiations with Croatia on the trade and cooperation agreement and suspended implementation of the PHARE aid programme for Croatia. The impact of this was recognised immediately in Croatia as being harmful for society and for transition efforts.[6] However, there was no policy change by Tudman; nor did Croatia respond positively to the series of reprimands and sanctions by the EU.

The EU's decision to increase its involvement in Croatia from 1995 largely depended upon Croatia's continuing support for the maintenance of UN troops on Croatian territory; only then would it be possible to continue with negotiations on an economic and trade agreement. The EU's firm adherence to this policy throughout the first three months of 1995 had the objective of avoiding the risk of military escalation (Agence Europe 10 March 1995). By April 1995 the European Council authorised the European Commission to commence negotiating a cooperation agreement with Croatia. The first round of these negotiations took place on 19 and 20 June 1995 and was seen as the 'first step towards Croatia's pure and simple accession to the EU' (Agence Europe 22 June 1995). The aim of these negotiations was to complete an agreement by the end of 1995, and the intention was that they would run alongside the PHARE programme. The decision to open negotiations on a trade and cooperation agreement and include Croatia in the PHARE programme placed the EU in a potentially transformative role in the summer of 1995 in Croatia.[7] However, these aims came to nothing as by August 1995 all negotiations with Croatia and its inclusion in PHARE were suspended because of Croatian activities in Krajina (Agence Europe 7 August 1995). In hindsight this marked a significant juncture for the EU in Croatia and indeed for Croatia's transition process. This is made all the more poignant by claims in December 1995 that the only way that peace could be established between Bosnia and Croatia would be through integration into the EU and NATO (Agence Europe 12 December 1995). Furthermore, these calls for EU and NATO enlargement to Bosnia-Hercegovina and Croatia were marked by contrasting calls from Bosnia, which argued that Serbia should not be accepted into the EU at the same time as Bosnia, Croatia and Slovenia (Agence Europe 10–11 June 1996).

Managing conflict

The major strategy for managing conflict in Croatia, Serbia and Bosnia was manifested in the Dayton Agreement which was settled in December 1995 when, after negotiations, Milošević, Tudman and Izetbegović agreed that Bosnia-Hercegovina would become a single-state entity with an international legal personality. Within Bosnia two distinct entities, Republika

Srpska and the Muslim-Croat Federation, were established. The immediate intention of the Dayton Agreement was to prevent violence and keep the conflict parties separate. However, in the medium term the management of the conflict over Bosnia and between Croatia and Serbia became much more ambitious. Rather than separating the parties, the medium-term plan was to engender cooperation between the parties to the conflict. According to Gow (1997: 298), the EC/EU engagement in securing the Dayton Agreement can be described as an 'initial well-meaning but hurried and ill-planned venture of the then EC troika [that] led seemingly ineluctably to the expansion of the EC role'. The EU promoted regional integration as an alternative to destructive *patterns of interaction.*

Following the Dayton Agreement in 1995, the EU actively encouraged financial and political rapprochement in the region which aimed to transform the conflict pervading regional relationships by promoting a more constructive and interdependent relationship. The EU launched a repackaged strategy for the Western Balkans in the form of the Regional Approach in 1996. Without the active participation of Greece, Turkey, Bulgaria, Romania and Slovenia the regional dimension was very much undermined. The Regional Approach was impaired by the fragmentation inherent in the approach owing to the exclusion of the Federal Republic of Yugoslavia (FRY) and compounded by Croatia and the FRY not qualifying for PHARE aid (Papadimitriou 2001: 79). The various regional initiatives in Croatia and Serbia were unsuccessful during the 1990s owing to the failure of Brussels to cement regional integration with EU integration and because the incentives to cooperate alongside neighbours with whom a country had recently engaged in violent warfare were insufficient.[8] The inability of the EU to take collective action which would have relied on consensus among its member states rendered the EU marginalised when a crisis in Albania occurred in 1997. According to Elsbani (2008: 5) the EU's inability to make a collective decision to form a common response to a crisis in Albania resulted in Italy leading a 'coalition of the willing'.

In 1997 it is possible to trace the emergence of a significant EU strategy and the enhancement of the EU's transformative capacity because of the development of its mechanism of political conditionality. In February 1997, in light of a fact-finding mission carried out by the Council and the Commission in Belgrade, the General Affairs Council decided to apply conditionality gradually with a view to developing a coherent strategy for relations with the countries of the region (Agence Europe 25 February 1997). The EU's conception of conditionality regarding the Balkans was defined in the Council Conclusions that applied to all future relations.

As Table 2.1 shows, in 1997 the European Council decided to grant autonomous trade preferences to the FRY in response to positive political developments within the FRY, namely the opening of political discourse between opposition and government parties and the opening of the media (April 1997 Council Conclusions). The EU aimed to promote economic revival and reinforce a trend towards democratisation. Despite the efforts made in the Regional Approach, the period between Dayton and the war in Kosovo can be described as unproductive. The intransigence experienced following the Dayton Agreement and the emergence of war in Kosovo signalled the failures, or rather the limitations, of the Dayton Agreement and the need for a clearer vision in the EU on what to do with the countries of the former Yugoslavia.[9] While it can be maintained that the EU was limited in its impact on Serbia since Serbia continued to pursue conflict-escalating policies, it can also be argued that, after Dayton, Serbia's policies were simply reactive. Therefore, the EU failed to have an impact on the reactions of the Serbian government post-Dayton largely because the Serbian government was locked into a knee-jerk and self-sustaining cycle of actions against which the EU's fractional and perceptibly prejudiced policies were ineffective. Indeed, Dayton could be perceived as a holding policy; only in 1999 after the war in Kosovo did the EU and the international community completely transform their approach to the region, and this was largely in response to the emergence of different faces in both Serbia and Croatia – faces the EU could more readily engage with.

Summary

This chapter has provided a historical context for the book and introduced the case studies by exploring the nature and development of conflict and relationships with the EU throughout the 1990s. The chapter draws on the main theoretical framework of this book, the conflict transformation approach, by establishing the impact or lack of impact that the episodic interventions by the EU had on the initiation, escalation and management of conflict in Croatia and Serbia. The chapter argues that the dominant and governing political elites were resistant to the diplomatic initiatives and the conditional political and economic carrots offered by the EU because of the overwhelming significance of the structures and relationships of conflict. During the escalation and management phases of conflict, EU member states and institutions were willing to negotiate with, but not offer any incentives (such as closer integration or membership), to the Milošević and Tuđman regimes because they saw them as responsible for the ethnic cleansing and the deployment of violent war

Table 2.1 Developing political conditionality under the regional approach

Furthering integration	What the aspirant must do	How the EU can assist
Granting of autonomous commercial preferences	Fundamental democratic principles and human rights as well as the determination of the countries involved to develop economic relations between them	Promote economic recovery and strengthen development towards democratisation
Participation in PHARE	Show proof of credible commitment in favour of democratic reforms and progress on human and minority rights. Respect the peace agreements and carry out economic reforms	Support democracy
Conclusion of bilateral agreements	Allow displaced persons and refugees to return, readmit nationals, respect peace agreements, undertaken democratic and economic reforms, respect human rights and hold regular free and fair elections Country-specific conditions	Beginning of negotiations, negotiation, conclusion of agreement and implementation

Source: Agence Europe, 17 May 1997

strategies. Arguably, the path-dependent traditional foreign policy instruments were unsuitable for dealing with the conflict once it had started to escalate.

This chapter allows several key conclusions to be reached about the EU's evolving capacity on conflict in Croatia and Serbia during the 1990s. The chapter has demonstrated that the EU became increasingly reflexive, in terms of developing its mechanisms of integration and enlargement, throughout the 1990s. However, this reflexivity came at the expense of failing to impact on the initiation, escalation and management phases of conflict in Yugoslavia, specifically in the two cases.

The chapter demonstrated that throughout the 1990s the EC/EU was very much a reflexive actor, aware of the effects of its actions and adapting its behaviour accordingly, learning from experiences gained both in the field and institutionally. Therefore, as an evolving actor the EU throughout the 1990s was full of contradictions. At times, the EU's engagement was constrained by internal dynamics such as member state and institutional preferences and path-dependency, yet at other times, when a more coherent strategy was developed it achieved little because of the inadequacy of the strategy combined with intransigence and lack of interest in Croatia and Serbia.

The chapter has demonstrated that because of its respect for state sovereignty and its own experiences of ethnic conflict, the EU's institutions and member states were initially reluctant to respond to Croatian demands for independence and preferred a containment strategy. At the outset, the EU also attempted to maintain a neutral stance and advocated that the UN should invoke a general arms embargo upon all the republics in Yugoslavia. This arms embargo had the impact of sustaining the authority of Serbia, which dominated the Yugoslav National Army (JNA), and removed the capacity for self-protection from Croat and Bosnian Muslim communities. The unintended negative impacts of the EU's strategy during the initiation and escalation phases of conflict compounds the notion that the Yugoslav crisis represents the EU's major foreign policy failure. As outlined above, the German decision to recognise Croatia, without the support of other EU member states (which later followed), and without Croatia meeting the conditions set out by Carrington, ultimately undermined not only the EU's international credibility but also its depiction as a neutral party in Serbia. Moreover, the Serbs further questioned EU neutrality when the EU lifted the trade embargoes against Croatia and Bosnia yet maintained the trade embargo against Serbia.

The EU's evolving institutional capacity and divisions between member state and EU institutional interests rendered the EU's attempts at dealing with the emerging conflict in Yugoslavia inadequate. Throughout much of the 1990s the EU was unable to reconcile the differences between member states not only about how to respond to the crisis in Yugoslavia but also, more significantly, about what the actual problem in Yugoslavia was. EU member states disagreed on how to respond to the Yugoslav crisis: France favoured the territorial unity of Yugoslavia, while Germany supported Croatian and Slovenian demands for independence; France favoured military intervention, Britain was reluctant (given its experiences in Northern Ireland and Cyprus) and Germany could not send troops unless under NATO auspices. In sum, this chapter argues convincingly that the structural make-up of the EU – which required intergovernmental decision-making, including member states – forestalled any ambitions to be a more effective international actor.

This chapter has shown that throughout the 1990s the EU's engagement in Croatia and Serbia was marginalised because of its episodic and often minimal nature. The EU's approach to the initiation, escalation and management of conflict throughout the 1990s was shackled by the intergovernmental nature of its foreign policy. Essentially, this policy required member state support for any foreign policy endeavour yet permitted an individual member state to pursue an individual policy outside the EU CFSP framework.

The EU's impact cannot be completely disregarded. The EU played to its strengths and experience in employing economic tools such as financing stabilisation projects in the region and investing economically in humanitarian projects. Arguably, the EU was at its most effective when targeting the humanitarian crisis by supplying economic assistance to those most in need. This can be explained by agreement on such measures across the member states. According to Dover (2005: 314), the explanation of this success lies in the fact that the member states had already committed finance to the EU for such projects and therefore it could easily be directed, which demonstrates that 'lowest common denominator intergovernmental politics' dominated the EU's approach during the early to mid-1990s.

Without military backing diplomatic strategies were rendered unproductive, especially when such strategies were lacking substance in the first place. This requires further clarification on why member states who were frustrated at the lack of being able to stop the violent bloodshed only two hours by plane from Brussels were ultimately unable to actually stop the violence, yet actually unable to establish an agreed course. Moreover, when the EU did agree a course of action in Bosnia following Cyrus Vance's negotiations in early 1992, not only did it fail to stem the escalation of violent conflict but it was culpable in helping to trigger the conflict in Bosnia. The EU's strategies were insufficient to stem the ethno-nationalist mobilisation during the initiation and escalation of conflict in Croatia, Serbia and Bosnia because all too often the EU was unprepared to take decisions and act on them.

It is also possible to conclude from this discussion that the EU was unlikely to impact the structures and relationships of conflict because of the timing, nature and design of its intervention. It was sporadic, inconsistent and purely economic. Therefore, the United States and Russia had greater success in their, similarly episodic, interventions. In particular the United

States could be more effective because of the military, economic and political power available to it. Furthermore, the EU came to accept its backseat role:

> The Community and its member states are in contact through the Presidency of the United States to bring pressure to bear on those responsible with a view to ending the atrocities and securing free access for international relief efforts.[10]

During the initiation and escalation of conflict the intergovernmental nature of the EU decision-making process doomed its strategies to failure. When Germany acted unilaterally to recognise Croatia in December 1991, this showed that many member states believed they could be more effective outside a CFSP framework.

Ultimately, this chapter has demonstrated that throughout the 1990s the EU was a reflexive actor. It ambitiously sought to develop a CFSP, but when the CFSP mechanisms failed to impact in Croatia, Serbia and Bosnia the EU adopted a mixed method: bringing CFSP and a quasi-integration strategy to the table. This strategy evolved further in 2000, which is the focus of the next chapter. The launch of a more intensified EU strategy in 2000 came after the breakdown of the Rambouillet negotiations over Kosovo and the NATO bombing of the FRY (March–June 1999); this denoted a turning point in EU relations with the Balkans. As has already been alluded to above, EU member states and institutions learn from their experiences, whether it be the Britain learning from engagement in Northern Ireland, or the Commission learning from the enlargement process in Central and Eastern Europe. Hence, we should expect that the EU has experienced reflexivity, which it could use to apply to its engagement in the Balkans at the dawn of the twenty-first century.

3

EU ENLARGEMENT

Evolution, Lesson Learning and Policy Impact

This chapter takes up the theme of the evolution of the EU's strategy and looks at how the EU attempted to develop a more coherent conflict transformation policy through its 'enlargement approach' after 2000. The year 2000 is taken as a year of change in EU policy in the Balkans and this chapter sustains sustained that view with empirical and qualitative discussion. The primary focus of the chapter is therefore to discuss the qualitative shift in the EU's approach and examine the institutional, operational and political implications for the EU that were played out in the decade that followed. The chapter focuses on how the nature, design and timing of conditionality and social learning changed over the decade as a result of institutional lesson-learning within the EU. In so doing the chapter describes the evolution of the EU's enlargement approach and the implications for its transformative power in Croatia.

A changing conflict

The EU's strategy toward the Western Balkan countries intensified in 1999 and 2000, with the result that a framework for integrating with the EU and a membership perspective of the EU both became much more visible. The intensified strategy was facilitated by significant contextual changes in Croatia and Serbia: the removal of the regimes which dominated the 1990s, and the emergence of a visible and organised alternative to the parties that had dominated the landscape for much of the 1990s.

In Croatia, following the death of Croatian President Tuđman and the emergence of a substantial opposition to the HDZ, the EU confirmed that it would continue to 'provide support to the country's efforts towards full integration into the European family' (Agence Europe 13 December 1999). The election of a President and Prime Minister, Mesić and Račan, who did not represent the HDZ, marked the 'beginning of a new era for Croatia' (Agence Europe 11 February 2000). This, with the pro-reform results of the parliamentary elections, led to the European Council establishing a Joint EU–Croatia Consultative Task Force in January 2000. The instrumentalisation and operationalisation of lessons learned from previous engagement in the Balkans began to emerge in early 2000, with the EU reviving instruments used in other non-member states – integration and enlargement in both cases. Early 2000 brought a flurry of activity in Brussels on the issue of Croatia, with talk of preparations being made for a Feasibility Study on a Stabilisation and Association Agreement, the upgrading of the Commission delegation to Zagreb, and the enhancement of Community assistance (Agence Europe 26 January 2000).

In Serbia, at the time of the policy turning point, the EU was faced with the challenge of dealing with the continuing bellicosity of the Milošević regime. While the EU was able to agree that Milošević's behaviour was 'unacceptable' and a matter for 'great concern', and confirmed its 'very strong condemnation of violence', no decisions were taken at the January 1999 General Affairs Council (Agence Europe 25 January 1999). Rather than dealing with the Milošević regime, the EU targeted its strategies at the opposition movement in Serbia. With the USA, the EU provided significant political and economic support to the opposition leaders in Serbia. When the EU foreign ministers met with Serbia's democratic opposition leaders in Kirchberg in October 1999, it became clear that the strategy of sanctions was feeding the nationalist rhetoric espoused by Milošević. Therefore, the EU interlocutors accepted that they should lift sanctions (Agence Europe 13 October 1999) as soon as the government of the FRY was under the political control of democratic forces. The EU promised to 'reach out to the Serbian people, who have suffered as a result of the detrimental policies of its leaders'.[1] In February 2000, the EU stated that it wanted to 'encourage the Serbian people in their struggle for democracy, reconciliation and the necessary political and economic reform'.[2] This was developed by Commissioner Patten in February 2000 when he pointed out that the 15 member states decided to adopt 'surgical and more effective' measures against Milošević (Agence Europe 16 February 2000). The EU's reflexivity in dealing with Serbia was manifested throughout 1999 and 2000. During this time, the EU increasingly recognised that isolating Serbia was a deficient and harmful strategy. The focus moved, therefore, to having an 'open Serbia' that had a 'society to society relationship' with the EU (Agence Europe 20 March 2000). By June 2000 the EU strengthened its links with and support for the democratic opposition in Serbia. This was indicated with Solana's meeting with Đinđić in June 2000 at which they agreed that there was the need for a 'real alternative to Milošević' (Agence Europe 22 June 2000).[3] Seeking to lend support to the opposition parties in Serbia, the EU stated the following objectives:

> to confirm that the countries in this region are bound to Europe; to clarify the reciprocal commitments between the EU and each of those countries; to remind them that the door will also be open to a democratic FRY, ready to cooperate and living in peace with its neighbours. Against this background the summit meeting will provide a chance to confirm the EU's support for civil society and for the Serbian democratic opposition forces.[4]

It was only after the removal of Milošević that the Zagreb summit went ahead with representation from Serbia in November 2000. Importantly, for both Croatia and Serbia, a timetable for advancement on integration remained elusive.

To recap from the earlier discussion, the transformation phase of conflict is predicated on a 'ripening' of the conflict, in which parties are seeking an exit strategy from the conflict (Zartman 1989: 15). It was in 1999–2000 that the situation in the Balkans appeared to be 'ripening'. Crocker (1992: 481) suggests that during such a phase it is necessary that the conflict should be positioned in the following ways:

(1) Give the parties some fresh ideas to shake them up.
(2 Keep new ideas loose and flexible and avoid getting bogged down early in details.
(3) Establish basic principles to form building blocks of a settlement.
(4) Become an indispensable channel for negotiation.
(5) Establish an acceptable mechanism for negotiation and an appropriate format for registering an agreement.

The development of the Stabilisation and Association process appears to embody all of these strategies. The Stabilisation and Association process provided fresh ideas in terms of offering a more coherent framework for achieving closer integration into the EU. The new ideas were kept loose and flexible, with each country being able to progress individually within an open time frame towards closer integration with the EU. The Stabilisation and Association process also established basic principles to form the building blocks of a settlement. It also acted as a channel and mechanism for negotiation between parties owing to the political conditionality and socialisation embedded in the process that provided opportunities and potential for registering an agreement.

At the heart of the intensified and more visible approach lay the Stabilisation and Association process that was developed and implemented to facilitate closer relations between the EU and the countries of the former Yugoslavia. This process represented a framework or a stepping-stone to eventual membership which in part reflected the lessons learned from the EU's experiences in the Balkans in the 1990s, and through this process these lessons were instrumentalised and operationalised. The EU's employment of the quasi-enlargement instrument as a method for dealing with the post-war situation in Croatia and Serbia was evident in 2003 at the Thessaloniki European Council, when the EU reiterated its commitment to the Western Balkans as follows: 'The Union's thus enriched Stabilisation and Association Process will remain the framework for the European course of the Western Balkan countries all the way to their future accession' (European Council 19–20 June 2003).

At the EU Western Balkan summit (21 June 2003) which followed the Thessaloniki European Council, the EU reiterated its 'unequivocal support to the European perspective of the Western Balkan countries. The future of the Balkans is within the EU' (European Council 19–20 June, point 2). The pre-accession strategy for the Western Balkans closely resembled that of the previous enlargement, combining financial assistance with membership conditionality. However, in the Western Balkans, issues of conflict transformation, state weakness and state building were still on the political agenda. As a result, the region was subject to extensive political conditionality and socialisation, which had traditionally been outside the scope of any EU policies.

While the EU's strategy became more intensive and a membership perspective more visible, eventual membership remained a distant prospect provisional on many conditions; the time frame for eventual membership of the EU was elusive. Thus, the countries of the Western Balkans would develop relations with the EU through assistance, association and eventually the process of accession. This was a guarded approach proposed by the EU and political conditionality and social learning mechanisms were its mainstay.

The evolution of the enlargement approach

The evolution of the enlargement approach can be traced empirically and chronologically. At its core were the EU treaties, which serve as a natural starting point for this discussion. This section identifies the period between 1999 and 2000 as a significant turning point in EU strategy in the Balkans and highlights the different approaches to understanding this shift, with attention paid to the suitability of the integration approach for Croatia and Serbia.

At the starting point of any discussion of the evolution of the enlargement approach, it is imperative to identify the fundamental treaty reform which made advancement in enlargement approach possible. The treaties of the EU – namely the Treaty of Rome (1957), the Single European Act (1987), the Treaty of Maastricht (1992), the Treaty of Amsterdam (1997) and the Treaty of Nice (2000) – have all asserted and preserved the open-door nature of the EU. While the Treaty of Rome was substantially concerned with matters relating to its own member states, it established a future scope for enlargement to other states. Each of these treaties progressively advanced the criteria for EU membership whereas the definition of what makes a 'European' state remained open. The Copenhagen European Council in 1993 stated that membership of the EU was based on:

> stability of institutions guaranteeing democracy, the rule of law, human rights and respect for and protection of minorities, the existence of a functioning market economy, as well as the ability to cope with competitive pressures and market forces within the Union, the ability to take on the obligations of membership, including adherence to the aims of political, economic and monetary union.[5]

Moreover, Article 49 of the Treaty on European Union as amended by the Treaty of Amsterdam stated that 'Any European state which respects the principles set out in Article 6(1) may apply to become a member of the Union'.[6]

Therefore, the basis of the European treaties permits any European state that meets the membership criteria to join the EU. Now that the basis for the potential of EU enlargement has been established it is appropriate to move on to consider how the EU's strategy towards the Western Balkan countries shifted in 1999.

The evolution of the EU enlargement approach in 1999 and 2000 marked a policy shift as a result of lessons learned from the EU's engagement in conflict, demonstrating an operationalisation and instrumentalisation of the new approach. Within the scope of the Balkans, the EU was still smarting from the colossal crisis in Kosovo and the FRY in 1999 and it recognised that there was a definite need for a more distinct European defence identity. Furthermore, as pointed out in the Introduction to this book, the EU had a range of experiences in conflict prevention, management and resolution before and during the Yugoslavian crisis. For example, EU intervention had resulted in mixed outcomes in Northern Ireland, Cyprus and the Central and Eastern European countries. As a result, from consistent engagement in various conflict situations in the EU, and from its experience during the 1990s in the countries of the former Yugoslavia, the EU refined its mechanisms for dealing with the situation in the Balkans, whether or not this was the most suitable way of dealing with Croatia and Serbia.

The Stabilisation and Association process marked the first example of the more intensified EU strategy in the Balkans that was followed by a multiplicity of interventions through a strategy of integration and offering membership. It is necessary to examine critically the EU's strategy prior to the shift in 1999 in order to contextualise and appreciate the nature of the change in EU strategy. This subsection focuses on the period 1999–2000 as a turning point which saw the EU develop its actorness and capacity in external relations, which ultimately resulted in the development of a more intensified strategy towards the Western Balkans, including Croatia and Serbia. Additionally, it traces the decision-making and agenda-setting activities of EU agencies such as institutions and member states that led to the realisation of a Stabilisation and Association process in 2000, and critiques the suitability of this approach for Croatia and Serbia. The account here highlights the way in which EU engagement moved from episodic and limited impact intervention during the 1990s to the EU becoming a consistently present actor in Croatia and Serbia after 2000. The period between 1999 and 2000 is regarded as the period of lessons learned for the EU from the 1990s conflicts in former Yugoslavia; the post-2000 period of democratisation in Serbia and Croatia is seen as the period of the instrumentalisation and operationalisation of these lessons.

Accepting Zartman's explanation that a conflict cannot be transformed until the parties involved are willing to engage in transformation processes, then ultimately the EU's engagement, regardless of the forms it took, would have been rendered ineffective since the parties to the conflict were hastily and wholeheartedly pursuing structures and relationships of conflict during much of the 1990s. Additionally, it was not in their constructed interests to engage in any meaningful relationship with the EC/EU. However, this impasse resolved and the situation gradually changed after 1995 at Dayton, more so during and in the aftermath of the war in Kosovo. Ultimately the situation in Croatia and Serbia changed with the removal of the Tuđman and Milošević governments from the political scene in 1999 and 2000 respectively. The timing of this coincided with, and was connected to, the EU realising a more intensive strategy in the Western Balkans.

During the war in Kosovo (1999), it became clear that the EU needed to reappraise its strategies towards the countries of the former Yugoslavia. The reassessment, based on knowledge gained from a spectrum of lessons learned, resulted in a shift in the EU's strategy towards the countries of the former Yugoslavia, which involved the decision to grant a membership perspective, therefore linking the transition trajectories of Croatia and Serbia to integration in the EU. As a reflexive actor the EU it responded to and evolved from engagement and experience in its external environment. This is a significant departure from the theory that EU actorness relied on its established toolbox: a central tenet of existing Europeanisation debate. Therefore, the turning point in 1999–2000 is explored within the framework of the EU relying in part on its established toolbox but departing from the traditional strategy of engaging with the countries of the former Yugoslavia, which signalled that the EU had learned from its engagement in the 1990s and, more significantly, that these lessons had been institutionalised, instrumentalised and operationalised. This argument is sustained by consideration of the insistence of Fischer and the German presidency that something radical had to be done because the existing EU approach was obviously not working (Elbasani 2008; Pippan 2004: 226–8). The Fischer Plan developed into the Stability Pact, which came about due to the war in Kosovo, the failures of the Rambouillet Conference and the bombing of Serbia. According to Pippan (2004: 228) the intention of the Fischer Plan may have been to offer an accelerated accession process, yet this would have 'resulted in a discrimination of the [Central and Eastern European Countries] … thus, in an inconsistent application of Article 49 [Treaty on European Union]'.

It is necessary to engage critically with the existing debates on reflexivity or, in other words, lesson learning. A compelling approach to lesson learning is provided by E. B. Haas (1990). According to Haas (1990: 26), when we say that 'an international organisation learns', it is

> a shorthand way to say that the actors representing states and members of the secretariat, working together in the organisation in the search for solutions to problems on the agenda, have agreed on a new way of conceptualizing the problems.

Conceptualising problems and searching for solutions to the problems is a process of change; change can be incremental and/or innovative. According to March (1991) incremental change refers to finding solutions to new problems without altering the fundamentals of a given institutional setting. Innovative change on the other hand refers to a fundamental alteration in structures of searching for and finding solutions. Levy (1994: 283) argues convincingly that learning refers to a 'change of beliefs (or the degree of confidence in one's beliefs) or the development of new beliefs, skills, or procedures as a result of the observations and interpretation of experience'.

Therefore, the lesson learning capacity of the EU relates explicitly and directly to the EU's reflexivity. However, this lesson learning capacity surely is predicated on the actor behaving rationally; rational behaviour is fundamental. According to Eriksen (1999: 223), actor reflexivity 'means the ability to adopt a reflective attitude, the ability to redeem presuppositions of knowledge, the possibility to learn, to alter behaviour and to change preferences when faced with better arguments'. Therefore, reflexive behaviour 'springs from an ongoing reflection about the action, its context, its effects on such a context and the feedback of those expected effects on the action' (Bicchi 2005). For the EU's lesson learning to have an impact on its transformative capacity, the lessons that the EU has learned must be institutionalised and implemented in policy. In addition, for lessons learned to be institutionalised and implemented, and incremental change to occur, organisational learning involves consensus building: in the EU's case, between the various EU agencies as well as member states. Yet limits to reflexivity must be considered. Potentially, problems of internal communication and cross-agency communication, as well as institutionalised and accepted practices, behaviours and norms within EU agencies, limit the EU's lesson learning. Furthermore, a lack of resources will inhibit the lesson learning process (Levinthal and March 1993).

This critical appraisal of the theoretical literature on reflexivity facilitates an analysis of the empirical changes in the EU's strategy in the former Yugoslav countries which occurred in 1999 and 2000. During the war in Kosovo EU discourse focused on the task of defining and implementing a post-war strategy for the Balkans. After the war in Kosovo the EU assumed the major role and presence in the future of the Balkans, which was a result of the shared past experiences and emerging common aspirations for the future of the Balkans within the EU member states.

From late spring 1999 and throughout 2000, the EU endeavoured to engender a more visible and coherent strategy towards the countries of the Western Balkans. The Centre for European Policy Studies (CEPS) (2000)

declared that the aftermath of the war in Kosovo was not a time for hesitancy and criticised a 'persistent tendency towards timidity in some EU
quarters'. This analysis by the CEPS suggested that the EU was apprehen-
sively following a path-dependent method which was inadequate in the
changing context in the Balkans. Evidence suggests that this argument was
overly critical. The EU was strategising and implementing a more intensified strategy in the Balkans from early 1999 in the form of the Stability Pact
and the Stabilisation and Association process.

The policymaking environment on the Western Balkans in 1999 was very
much determined by one EU member state in particular: Germany. The
German role was significant because of the drafting of the Fischer Plan, a
forerunner to the Stability Pact. The German presidency stressed the need for
'a common European policy' that would build on existing approaches and
instruments. What is more, the role of Germany in formulating and pushing
forward the Stability Pact was notable. Friis and Murphy (2000b: 770) reveal
that EU member states were 'stunned at the speed with which Germany
drafted the Stability Pact and the lack of prior consultation with them'. The
EU's change in strategy was impacted by the internally held sentiment that
the policy needed to be changed after some years of limited effect. It has been
pointed out that this is a common experience in EU policymaking circles.[7]
This institutionally driven change provides an important argument especially
in light of the accepted argument in existing literatures that the driving force
behind the shift in policy was essentially geo-strategic: the flow of refugees
and criminal networks into EU member states was an important motivating
factor (Gallagher 2005: 169). Therefore, this finding supports the reflexivity
inherent in EU policymaking staff and agencies.

The role that reflexivity in institutional agencies of the EU played in 1999
is crucial to understanding the shift in EU strategy toward the Western Balkans. The European Council, the German presidency and the Commission
played a central role in the development and implementation of a refined
approach, which had echoes of previous initiatives but still had a number
of fresh inputs. Clearly, the Stabilisation and Association process built on
lessons learned from the Regional Approach; it maintained conditionality
on regional cooperation yet offered a much more visible framework for integrating into the EU, whether it was appropriate to export this approach to
the Western Balkans or not.

The path-dependent nature of the EU was evident during the development of the Stabilisation and Association process. The EU had to honour
existing agreements and maintain previously agreed conditionality in the Stability Pact and the Regional Approach. The EU developed a Stabilisation and

Association process that was compatible with the Stability Pact, which sought to embrace the ambitions of the Dayton Agreement of 1995[8] and UN Security Council Resolution 1244 of 1999.[9] The Stability Pact was announced at a meeting of the EU Foreign Ministers during the German presidency in Cologne (10 June 1999). It stated that 'lasting peace and stability in South East Europe will only become possible when democratic principles and values ... have taken root throughout, including the FRY', and as Mr Fischer stated, by 'anchoring the countries of the region in the Euro-Atlantic community and providing them with the prospect of EU membership' (Agence Europe 28 May 1999).[10] Significantly, Gallagher (2005: 169) contends that the rhetoric at this meeting and at the launch in Sarajevo (31 July 1999) suggested that the Stability Pact 'would be a dynamic forum for transforming the Balkans into a genuine part of Europe rather than an uncomfortable appendage'. Clearly, the EU acted in a path-dependent way: the Stabilisation and Association process built on the association agreements that the EU utilised in its relations with the countries of Central and Eastern Europe. However, it was not simply path-dependent but simultaneously reflexive. Clearly, institutional learning occurred to deal with the situation in the Balkans: notably, a new component of the new generation of the association agreements was the inclusion of the stabilisation factor for the region (Pop 2003: 131).

During 2000 the EU made several momentous commitments to the countries of the Western Balkans, notably at the Santa Maria de Feira European Council (June 2000) and at the Zagreb Summit (November 2000). The Santa Maria de Feira European Council (2000) stated, 'All the countries concerned are potential candidates for EU membership'. The description as 'potential candidates' was important for the countries of the former Yugoslavia; while they were not ready to be considered by the EU as 'candidate' states, their 'potential candidacy' had political significance.[11] The creation of this new label of 'potential candidate' suggested that the EU was not prepared at this stage to offer full candidacy to the countries of the former Yugoslavia, with the prospect of getting locked into an accession process with more candidates.[12] When the 15 member states came together for the Zagreb Summit it sent a strong signal to the countries of the former Yugoslavia that they had a vocation as EU member states yet at the same time much was required of them before this could happen.[13] The Zagreb summit confirmed the EU's

> wish to contribute to the consolidation of democracy and to give its resolute support to the process of reconciliation and cooperation between the countries concerned. It reaffirms the European

perspective of the countries participating in the stabilization and association process and their status as potential candidates for membership in accordance with the Feira conclusions.[14]

This evidence suggests that the EU was not simply using methods similar to those it had used in the countries of Central and Eastern Europe, namely the integration and membership mechanisms. Rather, the EU recognised that earlier offers of an integration framework were inadequate to incentivise the political parties to transform; therefore, the veiled commitment of 'potential candidacy' was made, as it was deemed by the EU agencies to be the most suitable way of dealing with Croatia and Serbia in light of lessons learned.

To digress briefly, the adoption of a guarded approach created both difficulties and opportunities. In terms of difficulties, *second-class sentiment* materialised in the Western Balkans. The EU has clearly and consciously treated the CEEC and the Western Balkans differently, notably with regard to future membership; this fostered resentment among the general public in the region and created tensions within and for the elites. Furthermore, as the EU failed to firmly prescribe a path to membership there was a genuine fear that nationalist anti-EU sentiment could boil over as a result of disillusionment and disaffection with the EU (Batt 2003; ICG 2005). On the other hand, this guarded approach created opportunities: it facilitated a more conditional relationship with a series of intermediate rewards creating the opportunity for the EU and the political reform-minded elites in the Western Balkans to drive the reform process and manage public opinion. Additionally, it provided the EU with an option of choosing when to deploy the *big* carrot. In delaying the prize of membership the EU can bargain and negotiate from an enhanced position.

The appropriateness of offering a framework for integration and the possibility of EU membership can be debated, and, indeed, it was debated by EU agencies ahead of the various declarations in 2000. While the situation at the time would suggest that an offer of membership was highly inadvisable, given that no state was prepared for the obligations of membership, the EU did create the label of 'potential' member states for the countries. Why was membership then offered in 2000 for the countries of the Western Balkans? In their appraisal of the 'membership puzzle', that is, why the EU offered a membership perspective to the FYR, Macedonia, Albania, Croatia, Bosnia-Hercegovina and the FRY in 1999, Friis and Murphy (2000a) trace the 'turbo-charged negotiations' in which member states 'took a number of decisions that seemed to directly contradict their preferences'. Friis and Murphy argue that the decision to offer a membership perspective to the countries of the former Yugoslavia was a radical one because most EU actors were reluctant to do so and because it remained unclear to the decision-makers whether the enlargement policy was 'actually suited to the needs and capacities of the region' (2000a: 778). This is a strong and valuable argument. If the countries of the Western Balkans were so distant from achieving membership, was it appropriate for the EU to offer it, and more importantly, would the membership perspective be as attractive and thus have a transformative power?

To increase the suitability of the new approach for the Western Balkans the EU tailored the approach to include stabilisation as well as association. Phinnemore (2003: 103) notes that the EU 'created new forms of association' for the countries of the Western Balkans which were distinctively different from the previous forms of association. Motivated by frustration over its failures throughout the 1990s,[15] the EU reinvented the mechanisms of the enlargement process to deal with the situation in the countries of the former Yugoslavia. According to Phinnemore (2003), the European Commission 'was keen to differentiate between' the Stabilisation and Association Agreements and the Europe Agreements.[16]

Friis and Murphy (2000a: 771) found that offering a membership perspective to the countries of the former Yugoslavia was a cause for concern among the EU member states, who considered that it could go one of two ways: duplicate the existing initiative or get out of hand. The coolness toward offering membership can only be understood in the wider context of the enlargement process which was struggling with twelve aspirants including Romania and Bulgaria, whose position could be threatened if FYR Macedonia and Albania's status with the EU was upgraded (Friis and Murphy 2000a: 772; *The Economist* 1999). Despite the Stability Pact's ambitions to anchor the former Yugoslavia in Europe, the prospect of membership was watered down under pressure from the French and Spanish (Friis and Murphy 2000a: 772) to 'new contractual relations' (European Commission 1999). However, these new contractual relations did represent a substantive shift in the EU's strategy.

Whether integration with the EU and EU membership was the most effective way for the EU to engage with the Western Balkan countries and have a positive effect on the transformation of structures and relationships of conflict in the case studies remained doubtful in 2000. Indeed, the debate in the EU's institutions and agencies centred on the suitability of applying the membership perspective and integration process to the particular situation in the Western Balkans. The decision to offer a membership perspective to the countries of the former Yugoslavia represented a 'membership puzzle' in that the EU appeared to offer membership without really wanting to. Nonetheless, despite the Stabilisation and Association process being promoted as a framework for achieving EU membership, the Stabilisation and Association Agreements were textually and substantively different from the Europe Agreements, because the former were not seen 'as providing an appropriate framework for the countries' gradual integration into the EU' (Phinnemore 2003: 86).

This section has shown that the shift in the EU's strategy in the Western Balkans which occurred in 1999 and 2000 was only partially explained by the path-dependent approach most commonly proposed in existing literature. Rather, it is much more accurate to incorporate an argument of reflexivity that was apparent in EU policymaking processes to describe fully the reasons why the EU intensified its strategy in the Balkans in 1999 and 2000. Furthermore, it is impossible to complete this analysis without taking cognisance of the changing political context. The ripening of the conflict permitted and facilitated a shift in EU strategy.

The implementation of the EU's intensified strategy in Croatia and Serbia: instrumentalisation and operationalisation

This section explores the operationalisation of the EU's intensified strategy in Croatia and Serbia after 2000, and provides an empirical overview of the development of EU relations with Croatia and Serbia in this period in terms of the three phases of integration: assistance, association and accession. It focuses on the nature, design, timing, use and development of political conditionality and social learning mechanisms in each of these phases and draws out the potential successes and weaknesses of each mechanism during each phase. In this section, I establish which of the four pathways (enabling, constructive, connective and compulsory) of EU influence are most salient in each phase of integration. The section demonstrates that the relevance of political conditionality and social learning at various times throughout the process of gradual admission to the EU can potentially affect the transformation of structures and relationships of conflict.

Assistance, association and accession represent three phases that are distinct in terms of the salience of political conditionality and social learning. At the same time, each of these phases involved the agencies of the EU, more often than not the Commission, which used socialisation and conditionality to ensure the achievement of the desired impact. Nonetheless, the transformative capacity of these mechanisms has been subject to academic criticism (Smith 2003: 105). Anastasakis (2001: 201) argues that while the EU 'has devised strategies and directed funds and resources for the promotion of democracy in the countries of the region, the impact and effectiveness of its contribution is far from evident'.

Providing financial and technical assistance to countries has been a primary route for the EU to have an impact and transform societies, including those without a membership perspective. Throughout the 1990s financial and technical assistance targeting political and economic reconstruction was delivered to Croatia, Serbia and other Western Balkan countries through a number of different instruments, namely PHARE, ISPA, SAPARD and through the CARDS programme which rationalised assistance instruments of OBNOVA and PHARE.

Inherent in each of these financial and technical assistance programmes was political conditionality. The CARDS programme had four main objectives (European Commission 2002a):

(1) reconstruction, democratic stabilisation, reconciliation and the return of refugees;
(2) institutional and legislative development, including harmonisation with European Union norms and approaches, to underpin democracy and the rule of law, human rights, civil society and the media, and the operation of a free market economy;
(3) sustainable economic and social development, including structural reform;
(4) promotion of closer relations and regional cooperation among countries and between them, the EU and the candidate countries of central Europe.

The CARDS programme was available to Croatia and Serbia to finance democratic stabilisation, reconstruction, reconciliation and return of refugees, institution and legislative development, and economic and social development, as well as promoting closer relations and regional cooperation (Council Regulation (EC) No. 2666/2000). Pippan (2004) noted that the CARDS programme had an element of conditionality as it necessitated cooperation on various issues before permitting access to funding. On 5 December 2000, the European Council stated that European Community assistance was accessible upon meeting the following criteria:

(1) Respect for the principles of democracy and the rule of law, and for human and minority rights and fundamental freedoms is an essential element for the application of this Regulation and a precondition for Community assistance. If these principles are not respected, the Council,

acting by qualified majority on a proposal from the Commission, may take the appropriate measures.

(2) Community assistance shall also be subject to the conditions defined by the Council in its Conclusions of 29 April 1997, in particular as regards the recipients' undertaking to carry out democratic, economic and institutional reforms.[17]

According to Pippan (2004: 232), this reflected one of the 'most comprehensive conditionality clauses ever embodied in a Community legal instrument regulating external assistance'.

After 2007 the Instrument for Pre-Accession replaced all these instruments, bringing together for the first time a single instrument through a single framework to deliver assistance to candidates and potential candidates. According to the Commission, the Instrument for Pre-Accession was 'designed with five components to provide for targeted and effective assistance for each country according to its needs and evolution'. These five components are transition assistance and institution building; cross-border cooperation; regional development; human resources development; and rural development. As a candidate Croatia can access all these components, while Serbia as a 'potential candidate' is only able to access the first two components: transition assistance and institution building and regional and cross-border cooperation. Table 4.2 shows that Croatia and Serbia will continue to receive funds during 2007–13 via the Instrument for Pre-Accession Assistance.

With financial assistance the aspirant countries do get incremental benefits in the greater quality of funding available to them once the levels required for assistance are met. Essentially, when an aspirant demonstrates progress, a level of financial assistance is available to them. Therefore, the granting of assistance depends on the aspirant's capacity to meet the EU's conditions. Thus, in some respects EU assistance is a reward in respect of the efforts made. While this appeared to be a satisfactory method of providing assistance in terms of the post-war societies of Croatia and Serbia, it is arguable that its effect was limited. The impact was reduced in the early transition era because the aspirants did not have the capacity to absorb funds, even though the needs were very great.[18] Therefore, it is possible to surmise that the capacity of the aspirants to absorb and implement EU conditions and rewards is a central factor that can limit the EU's potential transformative capacity.

Croatia and Serbia are part of the Stabilisation and Association process which, as its title indicates, is not purely about association but includes stabilisation also. This is particular to the EU's strategy with the countries of the Western Balkans. The Stabilisation and Association Agreements negotiated with the FYR, Macedonia and Croatia set out the membership perspective as follows in the preambles:

> (the contracting parties recall) ... the European Union's readiness to integrate to the fullest possible extent the ... (associate) ... into the political and economic mainstream of Europe and its status as a potential candidate for EU membership on the basis of the Treaty on European Union and fulfilment of the criteria defined by the European Council in June 1993, subject to successful implementation of this Agreement, notably regarding regional cooperation.

The role of political conditionality and social learning are inherent in the Stabilisation and Association process. Political conditionality is inbuilt into achieving advancement in the Stabilisation and Association process. Also, the opportunities that arise for added interaction between the political elites and EU agencies facilitated an increase in social learning for Croatia and Serbia. The Stabilisation and Association process involved regular meetings between Croatia and the EU and Serbia and the EU. At the regular meetings it was possible for Croatia and Serbia to learn about EU practices, values and models which would affect the political elites.

According to the EU the aims of the Stabilisation and Association process focused EU intervention in three areas:

(1) Support for good governance and institution building, focusing on public administration reform, justice and home affairs (e.g. strengthening the rule of law) and customs and taxation;
(2) Economic recovery, regeneration and reform, focusing on energy, transport, environment and economic development;
(3) Social development and civil society, focusing on university education, enhancing regional co-operation, vocational education and training linked to employment generation and civil society strengthening.

From this it is possible to distinguish the admirable ambitions of the Stabilisation and Association process. However, there are limits to the success of association with stabilisation as a phase of integration in Croatia and Serbia, mainly because of the elite focus of the process. Association can be criticised for being elite-focused and neglectful of societal change. In essence, the entire process of integrating with the EU is a largely elite-focused and elite-driven process. The executive bias experienced during pre-accession and accession negotiations has been criticised as resulting in an elite-natured process which results in a Europeanised elite and a non-Europeanised and alienated electorate (Grabbe 2006). Potentially, this gap between elite and societal Europeanisation can therefore raise questions about the degree of Europeanisation occurring in an aspiring state.

The Stabilisation and Association process shares the asymmetrical element of other stages of integration, namely assistance and accession. This is the leverage necessary for accounting for the EU's transformative capacity. When the EU 'negotiates' with third states that are aspiring to receive assistance or become an associate of the EU the 'negotiations' are highly asymmetrical. The asymmetrical nature of the relationships between the EU and Croatia and Serbia is at the crux of understanding why the EU can cause transformation of structures and relationships of conflict through political conditions and socialisation.

The Copenhagen summit of the European Council in June 1993 laid the foundations for the EU's accession process with the countries of Central Eastern Europe and other aspiring member states (Schmitter 1995; Dimitrova 2002; Grabbe 1999, 2001 and 2002; Schimmelfennig *et al.* 2003; Vachudova 2001 and 2005; Schimmelfennig and Sedelmeier 2005). Possible membership of the EU relates to Article 49 of the Treaty of Europe, as amended by the Treaty of Amsterdam, which states that any European state which respects the principles set out in Article 6(1) may apply to become a member of the Union (Treaty on European Union). Commonly known as the Copenhagen criteria, these principles provide a commitment from the EU to the countries of Europe that they could accede to the EU once they could assume the responsibilities of membership, and additionally established a series of rules to be adopted and implemented ahead of accession. In 1993 this development was an appreciated departure from the previously criticised protectionist EU.[19]

The Copenhagen criteria are fundamental to understanding the EU's capacity to transform the structures and relationships of conflict. Clearly they are explicitly concerned with the structures and relationships of conflict. In terms of structures of conflict, the Copenhagen criteria discuss the 'stability of institutions guaranteeing democracy', which relates to the role that *parties* play in post-war transition, and in regard to *issues*, the criteria discuss the protection of the rule of law and human rights. In terms of *relationships* of conflict the Copenhagen criteria outline a 'respect for and protection of minorities', which speaks to the relationships between states, ethnic groups and the patterns of exchange between ethnic groups and parties to the conflict. Conditionality has been at the core of the EC/EU's strategy in engaging with third states since the EC–CMEA Joint Declaration in 1988 (Papadimitriou 2001: 82) which led to a multi-tier Eastern Europe.

Croatia and Serbia, like any state aspiring to join the EU, must meet the EU's conditions and assume the responsibilities of membership. However, the conditions and responsibilities of membership have evolved since the first statement of the Copenhagen criteria. In Madrid in 1995 additional criteria for EU accession were established, including the condition for the effective application of EU law through appropriate administrative and judicial structures in terms of competence, resources and stability. The conditions that Croatia and Serbia must meet as candidate and 'potential' candidate states have evolved since the Copenhagen and Madrid European Councils. Croatia and Serbia must also meet the conditions that were specified in 1997 under the Regional Approach, the Stabilisation and Association process and agreement conditions. For Croatia, a membership candidate, there are 35 chapters that embody the fields of EU competency in which Croatia must demonstrate capacity prior to accession to the EU. Therefore, as Croatia must meet the legal obligations of EU membership it is likely that the EU will become the primary point of reference for the entire reform process. Thus, potentially, the EU possesses a significant capacity to impact the reform process in Croatia through compulsory pathways. Accordingly, being subject to EU conditionality could give rise to deeper processes of social change (Börzel and Risse 2000).

Political conditionality and social learning
in an evolving enlargement approach

The nature of the EU's contractual relationships with aspiring member states has increasingly come to involve the mechanisms of political conditionality and social learning. Owing to the reflexivity inherent in the EU enlargement approach, the EU developed its application of political conditionality and social learning which has implications for the two cases. Since both Croatia and Serbia have experienced Stabilisation and Association Agreement conditionality it is important to explore the salience of political conditionality and social learning in the Stabilisation and Association Agreements.

Recent studies of conditionality have commonly framed this process within a rationalist choice framework, arguing that conditionality can be best understood as a bargaining strategy of reinforcement by rewards, under which the EU provides external incentives for a target government to comply with its conditions (Schimmelfennig and Sedelmeier 2005). The

EU has tried to deal with and target political parties in aspiring member states to internalise domestic political change in such states. Rationalist choice explanations of conditionality presuppose consensus between both sides on the content of EU rules and the benchmarks for their fulfilment. Vachudova's (2005) analysis of EU leverage clearly distinguishes between the active and passive leverage of the Union and the difficulties of grasping the latter. In response, analysts have argued that conditionality is better explained as a multiplicity of actors, perceptions, rewards and sanctions, including both its formal and informal features (Hughes *et al.* 2004). Consequently, the thesis understands political conditionality as a dynamic process, rather than as a clearly identifiable causal relationship.

The first political conditionality crafted for the accession process occurred in the mid-1970s with the Declaration on Democracy of the EU council adopting the proposition that maintenance of representative democracy and human rights are essential elements of membership in the European Communities.[20] As a result, some elements of conditionality were enforced in the accession of Spain and Portugal. Nevertheless, these attempts were far away from today's understanding of political conditionality, which developed primarily with respect to the post-communist candidate countries. As a result, the formalisation of the political conditionality began in the early 1990s. In June 1992 the Lisbon European Council stipulated the following conditions for membership in the Union: European identity, democratic status and respect of human rights.[21] Although membership criteria had not been alien to previous enlargements, the Copenhagen conditionality presented a more systematic and institutionalised set of rules whose gradual 'constitutionalisation' has resulted in their stricter application (Hillion 2003: 3).

Regarding the Western Balkans, political conditionality has been a feature of relationships with the EU. Even when, in the late 1990s, the EU introduced the regional approach for the Western Balkans, political conditionality focused on encouraging reforms in the political area, such as returns of refugees and interethnic reconciliation.[22] The regional approach, however, failed to provide the prospect of membership as the major incentive of conditionality, and did not deliver tangible results. This evolved in 1999–2000 when the Stabilisation and Association process was established. There were three main components of this process including the Stabilisation and Association Agreements, autonomous trade measures, and substantial financial assistance. Since the Agreements represented the primary contractual relations with the Western Balkans, the focus shifts to them at this stage.

Conditionality in the Stabilisation and Association Agreements was an evolution from an earlier form of association agreement, the Europe Agreements. These Agreements were different from the Europe Agreements because an added condition of regional cooperation was an explicit condition that must be met and which is found only in the Stabilisation and Association Agreements (Phinnemore 2003: 86). Also, while these Agreements did not include an explicit membership framework and in the Agreements the associates were named as 'potential candidates'. Furthermore, the EU had 'integrated the principle of conditionality' into the Stabilisation and Association Agreements (Pippan 2004: 230). Essentially Croatia and Serbia, as candidate and potential candidate states that have negotiated or are negotiating a Stabilisation and Association Agreement, are subject to two forms of conditionality. Political conditionality does not merely include acquis conditionality; conditionality is a multi-level phenomenon. First, as explained earlier in this chapter, there are the accession criteria as established by the Copenhagen European Council in 1993 and set out in Articles 6 and 49 of the EU Treaty. Second, there is the set of criteria that is specific to the Stabilisation and Association process and which includes 'full cooperation with the ICTY, respect for human and minority rights, the creation of real opportunities for refugees and internally displaced persons to return and a visible commitment to regional co-operation'.[23] The Stabilisation and Association Agreements required that the associates met the following conditions (European Commission 2002b: 1):

(1) respect for democratic principles, human rights and the rule of law;
(2) the establishment of a free trade area with the EU;
(3) and the achievement of rights and obligations, in areas such as competition and state aid rules, that allow the economies to integrate with the EU.

The Stabilisation and Association Agreement negotiations can only be concluded once the specific conditions of the process have been met. The Commission's annual country reports provide evidence of whether the prospective associate has met the criteria.[24] If the Commission deems the country to be fully meeting the Stabilisation and Association Agreement conditionality, the European Council then makes a decision, which is later ratified by the European Parliament, to conclude the Agreement.

Following the conclusion of a Stabilisation and Association Agreement, the path is clear for a membership application and the opening of accession negotiations. However, this too continues to be conditional on the continued implementation of the Agreement. The Stabilisation and Association Agreement that was signed with Croatia states the following:

> If either party considers that the other Party has failed to fulfil an obligation under this Agreement, it may take appropriate measures. Before doing so, except in cases of special urgency, it shall supply the Stabilisation and Association Council with all relevant information required for a thorough examination of the situation with a view to seeking a solution acceptable to the parties.[25]

This clause indicated that the progress of the Agreement would depend upon the continued implementation of the agreed terms. In addition to the Stabilisation and Association Agreements, the EU at the Thessaloniki summit in June 2003 introduced the common instruments for EU accession, such as the European Partnerships and the Progress Reports for the Western Balkans. The aim of the European Partnerships, inspired by the Eastern enlargement, is to identify political and strategic priorities 'with due consideration to the Copenhagen accession criteria and to issues particular to the Western Balkans' in order for the countries to carry out short- and medium-term reforms.[26]

EU conditionality in the Western Balkans is qualitatively different from that in previous enlargements; here we see the EU instrumentalising and operationalising lessons learned from previous engagements and enlargements. Most importantly, the political conditionality is not purely being applied to the acquis, but rather confronts issues outstanding from the wars, and therefore moves into the scope of conflict transformation. The evolving conditionality of the accession process is clearly evident in the employment of benchmarks. According to the Commission, benchmarks are a 'new tool introduced as a result of lessons learnt from the fifth enlargement' (European Commission 2006d). Benchmarks are linked directly to the acquis: the opening of negotiations includes taking preparatory steps such as action plans and fulfilling the contractual obligations of the acquis, and the closing of benchmarks involves the implementation of the acquis. A unanimous Council decision, on proposal from the Commission, is responsible for confirming that conditions have been met and opening further chapters. This means that at an earlier stage in negotiations the EU will monitor more closely and expect more from candidates than was the case in previous enlargements. For Croatia, a candidate that is also part of the Stabilisation and Association process, relevant benchmarks for opening chapters in accession negotiations also depend upon the fulfilment of commitments under the Stabilisation and Association Agreement (European Commission 2005). The implications for Croatia and Serbia and other aspirants are double-edged: it is much more difficult to become a member of the EU, but it will produce a better-prepared candidate. Pippan (2004: 227) noted that the introduction of benchmarks into the pre-accession process was inadequate and advocated that:

> Clearer benchmarks are needed, defining as precisely as possible the steps to be taken by each country in order to move to the next stage of the SAP. Indeed if the SAP is viewed as the 'road to Europe' for the Western Balkans, the countries concerned have to be provided with an appropriately detailed road map guiding them to their desired destination.

According to Smith (2001: 37), political conditionality entails 'the linking, by a state or international organization, of perceived benefits to another state … to the fulfilment of conditions relating to the protection of human rights and the advancement of democratic principles'. Political conditionality is utilised by the EU to transform politics and economics in third countries. Schimmelfennig and Sedelmeier (2005: 672) argue that the effectiveness of political conditionality relies on the size and speed of rewards, determinacy of conditions, the size of adoption costs and the credibility of threats and promises. Political conditionality can target political elites through supporting and strengthening pro-reform actors or by making the cost of non-compliance much too high. In an ideal world, the EU member states would hope to see all aspirants implement reform in the manner that the EU would specify. However, there are problems with this: the incoherence of EU conditionality and rewards and the nature of the receptor government and society. Additionally, EU conditionality can be vague and open to various interpretations. This relates to the intergovernmentalism within EU policymaking, which means that there are many traditions and practices within various policy fields making any single EU template impossible to import. Furthermore, EU conditionality can fail to produce compliance in transition states. Checkel (2000) criticises the hard conditionality applied by the EU as being less successful or not working in cases where it will have detrimental consequences for the future. For example, when domestic costs of compliance with EU conditionality are too high for the political elites, the political elites will refuse to cooperate with the conditionality, or do so only hesitantly and partially. Potentially, the incoherence and lack of specificity of EU political conditionality can restrict the impact of conditionality as an instrument for conflict transformation. Sadurski (2004: 378) points out that

> the degree of specificity of EU political conditionality varied from one domain to another, and so it might have been much more effective where there was a determinate set of rules that the candidate states were expected to observe, rather than in cases in which the criteria laid down could be at best characterised as a vague template.

Domestic factors have an important role to play in understanding the impact of political conditionality in Croatia and Serbia. This relates to the above point that in some instances, the condition is just too difficult for the aspirant to accept. However, domestic factors also relate explicitly to the role of society. If the condition being applied is perceived negatively by society and public opinion, given the governing elite's desire to retain power, it makes adoption of the condition awkward at best and impossible at worst.

Why do aspirants comply with EU conditions and what does this mean for the EU's transformative capacity? Schimmelfennig and Sedelmeier (2005: 3) propose an 'external incentive model' to capture the dynamics of political conditionality. In contrast to the logic of appropriateness the external incentive model is premised upon the logic of consequences. The logic of consequences supposes that the elites appraise, in a cost-benefit way, the rewards of membership in comparison to the costs of non-membership in order to decide if compliance with the EU's conditions is sufficient to cooperate. According to Brusis (2005: 293) conditionality is assumed to effect a policy change by influencing the cost-benefit calculations of domestic actors but may be combined with processes of learning and socialisation through which domestic actors adopt shared belief systems. Brusis (2005: 293) found that the EU's leverage appears to be particularly strong in states threatened with exclusion from the accession process. The EU can therefore threaten and reduce assistance, suspend association and/or delay the prospect of EU membership should the aspirant fail to comply with any of the EU conditions. It is this gatekeeping mechanism that can provide the EU with a more significant transformative power. In their analysis, Schimmelfennig and Sedelmeier (2005) move on to propose that given a domestic equilibrium in an aspirant the adoption of EU rules depends on certain circumstances: the size and speed of rewards; the credibility of conditionality; veto players and adoption costs; legitimacy of rules and processes; identity and resonance which fit with the external incentive model. This helps us to understand, in cases where society and elites support the case for EU membership, the ways in which the EU can maximise its transformative impact.

To move on, it is useful to examine the role social learning plays in the EU's capacity to transform Croatia and Serbia. Since the enlargement process of the 2004 enlargement the EU appears to have learned that strict conditionality or stand-alone dialogue does not work and is implementing this lesson in the Western Balkan countries. The EU institutions, in particular the Commission, recognise that strict conditionality cannot produce incremental change in the Western Balkans, and that any conditionality must be accompanied by progressive dialogue.[27] In the absence of explicit coercion, the EU changes attitudes and behaviours through persuasion. Persuasion can be defined as

> An activity or process in which a communicator attempts to induce a change in the belief, attitude or behaviour of another person … through the transmission of a message in a context in which the persuadee has some degree of free choice (Perloff 1993: 14).

This definition refers to the negotiation and argument that a person, state or entity such as the EU can employ to convince a third party, namely aspirant states. In his appraisal of conditionality and compliance, Checkel (2000) discovered that compliance with international institutions occurs through social learning involving knowledge and norm diffusion through learning and persuasion. Checkel identifies three 'modalities' of conditionality: pre-conditions, trigger actions and policy provisions. Pre-conditions involve the realisation of governments' actions which have been agreed upon during negotiations before the EU or an international institution approves assistance association or accession. Trigger actions, in the case of the EU's association, assistance or accession, involve adoption and harmonisation with the acquis communautaire. Finally, Checkel argues that policy provisions are the least likely to induce compliance yet involve socialisation of the aspirant. Checkel points out that while this can be the least binding aspect of EU conditionality it is often most effective in states that suffer from poor policy environments, where strict conditionality often fails. This is crucial to understanding the impact of the EU's conditionality in Croatia and Serbia, yet the impact of its tough line on certain conditions (such as ICTY cooperation) must not be ignored. This stringent and persuasive means of encouraging compliance shows flexibility in the EU's strategy, yet still limitations of conditionality remain. Gaps between conditionality and compliance do exist, which create problems for the EU in achieving its desired results. The completeness of transformation remains problematic. The degree of adoption and implementation of its conditions, or rather the gap between word and deed, represents a problem for the EU.

This extensive evaluation of the approaches to conditionality and social learning has suggested that the EU's transformative capacity very much relies on the rewards of closer integration and ultimately membership. However, in the case of Croatia and Serbia, for whom membership was a (semi-) distant prospect throughout most of the 1990s, how did the conditionality and social learning take place? Potentially, social learning and conditionality can occur in Croatia and Serbia because of the various mechanisms used by the EU to persuade and engage with Croatia and Serbia and monitor progress.

The EU employs various mechanisms to persuade and engage with Croatia and Serbia, as well as monitor their progress, which facilitate the processes of social learning and conditionality. As highlighted above, financial and technical assistance are a primary mechanism of encouraging social learning and compliance with EU conditionality. Inbuilt in the three phases of integration with the EU discussed above are the EU's mechanisms for encouraging Europeanisation. Identifiable mechanisms include annual Progress Reports, benchmarking, gatekeeping and continued engagement. Each of these is associated with the various pathways of EU influence, most significantly compulsory, enabling and connective.

Monitoring and scrutiny are key ways in which the EU encourages compliance with EU conditionality, as well as providing the opportunity for the EU to impact the political elites through social learning. This involves the compulsory and connective pathways. Highlighting salient problems or rewarding with a positive assessment, through monitoring and assessment the EU can continually provide a public opinion on the transformation processes in both cases and therefore induce a response in the political elites. Both cases in the thesis are open to ongoing scrutiny by the EU because of their involvement in the Stabilisation and Association process and, in Croatia's case, its status as a candidate state. In the Stabilisation and Association process, both cases had to achieve a positive Feasibility Study before furthering negotiations on a Stabilisation and Association Agreement (SAA). The Feasibility Study monitored and assessed progress in the two states on a variety of political, economic and legal matters. The Stabilisation and Association process also involves annual inspection of the two cases, the results of which are published in annual Progress Reports. The Progress Reports can both motivate and dishearten the elites in the aspiring states. On the one hand, they are helpful in that they highlight the challenges remaining and, therefore, focus attention on areas where reform is most needed in the short and medium term.[28] On the other hand, the revealing nature of the Progress Reports can cause offence or create dejection among the political elites in the aspiring states. According to Barroso (2006),

> Candidate countries are sometimes surprised by the level of scrutiny during the negotiations. But this is only natural as you get closer to the EU and we get closer to you. This means the Commission will continue to monitor and report on Croatia's progress towards meeting the requirements of membership. This monitoring is part of the Commission's formal responsibilities under the EU's Treaties.

In addition to the SAAs, the EU at the Thessaloniki summit in June 2003 introduced the common instruments for EU accession, such as the European Partnerships (EPs) and the Progress Reports for the Western Balkans. The aim of the EPs, inspired by the Eastern enlargement, is to identify political and strategic priorities 'with due consideration to the Copenhagen accession criteria and to issues particular to the Western Balkans' in order for the countries to carry out short- and medium-term reforms (European Commission 2003: 3). Consequently, while the EU uses the mechanisms of monitoring and benchmarking to assess the countries' progress on meeting EU conditions, the social learning aspect of this monitoring is crucial to understanding how the EU can impact aspiring members.

Acting as a gatekeeper, the EU can impact the aspirant's transformation by allowing or denying access to negotiations and further stages of integration with the EU, which has been described by Grabbe (2006: 86) as the EU's most powerful conditionality tool. Haughton agrees (2007: 223), saying the EU's 'transformative power is at its greatest when deciding to open accession negotiations'. Arguably, the compulsory pathway is most salient here. As part of the integration and accession processes for Croatia and Serbia the EU acts as a gatekeeper or a club-owner, determining the timing of opening and the speed of advancing EU integration process. As has been the case with previous accession processes, the decision to open accession negotiations or, in this situation, the Stabilisation and Association Agreement negotiations, depends on the decision of the EU. Additionally, the accession negotiation process is open-ended – meaning that at any time negotiations can be stalled or ceased. The member states or the Commission withhold the right to suspend negotiations with any candidate should the candidate's progress be unsatisfactory. Europeanisation and enlargement literature suggest that rewarding aspirants with progress or punishing aspirants with delays in progress is central to the EU's transformative power. It is also imperative to note that, as the rewards for advancement on integration with the EU improve incrementally at each stage of the process, the conditions associated with each stage can be specified to each stage too. Grabbe (2006: 87) points out that the main value of gatekeeping is to shame political elites into dramatically altering their policies. However, as is indicated in this book, gatekeeping ultimately relies on the aspirant government being committed to achieving EU membership.

In parallel with monitoring, benchmarking and gatekeeping, the EU has encouraged social learning through ongoing engagement and involvement. At the core of social learning lies interaction. Continued interaction, usually through negotiations or the presence of EU agencies in the aspirant countries, is reserved for an elite level and rarely permeates beyond this level. Contact with the political parties, government and institutional actors provides a direct line for the EU into policymaking structures and conflict transformation processes in both cases. According to Checkel (2003), the institutional environment of the EU is particularly well suited to socialising agents from within. Consequently, this is in keeping with what we would expect through a connective pathway. Both cases negotiate with the EU and in these negotiations there are opportunities for the cases to learn EU practices and techniques. Furthermore, the continued involvement with various EU agencies facilitates a networking between political parties, usually government, and their counterparts in the EU, which creates its own strategic benefits.[29] Crucially, social learning can result in a narrow socialisation of the political and conflict parties given that, usually, only members of the government will be involved in the socialisation process.

The various mechanisms of Europeanisation are significant to the argument I am putting forward here as they help illuminate how the processes of conditionality and social learning perform and effect transformation among the political elites. Furthermore, as this work has shown, since 2000 the EU's impact on both cases has been primarily elite-focused, which will have implications for the findings of the thesis. The mechanisms directed through compulsory, enabling and connective pathways have usually targeted the political parties. While the main appeal may be membership, it is these routes of influence that are significant to understanding the ways in which the EU can have a transformative impact on the political choices made by the elites in both cases. Clearly, these mechanisms are not new to the EU since they have been used in previous enlargements, so again we can see that the EU instrumentalised and operationalised lessons learned from previous experiences to have an impact on Croatia and Serbia.

Enlargement fatigue, the dynamic which (re-)emerged strongly in some quarters following the rejection of the Constitutional Treaty in May 2005 in France and the Netherlands, and again when Bulgaria and Romania joined the EU in 2007, politically threatened the enlargement project. The discord that followed the rejection of the Constitutional Treaty centred on the enlargement project and momentarily created a hostile environment for the future of enlargement. The vigilance about the future of enlargement was compounded when it was perceived that an ill-prepared Romania and Bulgaria joined much too quickly in 2007. The October 2004 and November 2005 Commission Strategy Papers on enlargement and the January 2006 Communication to the Western Balkans were the key documents that underlined the changing enlargement dynamics since 2004. These documents consistently reiterated the European destiny of the countries of the Western Balkans but indicated a tightening conditionality and a lengthened time frame for Western Balkans enlargement. According to the European Commission (2005b), the EU aimed to carry out a 'carefully managed enlargement process' that would address the EU public's 'legitimate concerns'; this suggests a weakening of opinion within the EU. The European Commission (2006d) made the following statements, which reflected the malaise and disenchantment with the future of the enlargement project: 'an institutional settlement should have been reached by the time the next new member is likely to be ready to join the Union', and '[account must be taken of] integration capacity – can the EU take in new members without jeopardizing the political and policy objectives established by the Treaties'. European Council statements made in 2006 revealed a lack of firm commitments to the countries of the Western Balkans. This indicated a reduced appetite for enlargement within the EU.

According to an interlocutor, the transformative capacity of EU enlargement was threatened by the incoherence, intangibility and inadequacy of the present enlargement project.[30] This interlocutor argued, rather, that the long-term prospect of membership was not enough and should be sustained by intermediate rewards for the aspirants such as Croatia and Serbia in order to keep reform-minded governments on track. So, what were the implications of this negative discourse on the future of the enlargement project for the EU's capacity to impact the transformation of structures and relationships of conflict in Croatia and Serbia? A key issue arises from this debate: can the processes of reform remain vigorous when the prospect of EU membership remains distant? For Serbia in particular, the prospect of joining the EU remains distant. Enlargement fatigue means that EU integration is no longer 'a case of calling and the EU will answer; rather it is a case of you call and the EU will think about answering'.[31] Possibly, this is not purely a consequence of enlargement fatigue but also a recognition that offering membership to Serbia is not achieving the EU's desired results.

The perceived implications for Croatia and Serbia of the changing nature of the enlargement process post-2004 were twofold: conditions for accession were both evolving (İçener and Phinnemore 2006) and tougher than for previous enlargements; moreover, the EU was less absorbent (*The Economist* 2006d). First, for Croatia and Serbia, compared with the experience of previous enlargements, the monitoring process is stricter. This was echoed by the EU's justice and security commissioner Franco Frattini, who stated that the aspirant's record on human rights, corruption and media freedom 'will be looked at with a more powerful magnifying glass' (*Guardian* 2005). Second, the time frame for eventual membership has been lengthened, and it is doubtful that such a distant membership perspective can be adequate for encouraging conflict transformation in Serbia in particular. While EU membership was credited as being the 'one glue' holding the region on the path of reform and stabilisation, the durability of the glue is questionable (Ashdown 2005). Stricter conditionality, and a lengthening of the time frame for accession is made clear in the November 2005 Enlargement strategy paper. In this strategy paper, the Commission establishes more staging posts and more steps on the path to accession. Perhaps the EU is seeking better-prepared candidates as a result of lessons drawn from previous enlargements. However, in some circles this is perceived with cynicism as a delaying tactic.[32] The introduction of benchmarking, more staging posts and more complicated steps reflects the institutional reflexivity within DG Enlargement and other EU agencies such as the Parliament and Council. The considerable experience of enlarging in 2004 and 2007 provided opportunities for the EU to learn how to avoid repeating mistakes and sidestep comparable pitfalls in Croatia and Serbia. Surely, this reflexivity is a sign of institutional learning, a departure from path-dependency, and also the development of an approach more tailored to the post-war circumstances of Croatia and Serbia.

The discourse about EU enlargement fatigue that emerged in the aftermath of the referendum on the Constitutional Treaty impacted in various ways on conflict transformation.

The discourse surrounding the future of the enlargement project had a negative effect on the political elites and political discourse in Croatia. Therefore, in order to bring Croatia closer the EU must have suitable instruments to provide immediate rewards, such as opening and closing chapters and visa agreements. In the aftermath of the rejection of the constitutional Treaty by the French and Dutch in 2005, the Croatian media picked up on the enlargement blues and considered the implications of this for their country, stating that Croatia may become 'collateral damage'. Furthermore, the Chairman of the foreign policy select committee of the Croatian Parliament, Neven Mimica, stated that the

> EU will now focus on internal programmes, not on enlargement. It is clear now how harmful it was that we failed to start accession negotiations on time. Had we succeeded in doing that, our position would have been easier now (*Transitions* 6 June 2005).

The trust issue between the EU and its candidates emerges at pivotal moments when the EU no longer can believe in the commitments and lip service paid to it.

Another key implication of the fervour of enlargement fatigue is the panacea selected by the Commission to ensure the momentum of reform in the aspiring member states continues unabated. The panacea takes the form of deliberate speech acts by EU elites to reaffirm that the final destination of EU membership was still possible. These speech acts were important since they were tangible and accessible for elites and also, importantly, societies in Croatia and Serbia. Speech acts were therefore a targeted method of preventing the reformist governments' efforts being destabilised. Most notable in these speech acts were DG Enlargement Commissioner Rehn and Council Conclusions. DG Enlargement Commissioner Rehn (2005) pointed out that enlargement 'is a two-way street – conditionality only works if the countries can believe in the EU's commitment on their eventual membership.' In 2006 the January meeting of the General Affairs and External Relations Council sought to 'make the European perspective more tangible' for the Western Balkans (European Council 2006a). However, under the Austrian presidency little was achieved to rectify the growing malaise and disenchantment with the EU enlargement process in the EU and beyond as the European Stability Initiative (2006) criticised the failure of the EU to 'calm concerns across the Western Balkans that the EU is backsliding on its promises'. At the March 2006 Salzburg meeting, the EU confirmed that the 'future of the Balkans lies in the EU', yet 'the EU also notes that its absorption capacity has to be taken into account' (Council of Ministers 2006). Overall, the attitude within the EU was that the promises that the EU has made must be adhered to (*Pacta sunt servanda*), and that 'it would be extremely counter-productive or extremely destructive to now halt this process' (*EU Observer* 2005c). Additionally, the legacy of the past conflict and the EU's role in this does continue to impact the EU's attitudes toward enlargement to the countries of the former Yugoslavia: 'As Europeans we cannot avoid a heavy share of responsibility for what happened' (Patten 2004). The negative discourse surrounding the future of EU enlargement has been largely neutralised by the agreed Draft Reform Treaty in 2007 (hereafter referred to as the Lisbon Treaty). Under the Lisbon Treaty, there exists a framework to institutionally incorporate further member states.

Summary

This chapter has shown that since 2000 the EU has selected and pursued the enlargement approach to deal with the unique circumstances of the aspiring member states in the Balkans. This critical analysis demonstrated that the suitability of the instrument of integration was questionable in the mid-1990s, which was reflected in the guarded and tailored way the EU ultimately chose to proceed in relations with the Western Balkans. The EU may have chosen to deploy an integration instrument but this instrument was not equivalent to what had been employed in preceding enlargements. Owing to the specific differences between Croatia and Serbia the EU recognised that any strategy needed targeted and tailored policies under the Stabilisation and Association process and enlargement process which would address the most immediate problems of dealing with conflict. This chapter presented an analysis of the evolution of EU political conditionality and socialisation in Croatia and Serbia, particularly in light of the institutionalisation and operationalisation of lessons learned from experiences gained during the 1990s.

Operating within the framework of Europeanisation and conditionality, understood as a dynamic process consisting of numerous formal and informal norms, this study has provided an analysis of the evolution and use of political conditionality and socialisation in the Western Balkans. The analysis demonstrates that an evolution of political conditionality has taken place since the 1990s, which indicates an incremental development of the criteria. The analysis of EU political conditionality and socialisation in the Western Balkans pointed to the mix of policies through which political conditions are channelled in the Western Balkans and under which pathways its influence could be most effectively directed at the structures and relationships of conflict in the cases. As noted in this chapter, the EU employed a unique mix of stabilisation policies coupled with the traditional mechanisms of accession, which helped to account for the potential transformative capacity of the EU's approach. The cases, therefore, point to the unique role the EU is acquiring in these countries through the combination of an active player and a framework approach.

In the critical evaluation of the instruments of change coming from the EU, it is possible to assess that political conditionality and socialisation can be more salient at different key moments during the phases of integration to the EU. For example, this discussion demonstrated that the strengths of political conditionality are more evident at times when EU leverage has increased, such as when decisions are being made to open negotiations either on a Stabilisation and Association Agreement or on accession. Therefore, if the EU chooses to exert explicit coercion on certain conditions ahead of opening negotiations it is more likely that these conditions will be met in the short or medium term.

This chapter has set out the various motivations and potential implications for the EU's intensified strategy in Croatia and Serbia between 1999 and 2000, and in doing so assessed the salience of political conditionality and social learning and the various pathways of EU influence in Croatia and Serbia on the structures and relationships of conflict. Chapters 4 and 5 move on to appraise the impact of the EU's intensified strategy since 2000 on the structures and relationships of conflict, which will ultimately provide us with valuable insights into the effectiveness of the EU in conflict transformation.

4

THE IMPACT ON CROATIA

This chapter focuses on the specific effects that EU intervention had on the conflict structures and relationships in Croatia. It discusses the transformation of political parties in Croatia, and builds on the insight that the past conflicts continue to affect the present; they are still a subject of debate among the political elites and remain open to political contestation. In other words, this chapter engages directly with the debate over the meaning of the recent past for the political parties and draws the lesson that unless the historical and institutional legacies of conflict are explored by the political parties in Croatia, the tendency will be to further marginalise experiences of conflict in Croatia. Following on from the conflict transformation narrative, this chapter examines the impact that the EU's intervention in the post-2000 period, framed around the prospect of EU membership, has had on the political parties and their readiness to deal with the legacies of wars, represent evolving structures of conflict and confront the ongoing political contestations in Croatia and the Balkan region. The chapter examines the key transitions of political parties through investigation of electioneering, electoral results, policymaking, primary sources and interview material. Certainly, the key issue of conflict – full cooperation with the International Criminal Tribunal for the former Yugoslavia (ICTY) – has been a key condition for Croatian membership, and this issue has served to divide and has dictated the response both to cooperation with the condition and to preparation for membership. Relationship transformation in Croatia is examined by investigating two linked micro-studies: the influence of Croatia on Bosnian Croats, and the return of refugees and displaced persons. These two empirical examples illuminate how conflict is being transformed in Croatia and the role that EU conditionality and socialisation is playing in this transformation.

Structural change: party representation and agenda issues

The structure of the conflict in Croatia has been transformed dramatically since the death of Tudman and the end of the HDZ-dominated regime in 1999 and the intensification of the EU's approach in 2000. This dramatic shift since 2000 helps us to understand the transformation of conflict in Croatia and Croatia's progression towards achieving EU membership.

Party representation transformation

A significant change in the conflict in Croatia after 2000 was the fresh focus on achieving EU membership and an abstinence from aggressive, violent nationalism. At the time when Croatia was engaged in a violent war for its independence, in Bosnia and the Krajina region, the Croatian political elites were largely focused on aggressive tactics and manipulated Croatian nationalism under the Tudman regime. A key turning point in Croatian party representation came in 2000, after the death of Tudman the previous year. The death of Tudman occurred at the time the EU was setting out a more constructive role in the countries of the former Yugoslavia, including Croatia.

The shift in party representation since the death of Tudman and the demise of his regime has been described as both 'substantial' and 'superficial'.[1] In this section I show that because of the increasing EU assistance, association and pre-accession processes and inbuilt incentive structures, evidence exists to verify that the transformation of parties has been more 'substantial' than 'superficial' since 2000. Additionally, and meaningfully, the processes of integration with the EU have decisively shaped this 'substantial' party transformation. Central to this argument is the role played by the EU's political conditionality and social learning. This transformation in party representation and, indeed, the transformation of the HDZ, were sustained in Croatia because Croatia, and importantly its political elites, have been locked into a process by virtue of its former potential candidacy and now its actual candidacy. Enclosure in the EU integration process is significant because there are few opportunities for the political elites to backtrack from commitments and transformation. Therefore they are compelled to continue transformation because of conditionality and socialisation pressures as well as pressures from societal expectations.

The EU's influence on party representation in Croatia since 2000 is most evident through compulsory, enabling and connective impacts. In terms of the *compulsory* impact, the EU provided direct incentives and policies for the political leadership of the various parties to the conflict. The key important party to the conflict, the HDZ, has encouraged a degree of transformation within the party in terms of policy output, relations with other parties and rhetoric. As for the *enabling* impact, the prospect of integration with and membership of the EU had an impact on the perceptions among the elite and in the institutions of the conflict parties. In Croatia, the EU had an enabling impact on the political elites when the EU supported a de-securitising framework by the local elites on contentious issues such as ICTY cooperation and refugee returns. The processes of integrating into and the prospect of joining the EU incentivised the HDZ to relinquish exclusionary discourses against refugees and minorities within Croatia. Finally, for the *connective* impact the EU assisted the parties perceived to be facilitating conflict transformation primarily through political and financial support after elections. This discussion demonstrates that party transformation is evident in terms of changes taking place within existing parties as well as the emergence of new players who have affected the balance of power in Croatia on the key agenda issue of ICTY cooperation. Therefore, this discussion explicitly links the transformation of the structures of conflict (parties and agenda issues) with the impact of the processes of integration with the EU and the prospect of joining the EU.

The death of Tuđman in December 1999 marked a change in the political landscape in terms of the balance of power between the conflict parties and their interests, representations and the agenda issues. As shown in Table 4.1, the HDZ were defeated in the parliamentary and presidential elections in 2000 and a coalition of six anti-Tuđmanist parties were the victors. Table 4.1 shows that Tuđman's nationalist HDZ government was replaced in 2000 with a centre-left coalition of six opposition parties, with Ivica Račan as prime minister. Račan's Social Democratic Party (SDP and ex-communists) won 44 seats and formed a coalition with five other parties on an anti-HDZ platform. Later, in 2000, moderate Stjepan Mesić was elected President of Croatia. How important was the EU to the shift in party representation in Croatia in 2000 and the balance of power between parties?

The EU's evolving presence in 2000 was a significant transformative force on the parties in Croatia. The electoral defeat of Tuđman's HDZ in the 2000 elections provided a window of opportunity for a rapprochement between Croatia and the EU. The changing domestic conditions in Croatia made it possible for the EU to evolve as 'a more fully fledged actor in Croatia'.[2] The enabling and compulsory impact of the EU was tangible during the presidential election in 2000 when the EU directly incentivised the emerging parties by offering closer integration, economic assistance and, later in 2000, a more intensified EU strategy.

The political agendas and rhetoric of the political parties in Croatia were transformed in 2000 when each of the presidential hopefuls contested the

Table 4.1 Croatian parliamentary and presidential electoral results, 2000

Parliamentary election results 2000

Parties	Votes	Percentage	Seats in the Parliament (total number 151)	Percentage
SDP, HSLS	1,138,318	40.9	71	47
HDZ	784,192	24.3	46	30
HSS, HNS, IDS, LS	432,527	15.6	24	16
HSP, HKDU	152,669	5.2	5	3.3

Presidential electoral results 2000

Candidate	Party	First round		Second round	
		Votes	Percentage	Votes	Percentage
Stjepan Mesić	HNS	1,100,671	41.1	1,433,372	56
Drazen Budisa	HSLS	741,837	27.7	1,125,969	44
Mate Granic	HDZ	601,588	22.5		

Sources: this table is compiled from the following: (a) http://www.parties-and-elections.de/croatia.html; (b) Central Bureau of Statistics of the Republic of Croatia 'Statistical Information 2004'; and (c) www.hidra.hr

elections on a pro-EU stance (*Financial Times* 24 January 2000). Significantly, the fact that all three candidates canvassed on a pro-EU ticket indicated that the prospect of EU membership was not a distinguishable feature which accounted for Mesić's electoral success (*Financial Times* 18 February 2000).[3] Nonetheless, the pro-EU agenda transcended the political party spectrum in 2000. This indicates that the prospect of EU membership facilitated a new discursive framework among the political elites. While the EU issue did not win or lose the presidential election for Mesić or the parliamentary election for the SDP and Opposition Six, the EU did provide a stabilising and supporting influence on the newly elected elites in 2000 because of the European Council decisions taken at Santa Maria de Feira in June 2000 and the Zagreb Summit in November 2000. In light of the election of pro-EU forces the EU set about offering support to the new government in the form of supportive speeches, financial rewards and increased political linkages. Here it is possible to see that through a connective pathway the EU was able to help consolidate the democratic reform process in Croatia by impacting party interests, representation and language in 2000.

In sum, the shift in party representation in 2000 was noteworthy for the following reasons. First, Mesić's election was important in that he represented an important departure from the nationalistic agendas of the HDZ, which was demonstrated in his support for cooperation with ICTY, dismantling Tudman's anti-democratic structures and Croatian withdrawal from interference in Bosnia-Hercegovina (Bideleux and Jeffries 2007: 217). Second, Mesić's presidency was stabilised by the political affirmations made by the EU, which were complemented by the EU strategy of offering highly visible political and financial commitments made in the Stability Pact, the Stabilisation and Association process, the Santa Maria de Feira European Council, and – crucially for Croatia – at the Zagreb Summit.

From 2000, Croatia began to avail itself of financial assistance from the EU which was explicitly linked to developing closer political ties in the form of the Stabilisation and Association process. In other words, for Croatia to receive economic benefits such as improved access to markets or economic assistance for the regeneration of war-damaged towns, Croatia had to engage politically with the EU and, therefore, meet the EU's political as well as economic expectations. The developing relations between Croatia and the EU under the framework of the Stabilisation and Association process continued between 2000 and 2002 and resulted in the submission of a membership application in 2003. In December 2002 all political parties in the Croatian parliament defined Croatia's accession to the EU as a strategic national goal and asked the government to submit an application for EU membership (which it did on 21 February 2003). With each political party in agreement, this signalled a 'consensus and determination of all political forces' in Croatia for EU membership.[4] Meaningfully, this resolution departed from isolationist Article 141 of the Croatian Constitution which Tudman had adopted and which prohibited Croatia from joining an association of states.

During the association phase of integration, when Croatia was part of a Stabilisation and Association process, a recipient of CARDS funding, a potential candidate for EU membership, and an applicant for EU membership, the EU had little impact on the balance of power between parties. It would be expected that the EU's influence in Croatia would result in continued electoral success for the party that had achieved so much in terms of structure transformation and integration with the EU (the SDP) in the

Table 4.2 Croatian parliamentary election results, 2003

	Votes	Percentage	Seats in the Parliament (total number)	Percentage
HDZ	840,692	33.2	66	43.7
SDP	560,593	23.3	43	28.5
HNS	198,781	8.3	11	7.3
HSS	177,359	7.2	9	6

Source: adapted from IFES Election Guide, Croatia, http://www.electionguide.org/results.php?ID=396.

early transition period from 2000 to 2003. Yet, despite the progress made in the three years since their election in 2000, the SDP did not experience the same electoral success in the 2003 parliamentary elections as in 2000. The re-emergence of the HDZ as electoral victors in 2003 represented one of the most significant indications of party transformation in Croatia since 2000, which ultimately affected the balance of power in Croatian politics. As Table 4.2 shows, the HDZ won 33.2 per cent of the vote in 2003, and 66 seats. The SDP won 28.5 per cent of the vote – a fall of almost 20 per cent since the 2000 parliamentary elections.

From 2000 to 2003 the shift in the political agenda, nature, language and political strategies of the HDZ indicated a significant party transformation in the wider context of integration with the EU. The HDZ responded to the changing context which was caused by the presence of the EU. By 2003 Croatia had applied for EU membership and was pressing for a positive avis from the Commission. According to one interlocutor, by 2003 the HDZ was 'totally incomparable to what it was', insofar as the HDZ was now dedicated to achieving the goal of EU membership.[5] Arguably, further investigation of this comment is necessary.

As a party, the HDZ had stated an ambition for EU membership, yet support for harmonising with the EU and meeting its conditions did not permeate all levels of the party. A notable occasion where we see a rift in the HDZ over the implications of closer integration with the EU was in 2003 regarding conditionality of ICTY cooperation. On the issue of ICTY cooperation the HDZ remained reluctant: when Dorothy Pack, speaking at the HDZ's Eighth General Assembly, stated that she 'hoped Gotovina would go to The Hague and so serve Croatia in peace-time as well, she was booed' (*World News Connection* 21 June 2003).[6] This indicated that the transformation of the HDZ party was not complete in 2003; factions within the HDZ did not favour EU conditionality or issue transformation. This was particularly significant given that the UK and the Netherlands had not ratified the Stabilisation and Association Agreement which had been negotiated under the Račan government because of Croatia's reluctance to cooperate with the ICTY.

It is useful to ascertain the credibility of the interlocutor's claim about the significant transformation of the HDZ. The role of political conditionality and social learning became increasingly salient in party transformation, particularly in advanced association and accession opportunities. The advanced and intensified processes of association and pre-accession dynamics resulted in increased relations between EU institutions and the political elites in Croatia as well as increased significance for EU conditionality. Therefore, the closer a country gets to the EU, in terms of association and accession, the stronger the case for transformation through social learning and conditionality. According to the interlocutor cited above, this was the case regarding the HDZ in Croatia.

Intensified association with the EU in 2003 led to an increase in meetings and interactions between Croatia and the EU, as well as the EU expecting more from Croatia in terms of meeting EU-specified conditions. Obviously, this would have a direct impact on the ruling parties in Croatia who were responsible for managing integration with the EU. Batt (2004: 1) contends that the HDZ was 'taking useful advice from Western European conservative and people's parties on how to revise its ideology and adapt to the demands of Europeanisation'. Therefore, according to Batt, there was a definite case of socialisation of the HDZ by elites and institutions within the EU. While the case for socialisation is compelling, it would be unwise to neglect other pressures and the wider context which the HDZ was responding to. It would be remiss to omit the domestic pressures for change experienced by the HDZ within the party and in Croatia. The transformation of the HDZ can be explained as a response to the changing political context in Croatia, a reaction to the electoral defeat in 2000, the failure of Račan's government to cope with the economic situation and to respond sufficiently to the expectations of the electorate since its election in 2000 (*Financial Times* 24 June 2002). Additionally, the re-emergence of the HDZ in 2003 represented a trend in post-conflict societies when the former ruling party could continue to have significant influence, not because of a change in orientation, but because the ruling elites have 'well-placed allies in both the private and state-run sectors of the economy, in the media, and in the judiciary and security services' (Batt 2003: 85).

EU agencies were also not convinced by the apparent transformation of the HDZ in 2003. The 2003 HDZ electoral success was not particularly well received by many in the EU because it had been less than a decade since the HDZ had pursued war in Krajina. Račan (SDP), who contested the elections against Sanader, amplified the concern about an HDZ victory. He contended that the HDZ had not moved from its nationalist agenda and thus a HDZ electoral victory would endanger Croatia's processes of integration with the EU (*Financial Times* 13 July 2004). Račan's comments can in hindsight be recognised as electoral politics rather than an accurate reflection of the situation. Since then, Sanader and the HDZ have pursued a democratic and pro-EU campaign which demonstrates the degree to which the prospect of EU membership has permeated the Croatian political landscape.

The transformation that Sanader claimed is evident in the following ways. First, the HDZ formed a coalition in this election with the Independent Democratic Serb Party – which was a departure from its previous attitude toward minorities (Jović 2006: 98). This was made possible because the HDZ adopted less exclusionary discourses about minorities and the return of refugees, which was largely encouraged by EU conditionality in the Stabilisation and Association Agreement. Second, the NGO Civic Committee for Human Rights confirmed that during 2003–4 the HDZ approach to human rights and ethnic reconciliation was 'a pleasant surprise' and was mirrored with a shift in rhetoric (*Financial Times* 13 July 2004). Third, the presence of the conservative-nationalist HDZ government that pursued a pro-EU agenda suggested that by 2003–4 democratisation was embedded in Croatia and the prospect of joining the EU had a transformative impact on the policies, rhetoric and agendas of the political elites (SEESOX 2007: 3). The transformation of the HDZ in 2003 was therefore substantial, but it was largely driven by the leaders of the party and had clearly not filtered down through the party ranks. This suggests, therefore, that the EU was much more effective at targeting and impacting the political elites, first through the compulsory pathway, and second through social learning. This is the case because increased interaction between EU institutions and agencies facilitated social learning among the engaged Croatian political elites. Additionally, EU conditionality aimed at the Croatian political elites required that the political elites (who had stated their ambition to join the EU) must meet EU conditions on minority rights and refugee returns. These two issues were at the cornerstone of the repackaged and 'transformed' HDZ. The shift in the HDZ's interests, policies and nature since 2000 can be explained by the widespread and accepted desire to become a member of the EU within the party and across the spectrum of political life

Table 4.3 Croatian presidential election results, 2005

| Candidate | Party | First round | | Second round | |
		Votes	Percentage	Votes	Percentage
Stjepan Mesić	HNS	1,089,398	48.92	1,454,451	65.93
Jadranka Kosor	HDZ	452,218	20.31	751,692	34.07
Boris Mikšić	Independent	396,093	17.79		

Source: IFES Election Guide, Croatia, http://www.electionguide.org/results. php?ID=68

in Croatia. To realise this ambition, the previously right-wing HDZ cast off its nationalist past and promised to move the country toward EU member-ship following victory in the parliamentary elections in 2003 (*Financial Times* 25 November 2003). Again, the salience of the EU as a transforma-tive influence on the parties in Croatia was evident in 2005. The 2005 presidential election featured the management of the EU accession proc-ess as a key issue on both the SDP (Mesić) and HDZ (Kosor) campaigns. However, Kosor's campaign was greatly weakened by the fact that Mesić was already bringing Croatia closer to the EU and thus 'drew much of the wind from her sails' (*Financial Times* 17 January 2005). The incumbent President Mesić won the 2005 presidential elections, which were held over two rounds on 2 and 16 January, gaining 66 per cent of the vote (European Commission 2005a).

As indicated above, the processes of integration into and the prospect of joining the EU emerged as an important aspect of party politics in Croatia after 2000 and featured significantly in electoral campaigns. Complying with the norms and rules of EU membership, which takes place during the pre-accession period, has the potential to weaken the domestic power base of the governing political parties. To clarify, the processes of integration with the EU present significant challenges and can potentially threaten the status of the governing political elites. Putman's concept of 'two-level game' is important here, as the political elites are answerable not only to the EU but also to their electorate. However, the threat posed by complying with and implementing unpopular policies in order to comply with EU demands was not realised in the post-2000 era in Croatia. Mesić was a prime advocate of integration with the EU and remained President of Croatia following electoral success in 2000 and 2005 (*EU Observer* 17 January 2005).

Evidence suggests that, in terms of the policies, relationships and rhet-oric the political parties of conflict in Croatia experienced 'substantial' rather than 'superficial' transformation. It is sensible to produce a counter-argument that the central political parties in Croatia failed to experience a qualitative transformation but were rather toeing the line as far as they needed to in terms of the integration with the EU process, without showing any substantial change.[7] However, the evidence gleaned through the empirical research conducted does not substantiate this counter-argument in a convincing way. The evidence presented in this section revealed that the EU has had an impact on party transformation in Croatia insofar as the agendas, relationships and interdependence are shaped explicitly by the integration with the EU process rather than by the conflict issues that dominated key party positions prior to 2000.

Agenda-issue transformation

The prospect of EU membership had a significant impact on the transformation of issues in Croatia. This was notable through the significant change in the conflict's political agenda; issues that had previously been highly controversial diminished in importance when other interests became more overwhelming. An indicator of agenda-issue transformation that is linked to the wars experienced in the 1990s was cooperation with the ICTY – an explicit condition for closer integration with and membership of the EU. The issue of cooperation with the ICTY is a useful indicator of conflict transformation in Croatia. Under Tudman, cooperation with the ICTY was a taboo subject. However, after 2000 it was widely discussed and the issue of ethnic cleansing featured in political discourse.[8] This did not mean that it had lost its contentiousness. Moreover, as the following discussion shows, its sensitivity had been amplified by the way in which the EU handled the ICTY condition – linking it to progress in integration with the EU. Therefore, while there was potential for the EU to positively impact the transformation of this issue, the outcome of the EU's practice was disappointing at times.

From the outset, indictments by the ICTY were hugely contentious and divisive among Croatian political elites and society because, for the majority of people living in Croatia, the war was recent, memories were vivid and the indicted war criminals were perceived as respected Croatian war heroes. While the EU did not deal out the indictments, the EU is perceived in Croatia to be closely linked to the ICTY because of its political (mis-)management of the ICTY issue. As stated above, the EU was quick to provide technical, economic and political incentives to the pro-reform governments after 2000; however, the indictments of Gotovina (8 June 2001) and Bobetko (23 August 2002) represented a challenge for the governments in their pursuit of EU membership. ICTY cooperation was a condition to achieve EU membership and integration. Therefore, by linking progress on integration with the EU to full Croatian cooperation with the ICTY, the EU had the potential to transform this issue. This was important in 2002–3 because the UK and the Netherlands refused to ratify the Stabilisation and Association Agreement over Croatia's perceived lack of cooperation with the ICTY. Therefore, regarding progress on integration with the EU and toward achieving EU membership, Croatia's pace was dictated by cooperation with the ICTY issue to a greater extent than any other condition. Between 2000 and 2003, the prospect of closer integration and the prospect of joining the EU failed to qualitatively change how the political parties dealt with the issue of ICTY cooperation. Instead the issue remained highly politicised and cooperation reluctant and partial. Gotovina was not transferred to the ICTY until after this period.

The EU's transformative capacity on how the political parties dealt with the issue of ICTY cooperation would potentially increase when Croatia came closer to integration into the EU. Therefore, after Croatia became a candidate state in 2004 it might have been expected that the EU's impact on the transformation of the issue of cooperation with ICTY would intensify. Instead, ICTY cooperation continued to dictate the pace of progress of Croatian integration with the EU. This was significant for two reasons: it revealed a protectionist and reflexive EU and it provided an opportunity for the EU to maximise its transformative capacity in a role of gatekeeper. On the first point, as a result of lessons learned from previous enlargements the EU had been applying stricter conditionality throughout the various stages of integration with the EU. As one interlocutor put it, pushing for full cooperation with ICTY ahead of opening accession negotiations was a way of 'getting the tough conditions out of the way earlier'. This demonstrated that the EU recognised the need to use conditionality more efficiently and more visibly earlier and earlier in the pre-accession processes, and encourage full compliance with the more difficult political rather than technical conditions earlier in the pre-accession process. Therefore, here we see a reflexive EU actively seeking to enhance its transformative capacity on conflict issues early in the pre-accession process.

On the second point, opening accession negotiations represented a major gatekeeping opportunity for the EU. Gatekeeping is a straightforward method of encouraging full compliance with EU conditions. In terms of EU relations with Croatia, this was the penultimate gatekeeping opportunity as delaying or stopping accession represents the final major gatekeeping opportunity. At a Foreign Ministers meeting on 12 December 2004, the debate over the decision to open accession negotiations with Croatia in March or

April 2005 centred on Croatia's continuing cooperation with the ICTY. Significantly, it was not explained precisely how this cooperation would be confirmed or defined (Agence Europe 13 December 2004). Ahead of the scheduled opening of accession negotiations on 17 March 2005, the EU increased pressure on Croatia to cooperate fully with the ICTY. Utilising the gatekeeping mechanism the EU attempted to ensure that the ICTY and its accession criteria were not undermined. As Grabbe (2006: 87) point out, gatekeeping is a 'blunt weapon that can be used judiciously for priority areas only'. According to Grabbe, its main value is as a shock tactic to embarrass applicant countries' governments into making dramatic changes owing to the domestic repercussions of failing to meet a major foreign policy goal (2006: 87). This helps to explain why the EU was motivated to act as a gatekeeper on this highly public issue. Additional supporting evidence that the strict conditionality of integration with the EU process had a transformative impact on party and issue transformation in Croatia since 2000 is particularly strong in 2003–4, when the previously nationalistic opponents of the ICTY, the governing HDZ, transferred more indictees to the ICTY than any of its neighbours in the same time frame (*International Herald Tribune* 28 February 2005).

The relationship between the ICTY and the EU merits further discussion at this point. EU conditionality fortified the clout of the ICTY in the Western Balkans. Importantly, for the first time a decision made by an external body, namely the ICTY, significantly influenced the EU's policy towards an associate and applicant: Croatia. Furthermore, this was also the first time that the EU had made a decision to postpone the opening of accession negotiations with an aspirant member. On 4 March 2005 ICTY Chief Prosecutor del Ponte stated in a letter to all 25 EU member states that 'despite all public and private assurances from Zagreb, Ante Gotovina remains within reach of the Croatian authorities, and until such time as he is brought to The Hague, it cannot be said that Croatia is co-operating fully with the international tribunal' (*International Herald Tribune* 2005b).

In the run-up to the 17 March deadline the EU made continued warnings that without better cooperation accession negotiations would not be opened with Croatia at this stage. There was no ambiguity. Here the EU acted very clearly and plainly as a gatekeeper. European Council President Junker summed up the situation rather bluntly:

> If Mr Gotovina is in The Hague by 17 March, negotiations will certainly begin on that day. If he is not there, there will be serious

difficulties, unless the Croatian authorities can prove that they have fully and entirely cooperated with the Tribunal (Agence Europe 12 February 2005).

The EU's decision to postpone the opening of accession negotiations with Croatia was significant in two respects: its implications for the wider region and future candidate states, and its effect on public support for the process of integration with the EU in Croatia. The EU's consistency on the demand for full cooperation with the ICTY was motivated by the regional implications of any perceived weakening of conditionality. This decision was made against the background of Serbia's deficient cooperation with ICTY. Additionally, the nature of conflict transformation in Croatia in terms of how political parties perceive ICTY cooperation and integration into the EU was impacted by the 16 March deadlock.

This experience lies at the core of the study: the link between Europeanisation and conflict transformation. The EU strictly maintained conditionality over ICTY cooperation and explicitly linked failure to cooperate to a stalling of the progress of integration into the EU. Therefore, at this crucial moment Croatian political parties had to deal with both the conflict legacy of war crimes and the ambition of becoming a member of the EU. Croatian political parties had to ask themselves a serious question: was the prospect of joining the EU attractive enough to cooperate fully with the ICTY condition and therefore deal with a very difficult legacy from the recent wars? Initially, the Croatian response to the weighty application of conditionality was to express a sense of injustice at the hands of the EU: Foreign Minister Grabar-Kitarović argued that failure to commence accession negotiations with Croatia on the 17 March 2005 deadline would put Croatia's application for EU membership in 'deadlock', stressing that Croatia was not able to transfer Gotovina to the ICTY because he was not in Croatia (*International Herald Tribune* 28 February 2005). Furthermore, the Croatian political elites were keen to remind the EU that such a decision was harmful for the EU's image in Croatia and indeed for the pro-EU forces within Croatia. As Grabar-Kitarović highlighted, during a period when support for EU accession was rapidly declining in Croatia (50 per cent in March 2005 from 78 per cent in March 2003), postponement of accession negotiations 'would definitely have a negative impact on the domestic political scene'. Not only this, but it would have wider regional implications and 'would give the hardliners a boost ... not only in Croatia but in the neighbourhood as well' (*International Herald Tribune* 28 February 2005). While these comments by Grabar-Kitarović on 28 February can be attributed to bargaining in the run-up to the 16 March 2005 decision, there is some significance in them as they help to capture elite-level concerns in Croatia regarding both conflict transformation and Europeanisation.

Later in 2005, when the EU opened accession negotiations on 3 October and Gotovina was still not in The Hague, criticisms were levelled at the EU. As one prominent MEP, Graham Watson, asked, 'What has suddenly changed?' (Agence Europe 5 October 2005). In terms of Croatia's response to the EU's earlier 17 March decision, much had changed. Croatia launched a more intensive campaign to capture Gotovina, which was combined with a more concentrated EU effort to assist, monitor and ultimately persuade Croatia to cooperate more fully with the ICTY by creating an EU task force. Developments between 17 March and 3 October 2005 reveal two important points about conflict transformation and Europeanisation. First, in terms of the EU's transformative capacity on conflict, the EU moved from a path-dependent approach and demonstrated reflexivity with the launch of a specified task force to deal solely with ICTY cooperation. This was an interesting shift in EU decision-making regarding its applicant countries, where ultimately the Commission plays the crucial monitoring role. Second, the transformation of the issue of conflict of indicted war criminals was visibly affected by the EU's conditionality and, therefore, the EU directly effected transformation among Croatian political parties and society on this conflict issue.

To digress briefly, the EU's impact on political parties and society in Croatia needs to be clarified further. When the EU made the decision to postpone the opening of accession negotiations with Croatia on 16 March 2005 because of Croatia's failure to comply fully with EU conditionality, it created a grey area between the individualisation and collectivisation of guilt in Croatia. As part of its purpose the ICTY upholds a fundamental aim of the Court and process of individual criminal responsibility.[9] Trust is a structural condition of conflict that is related to the ongoing issue of the collectivisation and individualisation of guilt. Quoted in the *International Herald Tribune*, Croatian President Mesić recognised that trust was a central tenet of restoring reconciliation through the process of individualising guilt rather than collectivising guilt: 'through the process of individualising the guilt, we have removed that scar. Croats and Serbs are being made accountable. It will put a stop to collective guilt' (*International Herald Tribune* 22 November 2005). Nonetheless, the EU's decision to prevent and postpone Croatia's progress towards EU accession because of its failure to transfer Gotovina to The Hague in March 2005 diminished the individualisation of guilt and transferred blame and punishment to the Croatian people. This negative impact of EU conditionality in Croatia had implications for popular support of EU membership and also challenged the stability of the political elites in Croatia.

The issue dominated EU–Croatia relations and conflict transformation in Croatia throughout 2005, culminating with the arrest of the much-wanted General Gotovina in December 2005. Following the opening of accession negotiations with Croatia, Gotovina was arrested in Spain on 7 December – the last of Croatia's indictees to be transferred to The Hague. While there is no indication that these two events were in any way linked it would appear to be more than convenient for both the EU and Croatia. Without Croatia's full cooperation and approval from the ICTY Chief Prosecutor, it is unlikely that accession negotiations with Croatia would have opened, despite pressure from the Austrian presidency.

While 2005 represented a key year in which the EU directly and obtrusively employed political conditionality to encourage what it perceived to be conflict transformation in Croatia, the EU remained uncertain that its impact was as thorough or as lasting as it had intended. The European Commission ascertained that 'little is said in public discourse about the need to establish the truth about who is responsible for the crimes for which Ante Gotovina and other Croatian generals are indicted' (European Commission 2006a: 14).

The European Commission naively associated the continued support for Gotovina and the general malaise about ICTY cooperation with the fact that 'the general public does not have easy access to objective information about the work of the ICTY' (European Commission 2005a: 14). This showed that in its pursuit of 'truth and justice' the European Commission and its member states had a limited understanding about the appeal of the military leaders who won independence for Croatia in the 1990s. This is significant for this book as it indicates that the EU's strategies may have unintended negative impacts that impede the transformation of conflict in terms of how political parties perceive the agenda issues. Are Croatian political parties adopting a superficial stance purely in order to achieve the greater benefit of EU membership? If so, does this diminish indications that conflict transformation occurred? Rather, the substantial and significant shift in how the political parties, particularly the HDZ government, responded to EU conditionality indicates convincingly that the EU caused the transformation on this issue.

Summary

At the crux of the discussion of issue transformation in Croatia lies the EU's intensified employment of political conditionality. This discussion demonstrated that the EU undoubtedly had an impact on conflict in Croatia, yet the transformation experienced was much more nuanced than the EU may have wished for. Acting as a gatekeeper, in addition to using the mechanisms of EU conditionality and socialisation, the EU denied and stalled progress towards advancement on EU relations because of incomplete cooperation with the ICTY. In Croatia, recognising the importance of meeting the requirement of ICTY cooperation, the political elites adjusted their rhetoric and attitude towards cooperation with the ICTY, albeit minimally and reluctantly. This demonstrated that through compulsory and enabling pathways the EU's conditionality and socialisation mechanisms were effective. The political will in Croatia to cooperate with the EU's condition of ICTY cooperation represented considerable evidence of the EU's capacity to transform the issues. The elites were party to and affected by the EU's bargaining strategy of reinforcement by rewards; for the most part, for all the conflict parties in Croatia, the cost of non-compliance outweighed the cost of compliance. However, one issue remained problematic: the EU making the opening of accession negotiations conditional on the transfer of General Gotovina, who the political elites maintained was not within the control of Croatian security services. Additionally, it is imperative to note that the shift in attitude towards cooperation was undermined by the elites using the EU as a scapegoat and transferring blame and enmity to the EU rather than accepting responsibility. Therefore, instead of having the desired impact of opening the ICTY/war crimes issue for appraisal in societal discourse, EU conditionality undermined any potential for issue transformation and had an unintended impact of fostering a sentiment of collective guilt in Croatia. This collective guilt was fostered because of the perceived punishment dealt by the EU, which denied Croatia the opportunity to commence accession negotiations.

Relationship change

Relationship transformation refers to how the political parties in Croatia interact with one another on key relationships of conflict. This is most usefully drawn out by an examination of the influence of Croatian political elites on Bosnia and Bosnian Croats, and the return of refugees. These two empirical examples illuminate how conflict is being transformed in Croatia and the role that EU conditionality and socialisation is playing in this transformation. Therefore, this section critically examines, first, how the political elites changed in their attitudes towards the conflictual relationships and, second, how these changing attitudes of the political elites in Croatia impacted on perceptions of conflictual relationships. Finally, the section examines how these changing perceptions impact on the patterns of exchange in the conflictual relationships.

As a signatory of the Dayton Peace Accords, and in view of EU conditionality focusing on good neighbourliness and the large number of refugees and displaced persons from Bosnia in Croatia, Croatia has a geo-strategic and historical interest in Bosnia and particularly in ethnic Croats in Bosnia. Hence Croatian political elites have consistently been engaged in the politics of Bosnian Croats as well as Bosnia. It is the relationship between Croatia and Bosnian Croats that is of chief interest here; more specifically, Croatia's capacity to influence Bosnian Croats.

During the 1990s ethnic mobilisation and propaganda politicised ethnic identities in Bosnia. While the ethnonationalist propaganda in the 1990s strengthened and sharpened ethnic intolerance, cooperation continued into the 1990s, despite the increasingly potent nationalist propaganda (Hodson *et al.* 1994). For example, according to Maček (2001: 208), in Sarajevo there was initially a strong resistance to the nationalist discourses but violence gradually forced people to accept the logic that members of other groups posed a security threat and their own security depended on solidarity with the national group. Therefore a manifest alignment between Croatia and ethnic Croats living in Bosnia came about during the 1990s and has continued. Since 2000, relations between Croatia and the Bosnian Croats have continued to be significant, particularly for the Bosnian Croats. The relationship between Croatia and Bosnia was institutionalised with the creation of the Croatian-Bosnian Council for Cooperation, with a stated ambition to incorporate European ideas into the settlement of the two countries' relations. The HDZ funded and assisted ethnic Croats in Bosnia. This is interesting, as the levels of support provided by the HDZ had to be balanced between its level of obligation towards the Bosnian Croats and the level it believed the EU would consider appropriate without being too intrusive or destabilising. Therefore, it is possible to state that the EU had the capacity to encourage Croatia to act as a stabilising and pro-EU force in Bosnia.

In view of this, it is appropriate to ask the question: have the processes of integration with and the prospect of joining the EU provided an increased transformative capacity for Croatia to act as a pro-EU force or perceived stabilising force? While Croatia continued, after 2000, to have a significant role in Bosnia because of its financial and political support for the Bosnian Croats under President Mesić, a significant refinement in the scope of this support occurred. Mesić advocated a change in Croatian policy toward Bosnian Croats which resulted in the successive governments of Croatia ending financial assistance for Croats in Bosnia and also limited political-level interference in Bosnia. This had an implication for how the Bosnian Croats perceived the HDZ and Croatia. Bosnian Croats too began to move away from the HDZ and bring to an end the reliance demonstrated throughout the 1990s. The EU did play a significant role in the shift in relations between Croatia and Bosnian Croats, primarily through the agency of the EU's High Representative in Bosnia. Owing to the Office of the High Representative's mandate for pushing through reforms in Bosnia a distance was established between Bosnia and Croatia. The presence of the High Representative and the successive governments in Bosnia undermined the political and financial muscle of Croatia in Bosnia. Furthermore, the EU actively pressed the HDZ and the Croatian political parties to limit their relationships with Bosnia in this respect and, through a connective pathway, facilitated relationships through transnational linkages across the region rather than direct Croatian–Bosnian Croat linkages. Due to the ambition of the HDZ to stay in government and to make progress on EU membership, the HDZ was prepared to alter its interests in Bosnia and use its influence to discourage secessionist discourse in Bosnia and encourage implementation of the Dayton Agreement. Hence, it is arguable that through the membership perspective, particularly through enabling and connective pathways rather than compulsory pathways, the EU transformed the relationship of conflict.

While there is evidence that a compulsory pathway was present, it is clear that the EU did not condition Croatia's integration with the EU, or cause Croatia to refine either its attitude toward Bosnia or, importantly, its relationships with Bosnian Croats. It is interesting to note that, while it was not an explicit condition or politically salient issue which dominated the agenda in Croatia or at the EU level, through socialisation and political conditionality the EU did persuade the HDZ that a more appropriate relationship between the HDZ and Bosnia's Croats needed to be established and that any influence should be used to advance the Dayton Peace Accords.

The processes of integration with and the prospect of joining the EU can transform conflict through more than strict conditionality. The way that the technical negotiations interplayed with the political socialisation pressures coming from EU agencies such as member states and institutions resulted in the HDZ altering its attitude and role in Bosnia quite significantly. This is not to diminish the continued salience of the ethnic ties and interlinkages between Croats in Croatia and Bosnia, but what is significant at a political level is that the political elites in Croatia have actively demonstrated a refined approach to Bosnia and therefore to Bosnia's Croats. In sum, the socialisation pressures of the EU's contractual relations with Croatia played a determining role in the shift in Croatian attitudes and policies toward this relationship.

One source of conflict in Croatia during the 1990s was the relationship between the Croatian government and the Serb minority communities in Croatia. Throughout the 1990s the relationship between the HDZ government and the Croatian Serb communities was highly destructive, and this was manifested in the depletion of the Croatian Serb population in the 1990s. During Operation Flash and Operation Storm in May and August 1995 approximately 84,000 Croats fled from areas under Serbian control and 70,000 ethnic Serbs (Blitz 2005: 366). Given the political salience of the refugee issue and the EU's stated ambition that ethnic cleansing would not be successful in the Balkans, refugee return has been at the cornerstone of the EU's intensified strategy in the region.[10] The EU employed the processes of integration with and the prospect of joining the EU to incentivise the Croatian political elites to transform their perceptions and attitudes towards refugee return. It was a top-down process of pressuring elites to publicly transform their attitudes to the returns process.

As with the political conditionality of full cooperation with the ICTY, the EU conditioned the evolution of relations with Croatia on achieving success and progress on the issue of return of refugees. The refugees in question are not only the Croatian Serbs who fled during wartime but also ethnic Croatians who were displaced during the wars. The returns process was not a straightforward issue for transformation in Croatia, as became evident in early 2000. Following the electoral victories of Mesić and Račan, both leaders advocated the return of refugees and displaced people 'regardless of their ethnicity' (*Financial Times* 2000c). Attempts to encourage the return of refugees in Croatia stand in marked contrast to the approach favoured in 1995 by Tuđman, who introduced the 'law of temporary takeover' to formalise the rights of Bosnian Croats to settle in formerly Serb-dominated towns and villages in Croatia. Previously, the electoral law which was adopted struggled to deal with the enfranchisement of Croatian Serbs and seats for minority groups. This was confirmed in a report by the International Crisis Group (2002), which concluded that the newly elected government and president in 2000 inherited an 'unsatisfactory legacy of discriminatory laws and practices from its predecessor, to the detriment in particular of ethnic Serb displaced persons and refugees'. Therefore, in spite of pressure and political and financial support from the EU, institutional and legal obstacles to the integration of national minorities prevailed because of inadequate electoral laws.

Since 2003, we can see the HDZ government and PM Sanader seeking to improve relationships with the Croatian Serb community in three, largely symbolic, ways: Sanader publicly asked Serb refugees to return; he attended the Orthodox Christmas reception party of the Serb National Council in Zagreb; and he made a visit to the concentration camp at Jasenovac where Serbs were murdered during World War Two. At the end of 2002 the European Union pressurised Croatia to increase the return of refugees and facilitate the integration of national minorities. In 2003 the Croatian government adopted the Constitutional Law on the Rights of National Minorities and important legislative modifications were adopted to facilitate refugee return. Obviously, Sanader's more conciliatory attitude towards refugee return and national minorities, combined with a shift in the HDZ stance on these issues, ultimately created the opportunity for an increase in refugee returns in 2003: 108,000 had returned by the end of the year (European Commission 2004a: 27).

Furthermore, EU socialisation and conditionality was notable in 2004, after the EU had criticised the Croatian government in 2003 for having made 'only limited progress' in the return process and de facto integration of the Serb minority. This reprimand was underlined by EU pressure for enhanced regional cooperation between Serbia and Croatia, which the EU perceived to be crucial to the return process and the integration of national minorities in both Croatia and Serbia. EU conditionality and socialisation on this issue resulted in a joint endeavour in 2004 by Croatian PM Sanader and Serbian PM Koštunica on a bilateral Agreement on the Protection of Minorities.[11] In part, this rapprochement was fuelled by the sentiment that 'we can cooperate; we can do this in order to become a member of the EU'.[12] Institutional and legal transformations have occurred as a result of a shift in attitudes of the Croatian governments since 2000. The Croatian government has financed over 90 per cent of all return projects and compensated property owners, but the most important signal of transformation was when the HDZ government signed an agreement with the Independent Democratic Serbian Party (SDSS).

The limits of EU conditionality and socialisation on the returns process and the integration of national minorities became evident in 2005, when continuing discrimination against the Serb and Roma communities in Croatia in terms of access to employment and housing led the Commission to state that Croatia must foster as an urgent priority a 'receptive climate in the majority community' towards the Serb and Roma communities. As suggested above, the process of highlighting and criticising shortcomings of the reform process in an aspirant state potentially equips the EU with a significant transformative capacity. However, in certain areas it is evident that the progress reports have had limited impact as the discrimination issue featured again in the 2006 and 2007 Commission Progress Reports.

On the matter of the returns process, the EU has faced much criticism in academic scholarship. Most notably, according to Belloni (2007: 464) the processes of integration with the EU were 'centred on the ability of the European states to keep civilians within war or war-ridden zones'. Additionally, Belloni (2007: 464) argues that the policy of refugee return in the former Yugoslavia has replaced 'voluntary repatriation with the concept of "safe return" which involves the return of refugees often against their wishes, and even before peace has been achieved and consolidated'. Undoubtedly, there is merit in Belloni's arguments. Returnees still faced difficulties in gaining access to housing and employment, which denoted a lack of transformation on how the minority communities are perceived in Croatia. Additionally, a report by the Serbian Democratic Forum stated that it was 'frustrated' with the results of the HDZ government on refugee return. An indicator of the limited success of the return of refugee policy in Croatia is marked by the fact that in 1991 Serbs comprised over 12 per cent of population but in 2006 they represented only 4.5 per cent of population (*Balkan Insight* 19 October 2006).

In Croatia there is a gap between promises and implementation regarding the return of refugees. The HDZ signed an agreement in December 2003, yet three years later there was still cause for concern over the return of Croatian Serb refugees. Significantly, the December 2003 agreement on the return of refugees did nothing to improve the Croatian Serb position in Croatia, yet it served to lend crucial credibility to Croatia's image when negotiating with the EU. This section has shown that the processes of integration with and the prospect of joining the EU impacted the transformation of rules in Croatia since 2000. The changing narratives in Croatia have shown that the prospect of EU membership has had an impact on relationships between political elites in Croatia and across the region.

Conflict transformed?

This analysis has revealed that at various stages of transformation the process of integration with the EU has had a transformative impact on conflict in Croatia. This chapter has also demonstrated that the mechanism of political conditionality had greatest impact on conflict transformation in Croatia, particularly with regard to party, issue and relationship transformation – especially as conditionality increased in salience when Croatia progressed toward EU candidacy. It became clear in this chapter that the EU's transformative capacity relied on the domestic parties' ambition for Croatia to become an EU member state.

During 2000 and 2001, when Croatia was adjusting to life after the HDZ regime, the prospect of signing a Stabilisation and Association Agreement was a motivating force for the political elites, and the commitments made at Santa Maria de Feira and Zagreb had a political impact. This chapter has shown that the early stages of integration with the EU, in the form of negotiating and signing a Stabilisation and Association Agreement, had an impact on stabilising and orientating the Croatian political elites toward the EU. However, by 2004, with a stricter application of conditionality and need for compliance as Croatia came closer to integration with the EU, the European Commission was more ready to highlight the reforms necessary before membership could be achieved. Therefore, the closer to membership it came, the more scrutiny Croatia faced, with a similar increase in the EU's transformative capacity.

The transformation of actors in Croatia has occurred and this analysis showed that this was a direct result of EU conditionality and socialisation. This chapter has shown that as increasing integration with the EU became more evident the Croatian political elites orientated their language and policies along a pro-EU line. The processes of integration with and the prospect of joining the EU bridged the ideological gaps among the political actors in Croatia. Cross-party support for EU membership in Croatia has streamlined political debate across the party spectrum. Cross-party support for EU membership in Croatia is indicated by the electoral campaigns which took place between 2000 and 2007. During these elections, parliamentary and presidential, all contending parties campaigned on a pro-EU stance. As argued above, this creates challenges for party transformation in Croatia. It is the political actors who are central in determining the future trajectory and projection of the conflict, as well as determining the pace and nature of integration with the EU. Therefore, the norms and accepted behaviour of the conflict are centrally in the hands of the political elites. Because of cross-party support for EU membership there is not much opportunity for the main political parties in Croatia to move left or right on the political spectrum since they all have the agreed position of EU membership. Rather, the political relationships and discussion across the party spectrum in Croatia focus on *how* Croatia's EU accession process will be managed; not *whether* Croatia should be a part of it. EU financial, technical and closer relations incentives have helped to 'streamline political debate' in Croatia.[13] The political configuration in Croatia is centred on EU membership; there is no party against EU membership.[14] This shaped and altered the ways in which the actors to the conflict behave, and norms have been transformed. The streamlining of political debate on EU issues across the political party spectrum in Croatia means that the 'success on the path to EU membership is not rewarded in votes'.[15]

The transformative capacity of the processes of integration with and the prospect of joining the EU were less successful on the issues of conflict in Croatia after 2000. A limit of the EU's transformative capacity was evident when Croatia failed to cooperate sufficiently with the ICTY until December 2005. This was not so much the fault of the EU's transformative capacity but rather an indicator that the processes of integration with and the prospect of joining the EU have a limited power on certain confining conditions within an aspirant state. ICTY cooperation was a key issue that the EU was keen to see resolved earlier rather than later in the accession process.

In sum, this case study has proven that closer integration with the EU, the perceived closeness of integration with the EU, and the prospect of joining the EU have had a transformative impact on the structures of conflict in Croatia since 2000 and, to a lesser degree, an impact on the relationships of conflict. This chapter has also shown that the EU learned and implemented lessons from its engagement in Croatia.

5

THE IMPACT ON SERBIA

As was made clear in Chapter 4, since 2000 Serbia has experienced the same set of EU instruments, policies and initiatives as Croatia. However, Serbia's progress towards closer integration and to EU candidacy has lagged behind Croatia's. This chapter examines the conditions which have prevented Serbia's advancement towards integration into and institutional membership of the EU, given the similar pre-accession pressures and opportunities. The chapter also examines the EU's role in conflict transformation with a particular focus on the case study of Serbia, to demonstrate the mixed impacts of the Europeanisation/enlargement processes on conflict transformation, and it offers explanations for the varied outcomes. In doing so the chapter makes the argument that the EU's impact has been more significant at certain times and on certain aspects of conflict, as a result of determining domestic factors within Serbia as well as inherent limits in the EU's capacity owing to the nature of its contractual relations and agency structure and the mismanaged delivery of its mechanisms.

Structural change: party representation and agenda issues

The structure of the conflict in Serbia has been transformed noticeably since the removal of the 1990s regime and the intensification of the EU's approach in 2000. An empirical examination of the impacts of EU influence on party representation and agenda issues between parties elucidates the EU's transformative capacity on conflict in Serbia. Party transformation is detectable through examination of the change in party representation and interests in Serbia. As the following discussion highlights, the absence of cross-party support for EU membership in Serbia simultaneously demonstrates and explains the limits of the transformative power of processes of integration in Serbia. So, have the incentives of closer integration and EU membership qualitatively transformed the parties of conflict in Serbia?

Since 2000 pro-reform and pro-democracy parties have been consistently successful in elections in Serbia. The disintegration of the Milošević regime in Serbia was confirmed with the 23 December 2000 elections to the Serbian Skupština (parliament). These elections resulted in success for the Democratic Opposition of Serbia (DOS), which linked the highly fragmented democratic opposition groups in Serbia. The democratic opposition, comprising Đinđić's Democratic Party and Koštunica's Democratic Party of Serbia, won 64.4 per cent of the votes. The EU's role in this initial seismic shift in government was significant. Although the vote for pro-reform, anti-Milošević parties was important, it did not follow that democratic consolidation and/or conflict transformation would occur quickly. Rather, the changes in 2000 in Serbia were fuelled largely by a widespread disaffection for the Milošević regime combined with international pressure following the war in Kosovo.

As the EU's strategy in Serbia intensified, the EU became more influential in the country. By 2003 the EU's role had become substantive. It is possible to trace the impact of increasing EU pressure on Serbian electoral politics. Conditionality and social learning were not the main instruments for ensuring change in Serbia; rather, the EU attempted to incentivise and bargain with both the electorate and the pro-reform elites in order to maintain a pro-EU government in Serbia. One way in which the EU influenced Serbian elections was by demonstrating public support for the pro-EU parties, calling for the electorate to support these parties and offering political and economic incentives if the election resulted in a pro-EU government. This has occurred during successive elections since 2000, demonstrating that the EU was conspicuously seeking to impact and transform parties in Serbia. It can be argued that these attempts to influence Serbian politics were little more than 'wishful thinking' on the EU's part, but arguably the May 2008 results proved to be more than wishful thinking.[1]

A prime example of the EU's prominent attempts to influence the outcome of electoral politics in Serbia occurred in 2003. The democratic parties in Serbia were not as cohesive as they appeared in 2000, and following a troublesome electoral campaign the democratic parties together won a majority of the votes. The Serbian Radical Party (SRS) won 27.3 per cent of the votes and 81 seats but was unable to form a government. According to Batt (2004) the 2003 elections in Serbia were characterised by 'deep division and personal animosity between the democratic government' members. In part this helped to account for the electoral success of the SRS. The democratic parties separately gained the majority of the votes and were able to form a government based on a coalition. Following the elections Solana called on Serbia to form a new government 'based on a clear and strong European reform agenda' (Agence Europe 31 December 2003). Despite the success of the pigeonholed pro-reform pro-EU parties in Serbia, the EU's desired outcome was far from realised. Bandović (2004: 218) argued that the election results of December 2003 showed a 'restoration of the values from the Milošević period: traditionalism, nationalism and denial of the war crimes', owing to the reluctance of the pro-reform parties to respond to international obligations such as cooperation with the ICTY.

The election of the pro-EU and pro-reform parties to government, and of Tadić to the President's office, provided an indication that a qualitative level of conflict transformation had occurred in Serbia. The main parties pursued a strategy of compliance, respect for and maintenance of the rule of law and constitutional law.[2] The shift in parties' interests and representation was marked by an adherence to pro-reform interests such as cooperation with ICTY and a disinclination to mobilise ethnically or use state violence, particularly regarding the Kosovo issue. During his investiture speech President Tadić confirmed that during his presidency ICTY cooperation would be a 'priority' as it symbolised Serbian attachment to European values (Agence Europe 12 July 2004). Following the election of Prime Minister Koštunica in 2003 and in response to the emerging violence in Kosovo in March 2004, the EU pressured Koštunica to use his authority to quell violence in Kosovo as well as to continue to cooperate with the ICTY – which Prodi stated was an 'absolute necessity' (Agence Europe 23 March 2004).

The EU's ambition to see a pro-reform, pro-EU stable government in Serbia through socialisation and bargaining instruments was not entirely achieved by 2007, as the January 2007 elections indicated. Rather, the interests of the main political parties and their political representation were identifiably rooted in the past conflict. This suggested that the EU's transformative capacity, or rather its favoured tactics of bargaining, conditionality and socialisation, could only reach so far. The EU's bargaining method continued ahead of the 2007 elections. Ultimately, this continued bargaining strategy had an unintended impact. The EU's barter of offering closer political relations, economic benefits or relaxing of visa restrictions increasingly came to be perceived by the Serbian electorate and political elites as a series of false promises and an attempt at blackmail.[3] During the run-up to the 2007 elections, the EU took every opportunity to remind the Serbian political elite and society that the EU was ready to resume Stabilisation and Association Agreement negotiations as soon as a democratic government was formed and cooperation with the ICTY improved.[4] The pro-Western parties and EU media framed the election as a clear choice between a future in the EU or a return to the dark and nationalistic past; when calling for elections Serbian President Tadić stated:

> I expect a victory of the democratic political forces, a victory for a policy that is defined by one goal – membership in the EU and improvement of citizens' lives … I will not let the political forces and the representatives of the ideas pulling Serbia back into the past (win).[5]

Likewise, the EU echoed this when Rehn (2007) referred to early 2007 as a 'very sensitive and challenging moment in its [Serbia's] history' and continued to stress that the EU should 'help it leave the nationalist past behind and turn towards a European future'. Such statements revealed an EU that was concerned with the ongoing transition in Serbia and was prepared to attempt openly to influence electoral politics to achieve an outcome suitable to its objectives. Therefore, we can see that the EU had intended outcomes and was utilising enabling and connective pathways to realise its aims.

Following the formation of a pro-democracy government in Serbia on 15 May 2007, the EU initialled a visa facilitation and readmission agreement with Serbia and resumed Stabilisation and Association Agreement negotiations with the country (13 June 2007) following Serbian activity on ICTY cooperation. This indicated that the newly elected key political actors, heartened by their electoral success, were motivated to move forward towards integration with the EU. Moreover, the electoral success facilitated a window of opportunity for the Serbian elites to cooperate with the ICTY. The pro-EU nature of the newly formed government was evident in Prime Minister Koštunica's keynote address, which stated that integration with the EU was the second key principle of the government's policy.[6] This was linked explicitly to the government's third key principle: to pursue complete cooperation with ICTY. If measured simply in terms of advancement through the phases of integration, 2007 may have indicated that party transformation in Serbia had taken place when the Commission initialled a Stabilisation and Association Agreement with the EU. This decision was significant because it represented a departure from the derisory *demarche* issued a week earlier by the UK, France, Germany and Italy (and the USA) criticising Serbia over its linking of the future of Kosovo and Bosnia. Interfering in Bosnian politics as well as angering the various member states, Koštunica argued that if Kosovo became independent the Dayton Peace Accords would be undermined, hinting at a revision of Dayton with obvious support being given to the Bosnian Serbs.

The backdrop of Kosovo's status and the presidential elections in 2008 tested the extent to which the EU was able to influence parties in Serbia. For some, the violence in Belgrade on 21 February 2008 provided evidence that Serbia had not yet come to terms with its past and a political culture steeped in blame and denial (Moore, Radio Free Europe/Radio Liberty 22 February 2008). It remained clear that the situation in Serbia was far from stable, and that the EU's strategy of stabilising and integrating Serbia through a quasi-enlargement strategy was proving to be inept. All political parties in Serbia were against Kosovan independence, yet the response of Prime Minister Koštunica and President Tadić revealed a schism over the future of Serbia. Both were united in their opposition to Kosovan independence, but Tadić argued that this opposition should not interfere with Serbia's EU membership ambitions. Koštunica disagreed. This was significant for two reasons. First, it demonstrated that among the pro-reform, pro-EU parties in Serbia, the issue of Kosovan independence had the capacity to create a deep schism. Second, it demonstrated that the hard-core nationalists could exploit the situation over Kosovo to threaten the democratic and pro-EU ambitions.

Ahead of the signing of the Stabilisation and Association Agreement in April 2008 the question for the EU was 'How do we deal with Serbia?'. In early 2008 Brussels may have asked 'Who lost Serbia?'.[7] This question arose because of Koštunica's retrenchment from pro-EU discourse in light of many EU member states moving to recognise Kosovan independence. The question must be posed: was the EU responsible for Koštunica's retrenchment? Should the EU feel responsible for not being clearer about conditionality, the steps that must be taken in order to become an EU member? Ultimately, it is easy to lay blame with Brussels, but Serbia too must shoulder responsibility for its situation.

Given the EU's lack of capacity to deal effectively with conflict and chaos, is it likely that the awkward situation in Serbia will lead to an ineffective, inadequate and untidy response by the EU?[8] Indeed, the situation in Serbia is increasingly seen as a separate and unique one: Solana said Serbia was in an 'exceptional situation', adding that it needs 'exceptional solutions' (RFE/RL Newsline, 10 April 2007). The argument developed in this thesis is that the EU has demonstrated that it is a reflexive actor which has used the learning from previous experience to enact a more intensified and visible strategy in the Balkans through integration and the quasi-enlargement approach. Yet, when faced with the emerging crisis in Serbia, the EU had partially failed to achieve its intended ambitions of keeping Serbian political parties on a pro-EU, pro-reform track. Therefore, doubts remain about the EU's capacity to impact conflict transformation during an initiation or escalation stage. However, what we can discern is that the socialisation influence brought about by the presence of the EU in Serbia did affect the decision by the Serbian government not to respond militarily to Kosovan independence.

The EU's bargaining mode entered into full flow ahead of the 2008 elections when the EU tabled a 'political agreement' that lacked legal force. This agreement did not amount to signing a Stabilisation and Association Agreement but it represented a significant symbolic advancement in integrating Serbia into the EU. Essentially, the EU offered an agreement which would facilitate easier trade and travel between Serbia and the EU. This was a blatant intervention in the pre-election period. Solana summed up the EU's intentions: 'We want to send a clear message to citizens of Serbia that their future lies in the European Union' (*Guardian* 29 January 2008). This EU initiative was a direct intervention for the EU to affect the outcome of domestic electoral politics. Significantly, it is possible to compare the precarious nature of Serbian electoral results with the more steady electoral politics in Croatia. For example, the elections in November 2007 in Croatia represented the first in 20 years in which voters could be sure that the winner would not impede Croatia's EU ambitions. This is clearly not the case with Serbian elections. Voters, politicians and the EU recognise this. Why is this the case, and what are the implications of such uncertainty?

Across the political spectrum in Serbia, political parties were not agreed on Serbia pursuing EU integration and EU membership. This is different from the situation in Croatia. This indicated that the processes of integrating and the prospect of becoming a member of the EU have perhaps only recently begun to transform the political parties qualitatively in Serbia. Despite consistently high levels of public support for EU membership in Serbia (most recently at 75 per cent in January 2008), support for EU membership among political parties is far from clear cut.

The main implication of the uncertainty of electoral results in Serbia is that it jeopardised Serbia's progress on integrating with and joining the EU. For example, electoral success by the SRS could diminish Serbia's political working relationships with the EU and result in an increased detachment between Serbia and the EU. Therefore, this has a further consequence of impacting the nature, design and timing of EU engagement in Serbia. This was made clear ahead of the second-round elections in January 2008 when the EU had offered a political and symbolic agreement to Serbia. The EU tabled the agreement before the elections but decided against signing it until after the election results were known. This was a delicate balancing act by the EU: on one hand it was offering Serbia an incentive to vote pro-EU, but because of the anticipated closeness of the electoral results and against the backdrop of the Kosovo status decision, the decision was taken to delay the signing of the agreement. Furthermore, discord between EU member states about how to proceed with Serbia affected this decision. For example, the Dutch were adamant that closer relations could not take place without full ICTY cooperation.[9] This balancing act suggested that the EU was fully aware of the possible implications of signing an agreement ahead of the elections. First, such a direct intervention could be perceived as patronising by Serbian voters and undermine Tadić's chances of electoral success. Second, the EU would be perceived as weakening its traditional method of political conditionality over the ICTY issue; this would, therefore, diminish the credibility of the EU's transformative capacity. Related to this, third, the EU would effectively be reneging on its consistent support for the work of the ICTY. Finally, if Nikolic won the election it would be difficult for the EU to ratify the agreement (in the best-case scenario), and might impede future progress with Serbia.

The qualitative transformation of success of party representation in Serbia must be tempered with an examination of the solid electoral success of the SRS. The SRS has maintained a consistent representation in parliament and a substantial showing during presidential elections. It is the qualitative shift in the interests, policies and language of the SRS that has provided compelling evidence about party transformation in Serbia. During the 1990s the SRS was largely supportive of the Milošević regime and was keen to pursue war and violent suppression of ethnic minorities in its pursuit of a Greater Serbia. However, since 2000, the changing context caused by the end of the war in Kosovo, the removal of Milošević and the intensified EU engagement have affected the development of the SRS.

It is helpful to clarify and account for the electoral success of the SRS since 2000. Since 2000 the SRS have posited themselves as opponents of Serbia's EU membership and projected themselves as Serbian 'patriots', therefore maintaining an appeal among their 1990 support base and building by seizing what were previously Milošević and Socialist Party of Serbia (SPS) votes. In the January 2007 elections the SRS won 28.59 per cent of the vote. As in 2003, the 2007 electoral success by the SRS failed to secure enough seats for the party to form a government. A post-2007 election report from the National Democratic Institute (2007) argued that 2007 election results showed that the SRS and the SPS did not show similar growth. Support for the SRS remained steady (34.8 per cent in 2003 and 34 per cent in 2007). The steady level of support for the SRS can be explained by a variety of factors: the perceived corruption and failures of the pro-reformist governments; apathy toward the pro-reformist parties; continued high levels of unemployment and low standards of living; and decline in support for the SPS. The changes within the SRS can be described as akin to those experienced by the HDZ in Croatia, since we see that when each party adopted a less radical standpoint and moved from a rejectionist stance on EU integration, their support increased.

The qualitative shift in the SRS is evident from the electoral results of the SRS, which throughout the 1990s and even during the period 2000 to 2005 had campaigned on an isolationist, anti-EU, anti-Western platform. While the SRS has not adopted a pro-EU stance, its position has become much more nuanced. While this section utilises electoral propaganda as evidence it does so cautiously, mindful of the difficulties of dealing with electoral campaign speeches and propaganda. In the run-up to the 21 January 2007 elections the SRS developed its strategy and profile on economic issues rather than on nationalism. This was a significant qualitative shift. Furthermore, Nikolic supplanted Šešelj as leader of the SRS, as Šešelj had been indicted and put on trial in the ICTY. The SRS fought the 2007 election on an economic reform platform which generated support in the economically depressed areas with high refugee populations. However, this does not accurately reflect the SRS's support base. Rather, during the 2007 elections the SRS drew support from well-educated people with a high standard of living. According to Kovacevic (2007), the growth in support for the SRS is 'alarming' because it has come mostly from well-off districts in Belgrade; although it remains true that the young and the less well educated consistently vote for the Radicals. Rather than targeting this area where it is clear that the Radicals can mobilise support, it appears that the EU incentives and policies are failing to target these issues, engage with this section of the population or assist the pro-EU parties to deal with these issues sufficiently. While the SRS has transformed qualitatively in response to the changing context in Serbia it has remained ardent in its anti-EU membership stance and the EU has failed to attract or incentivise the SRS and its support base. In sum, the EU's response to the continued popularity of the SRS has been dismal. Ahead of the January 2007 elections concern mounted within the EU: 'if you have radicals at the wheel it will always make (EU integration) more difficult' (*EU Observer* 2006d). This suggested that the continued popularity of the SRS does not fit well with the EU's agenda for Serbia. Furthermore, the EU does not meet or talk with SRS representatives.[10] This indicates a missed opportunity to engage with the single most popular party in Serbia, which would have the potential to transform the SRS and thus parties in Serbia.[11] Moreover, it confirmed why the EU's bargaining in Serbia is ineffective and limited in scope and is ultimately mobilising support for the SRS – not an intention of the EU. In 2008 the SRS softened its nationalistic rhetoric in order to help boost support for Nikolic in the presidential elections, stating that under his presidency Serbia would never wage wars (*Balkan Insight* 16 January 2008).

The rise of the SRS does not paint a complete picture of the 2007 results and their implications for party representation transformation in Serbia. It is suggested that for actor transformation to occur new actors must emerge. The G17+ party emerged as a new actor in the political landscape in the 2003 elections. The 2007 results saw the emergence of the LDP, which won over 5 per cent of the vote. According to Gowan the LDP is a 'refreshingly pragmatic and forward looking' party (Gowan 2007: 2). This indicates that actor transformation is occurring in Serbia with the emergence of new parties, which are having an impact on the government of Serbia. The processes of integration with the EU and prospect of joining the EU had a conclusive impact on the key political actors in Serbia in terms of their ambitions, orientation and electoral campaigning.

The May 2008 elections and results demonstrated that the EU's transformative capacity could be considered to have been effective. Prior to the election the EU signed the Stabilisation and Association Agreement with Serbia, but with the possibility of delaying ratification depending on Serbia's capacity to meet EU conditionality. This decision made by the EU was significant given the possible repercussions on Bosnia, also waiting to sign its Stabilisation and Association Agreement. Campaigning 'for a European Serbia', Tadić's party secured 38.7 per cent of the vote, decisively beating the second-placed SRS with 29.1 per cent of the vote. Clearly, the election results suggested a victory for pro-EU forces in Serbia, but a closer examination of the election campaigns and results is valuable. First, the continued success of Tadić's party relies on its ability to form a government and (at the time of writing) its possible partners are Milošević's ex-party, the Socialists. Therefore, the balance of power in Serbia presently lies with the Socialists. The Socialists demonstrated a post-Milošević outlook in the elections, but the party is torn over the EU issue especially because of the ICTY condition. Party leader Dacic stated 'we're facing a complicated political moment and decision on whether we should take a traditional or fresh, uncertain path … It is not easy to create a coalition with ones who had been arresting us' (*Balkan Insight* 20 May 2008).

A second significant implication of the May 2008 election was that the result may have positioned Tadić's party first, but it also demonstrated a deeply polarised Serbia with the SRS and Koštunica's Democratic Party of Serbia–New Serbia alliance on the opposing side to Tadić with a healthy share of the vote. The election results on the surface appeared to be a clear victory for the EU's transformative impact on conflict parties in Serbia, yet the underlying tensions in Serbia have not been resolved.

The EU has had a transformative impact on party representation in Serbia since 2000. This was a direct result of the EU's more intensified strategy through the enlargement approach. However, the EU's impact has not always produced the outcomes that the EU intended or wished. The EU has been most successful at transforming the agendas, nature, representation and balance of power between the conflict parties in Serbia because of the conditionality and social learning opportunities provided in the EU pre-accession process. Therefore the EU has been most influential on conflict parties through a compulsory and enabling pathway. However, it remains the case that in light of the difficult political determinants in Serbia, specifically over Kosovo, Montenegro and ICTY cooperation, the EU's transformation of the political parties has been impartial and less than the EU would have expected or wished. The EU's impact has been limited in Serbia not because the attractiveness of EU membership has not pervaded political parties across the political spectrum, but rather because of the way the EU has managed the relationship with Serbia. The EU's political management has been detrimental because of the preference to bargain rather than negotiate with the conflict parties at politically contentious moments such as presidential elections ahead of Kosovo's declaration of independence. This finding suggests that the EU should negotiate with the SRS not with the purpose of 'Europeanising' the SRS but rather so that the EU can experience social learning so it would be better informed about the people, attitudes, motives and strategies of the SRS and therefore more equipped to deal with a SRS government. The EU must widen its perspective to broaden its scope of influence and understanding of the conflict parties in Serbia in order to realise its potential impact.

Agenda-issue transformation

The 'transformation of agenda issues' refers to how issues that are central to the conflict are dealt with and involves an examination of the processes in which controversial issues are reduced in importance when other interests become more important. This section reveals how the processes of integration with and the prospect of joining the EU impacted the central agenda issue of cooperation with the ICTY, which has dominated the political agenda in Serbia since 2000; its relative dominance was shored up because of the salience of EU political conditionality. The processes of integration with and the prospect of joining the EU changed the political discourse, issues of interest and debate in Serbia on ICTY cooperation, which in turn changed the focus of discussion about the rule of law and reform.[12] This demonstrates that EU conditionality, through compulsory and enabling pathways, affected political issues in Serbia.

In Serbia, Milošević's transfer to the ICTY in 2000 was a watershed moment in EU–Serbian relations and in the transformation of conflict in

Serbia.[13] According to Bideleux and Jeffries (2007), under pressure from EU foreign ministers the EU conditioned Serbia's receipt of aid and participation at a donor conference on the transfer of Milošević to the ICTY in 2000. Serbia's participation in the Stabilisation and Association process was conditional on meeting the EU's conditions, which included cooperation with the ICTY. The justification for the persistence of political conditionality over ICTY cooperation lies in the belief that ethnic cleansing should not be perceived as a successful method of conflict management as pursued in the former Yugoslavia during the 1990s. According to Gow (2003), after the end of the war in Kosovo 'peace and justice were intertwined'.[14] Gow (2003) contends that all governments including EU member states have a responsibility to ensure that all indicted war criminals stand trial and the legacy of war crimes is dealt with.

While full cooperation with the ICTY has long been a condition of the Stabilisation and Association process, since 2002 the political elites in Belgrade have sensed increased pressure from the EU for Serbia to cooperate with the ICTY issue.[15] This was made clear in the consistent calls made by the EU for full cooperation, as well as the threatened delays in the progress on integration with the EU. This 'increased pressure' from the EU does not *appear* to be the case, as arguably the condition was always present, but it can be better understood in terms of Belgrade's political elites' recognition that more could be lost, in terms of their progress in integration with the EU, when not cooperating.

Elite willingness to cooperate with the ICTY was limited by the continued reluctance to cooperate prevailing in Serbian society. In 2003 cooperation with the ICTY was perceived by society as 'trade with the West'.[16] Between 2002 and 2005 the EU's relations with Serbia moved slowly toward the realisation of a positive feasibility study on opening Stabilisation and Association Agreement negotiations by the Commission in April 2005. Following the assassination of Đinđić the EU upped its efforts in Serbia with extra financial assistance and the Commission decision to launch the Feasibility Study on a Stabilisation and Association Agreement (Agence Europe 5 September 2003).

The EU's transformative capacity in Serbia on the issue of cooperation with the ICTY was most notable at the beginning of 2005, ahead of the expected issuing of a feasibility study on Serbia and Montenegro's preparedness to negotiate a Stabilisation and Association Agreement by the Commission. Croatia struggled to meet the EU condition for full cooperation with the ICTY ahead of accession negotiations. During the same period Serbia was actively cooperating with the ICTY, in stark contrast with Croatia. In early 2005 Serbia transferred six indicted war criminals to the ICTY. Following Serbia's transfer of General Lazarovic to the ICTY in January 2005, Enlargement Commissioner Rehn pointed out that by 'cooperating with the ICTY Serbia and Montenegro removes obstacles to the country's rapprochements to the EU' (Agence Europe 31 January 2005). However, the EU was quick to reassert that continued cooperation was necessary for Serbia to continue to make progress. With the publication of the feasibility study looming the EU stressed that without 100 per cent cooperation with the ICTY there would be no prospect of Serbia coming closer to the EU (Agence Europe 1 February 2005). On the day of publication of the positive feasibility study, Rehn stressed that 'until the very last person responsible for war crimes committed has been caught', it would be impossible to contemplate membership (Agence Europe 13 April 2005). Serbia's cooperation with the ICTY in early 2005 suggested that the prospect of coming closer to the EU encouraged Serbia to cooperate more fully with the ICTY. The political elites in Serbia were motivated to cooperate with the ICTY since they were keen to have a positive feasibility study and make progress on a Stabilisation and Association Agreement. This showed that in early 2005 the prospect of closer integration with the EU had a transformative impact on the issues of conflict in Serbia. It was the central interest of the political elites in Serbia at this time to make progress toward integration with the EU and therefore they facilitated Serbia's cooperation with the ICTY.

Serbia (and Montenegro) received a positive feasibility study in April 2005. Throughout this period, the EU's consistent application of conditionality was communicated plainly to the political elites in Serbia. The clear and constant communication showed a coherent and unswerving EU stance on the issue of ICTY cooperation. According to the International Crisis Group (2005), Serbia's cooperation with the ICTY in early 2005 was an indication of the successful conditioning assistance and integration into Western institutions on cooperation with the ICTY. However, after the Commission issued a positive Feasibility Study, cooperation with the ICTY declined and Belgrade failed to keep up momentum. This downturn in ICTY cooperation suggested that without the pressure from EU conditionality that it had experienced in the run-in to the Feasibility Study Belgrade would not have achieved as much as it did. This event prompted one interlocutor to state: 'without the anchor of EU integration, Serbia would've done even less than what has been done'.[17] In June 2005 the EU believed that indicted Serbian General Mladić was within the grasp of the Serbian government and Rehn continued to pressure Koštunica and the Serbian authorities to transfer Mladić to the ICTY. Yet Koštunica denied that Belgrade had this capacity, stating: 'We are not in contact with him and we are not negotiating with him' (Agence Europe 16 June 2005). This situation revealed a gulf between the EU's expectations of Belgrade and Belgrade's capacities. For the EU, on the assumption Mladić was indeed inside Serbia, Belgrade either was unwilling to cooperate with the ICTY in summer 2005 or was not in control of its territory; either reason was sufficient for alarm and the cessation of progress.

The schism between the government in Serbia and the EU member states, which insisted on full cooperation, continued to plague Serbia's progress on integration with the EU in 2006. While the EU opened Stabilisation and Association Agreement negotiations with Serbia in October 2005, the continued absence of Mladić in the ICTY had repercussions for progress in May 2006. The EU decided to postpone negotiations with Serbia and Montenegro on 3 May ahead of the scheduled third round of negotiations because of Serbia's failure to meet EU conditionality over the rule of law. Enlargement Commissioner Rehn asserted, 'Serbia must show that nobody is above the law and that anyone indicted for serious crimes will face justice' (*Financial Times* 2006b). Serbian Prime Minister Koštunica complained that the EU was deeply wrong in its policy and attitude towards Serbia following the EU's decision to stall Stabilisation and Association Agreement negotiations with Serbia.[18] As is highlighted in the next section, the EU's decision to postpone negotiations with Serbia and Montenegro occurred just three weeks before the referendum on independence in Montenegro.

In 2007, the issue of cooperation with ICTY remained the main hurdle for Serbia's progression on the road to EU membership and had momentarily interrupted Montenegro's progress. While Serbia has transferred many to the ICTY over the past years, four of the highest-ranking officials to have been indicted are still to be transferred. While the international community expected Serbia to be ready to cooperate with the ICTY as a means of signalling a clean break with the past, Serbian politicians perceived cooperation with ICTY as a destabilising threat to a fragile democracy, which was propagating the collectivisation of guilt in Serbia. The Serbian government launched an Action Plan aimed at achieving full cooperation with the ICTY in July 2006. In keeping with what might have been expected the EU remained unconvinced about the Action Plan and favoured actual results over new strategies and documents (*EU Observer* 2006c).

In addition to the positive contribution to the transformation of this issue of conflict, the EU's conditionality was double-edged and had a negative impact on conflict transformation. According to Simeunović (2007) the EU's insistence on cooperation with the ICTY as a condition for progress towards integration with the EU employed and propagated a notion of collective guilt in Serbia. Commenting on when the EU stalled Stabilisation and Association Agreement negotiations with Serbia between May 2006 and May 2007, Simeunović (2007: 15) argues that 'though there are lists of individual Serbs accused of war crimes, at the same time the entire Serbian nation is being held guilty for those same crimes'; therefore, the 'only way out is the individualisation of crime'. Analysis from outside Serbia offers a different reading of the protracted cooperation with ICTY. For example, Gowan (2007: 2) argues that 'a deeply ingrained sense of affront and injustice explains why Serbian politics clings so fiercely to the past'. Gowan's sentiments show a misinformed reading of the situation in Serbia. Serbia has made a substantial contribution to cooperation with the ICTY since 2000, such as the transfer of indicted persons, adoption of the Law on Freeze of Assets of ICTY fugitives (February 2006), and the opening of archives of the Ministry of Interior, the Ministry of Defence and the Serbian presidency to the ICTY (May 2006). Despite the internal pressures, which make it difficult for the willing as well as the reluctant members of the Serbian government to cooperate with the ICTY, Serbia has made significant gestures of cooperation with the ICTY, which should not be underestimated. It is a convincing indication that the Serbian government and people accept that such cooperation is a condition that must be met if they are to realise their ambition of securing EU membership for Serbia.

The issue of cooperation with the ICTY must be understood in terms of the wider political issues that have dominated the agenda in Serbia, especially the status of Kosovo. A media report in June 2007 revealed that the Mladić issue was being utilised as a bargaining tactic by the Serbian political elite against the backdrop of the Kosovo final status negotiations. This report argued that the transfer of General Mladić to the ICTY was not a technical issue but a question of political will, and the primary reason explaining why Mladić had not been transferred to date was that he remained an 'asset' or rather a bargaining chip (Balkan Investigative Reporting Network 2007a). The idea that Mladić was being used in this way was strengthened by the ICTY Chief Prosecutor's call for delaying a decision on Kosovo in favour of facilitating Serbia's complete cooperation with ICTY. The continuing dominance of the ICTY issue limits any impact that the EU or the prospect of EU membership can have on transforming conflict in Belgrade. According to Schuvelbusch (2003), Serbia seems to be moving through a period of mental adjustment characteristic of nations trying to come to terms with defeat. This insight helps explain why Serbia's experience of integration with the EU is so different from the experiences of previous accession countries, including Romania and Bulgaria. This discussion has shown that EU conditionality and engagement in Serbia transformed the central issue of ICTY cooperation to a certain degree. The limits of the transformative capacity are recognisable in the failure of Serbian society to understand the role of the ICTY and its independence from the EU, as well as the persistence of the collective guilt discourse that is perpetuated by EU conditionality in Serbia.

Despite Serbia's continued cooperation with the ICTY, it has not been enough to satisfy critics of the Serbian government since 2000; the EU demands full cooperation with the ICTY. According to Gowan (2007: 2) 'successive governments since 2000 have used strong nationalism to justify indecisiveness, for instance over Mladić ... there has been no clear break within the political elite'.[19] Blame for Serbia's failure to transfer Mladić to the ICTY has also been pinned on the EU. On 2 April 2007 an amalgamation of Serbian NGOs recorded their concerns about the perceived weakening of EU conditionality against the backdrop of Kosovo status negotiations:

> If the EU fails to maintain its insistence on Serbia's full cooperation with the ICTY as a condition for resuming Stabilisation and Association Agreement talks, it will encourage extreme nationalists who adamantly and openly oppose trials for 'Serbian heroes'.[20]

This criticism arose from the perceived softening of the EU's stance on Serbia's ICTY cooperation, which featured in a meeting of EU foreign ministers on 12 February 2007. A survey compiled for the Serbian European Integration Office (June 2007) found that 49.1 per cent of persons polled believed that the 'constant conditioning and blackmailing of the EU' in relation to Serbia was a reason why Serbia's journey toward the EU had been obstructed. In this same survey, 20.1 per cent felt that blame lay with Serbia's incapacity to meet international obligations and 13.9 per cent blamed the incompetence of local leadership. The EU foreign ministers concluded that Stabilisation and Association Agreement negotiations with Serbia could be restarted if the newly elected government took 'concrete and effective action for full cooperation' with the ICTY. The ambiguity in the phrase 'concrete and effective action' suggested that Stabilisation and Association Agreement negotiations could be restarted without Mladić or Karadžić in the ICTY. The Foreign Affairs Minister of Slovenia raised this point: 'by continuing blocking Serbia's Stabilisation and Association Agreement we may in fact further undermine the ICTY process' (*EU Observer* 12 February 2007b). Stabilisation and Association Agreement negotiations were recommenced with Serbia following the establishment of the new government as well as the arrest and transfer of an indicted Bosnian Serb general in May 2007. A survey by the Serbian European Integration Office (June 2007) discovered that 54.1 per cent remain opposed to cooperation with the ICTY and, of these, 26.6 per cent would support it if it were to further integration with the EU. Therefore, according to this poll, the prospect of closer integration with the EU and EU membership was a motivating factor for 26.6 per cent of those opposed to cooperation with the ICTY to change their opinion and support cooperation if it facilitated integration with the EU.

Undoubtedly, the issue of cooperation with the ICTY has shaped the pace and nature of Serbia's integration with the EU since 2000. The prospect of closer integration with the EU has encouraged Serbia to cooperate with the ICTY. Nonetheless, in the years since Milošević was transferred to the ICTY public and elite support for the ICTY has remained low in Serbia. This indicates that although some issue transformation has taken place, it has not been complete. Therefore, while on occasions (such as in early 2005) the EU has encouraged, facilitated and rewarded Serbia's cooperation with the ICTY, for the most part the process of integrating with and the prospect of joining the EU has not fundamentally transformed this issue of conflict in Serbia.

Relationship change

Serbian and Bosnian Serbian nationalistic rhetoric in the 1990s focused on religion, history and national affiliation. Since 2000, politicians in Bosnia have often resorted to nationalist rhetoric to defend their interests. For example, Bosnian Serb leader Karadžić invoked propaganda from the battle of Kosovo.[21] Moreover, religious monuments and symbols became the target of nationalist forces during the period of ethno-mobilisation and escalation of political violence in Serbia, Bosnia and Croatia. The targeting of mosques and cultural buildings during the war sought to rewrite history and deny that the different ethnic categories had ever lived together peacefully (Chapman 1994; Riedlmayer 2002). According to the International Crisis Group, 'politicians continue to pursue wartime aims, often using the language of fear that so effectively mobilized national populations during the 1990s' (2007: 7). Essentially, for Bosnian Serbs, this meant an independent Republika Srpska or union with Serbia. For Bosnian Croats, it meant their own entity. Despite the continued rhetoric, relationships between Bosnian Serbs and Serbia underwent a shift rather than a transformation after 2000, which is in part explained by the EU's engagement. This shift in relations between Bosnian Serbs and Serbia emerged under the premiership of Đinđić. Đinđić's attitude toward Bosnian Serbs resulted in a normalisation of relations. Đinđić was killed on 12 March 2003, and on 23 May 2007 the Belgrade Special Court for Organised Crime found 12 men guilty for arranging his murder. However, since his assassination, the Serbian attitude toward Bosnian Serbs has arguably continued to be dominated by Serbia's interference in Bosnian politics, particularly on the politics of the Bosnian Serbs.

An interesting example involving the EU, Bosnian Serbs and Serbia occurred in late 2007. High Representative Lajčák, backed by the Peace Implementation Council, proposed contentious reforms to streamline Bosnia's decision-making process. These reforms were perceived to disband the quorum of votes between Bosnian Croats, Bosnian Serbs and Bosnians in order for a bill to pass. Therefore, this could remove or diminish the veto held by any one of the three groups in Bosnia as agreed at Dayton. In response to these proposals, the head of Bosnia's federal government, Spiric, resigned his post in protest that these reforms would undermine Bosnian Serbs rights and influence in Bosnia. In this situation the Bosnian Serbs, Serbia and the EU were locked into a dispute which was not impacted by the prospect of EU membership. In November 2007 Britain, France, Germany and Italy (as EU member states) and the United States lodged a letter of protest with the Serbian Foreign Ministry, following Serbia's criticism of the role played by the international community in Bosnia. This was in relation to Prime Minister Koštunica's comments that High Representative Lajčák's reforms were undermining rights secured by Bosnian Serbs in the Dayton Accords. However, the fact that Serbia is a guarantor and signatory of the Dayton Accords means that it has a role to play in the future of Bosnia. The Serbian influence was not only from Koštunica and the DSS party; cross-party support for Bosnian Serbs emerged across Serbia. Likewise, Tadić refused to host a meeting of NGOs from the three countries. This controversy threatened to destabilise and harm relations between Croatia, Serbia and Bosnia despite a series of attempts and initiatives sponsored by the EU to normalise relations. The debate continued with the involvement of the Bosnian Croats in the dispute when Bosnian Croat parliamentary member Komšić warned that Serbia should 'keep its hands off Bosnia' (RFE/RL Newsline, 26 October 2007). As pointed out in Chapter 4, this was in contrast to Croatian President Mesić, who openly stated that he would reduce and eradicate Croatian government funding for Bosnia's Croats. Koštunica or Tadić had not made similar statements or indicated intentions in this area.

It is instructive to analyse the issue from a different perspective: that of Bosnia. Bosnia received a positive feasibility study in 2003 that altered Bosnian Serb attitudes towards Serbia and towards the structures and relationships of conflict. With the EU's feasibility study in 2003, the Republika Srpska issued a public apology for the Srebrenica massacre as well as upgrading its cooperation with the ICTY.[22] This was a significant transformation; previously, politicians in the Republika Srpska had been hesitant at best to implement the Dayton Agreement, and the elites in Serbia supported this hesitancy. According to one interlocutor, Koštunica's government continued to demonstrate political and, significantly, financial support for any Bosnian Serbs disinclined to implement the Dayton Agreement and reforms.[23] It is important to note that in part, Serbia's funding of Republika Srpska is not transparent and is not mentioned in budgets of the Serbian government; however, it has been argued that funding occurs through 'black' funds. Therefore, while the EU's influence in Bosnia increasingly appeared more significant, Serbia's influence continued to undermine any EU impact. This prompts the question: why did the EU not attempt to have a stronger impact on Serbian conflict parties' attitudes toward Bosnia? It is clear from the above discussion that the successive governments in Serbia since 2000 have openly and actively opposed the reform process in Bosnia. The significance of this opposition lies in its sustaining influence on anti-reform forces and the Serbian Democratic Party in Republika Srpska, which has created a destabilising impact on Bosnia.

The EU has not influenced the Serbian governments' attitudes toward Bosnia and Bosnian Serbs, which have continued to be a dominant force in Bosnia with an effect of limiting the reform process. So why has the EU not focused more attention on this area, since it is of vital interest to EU conditionality on good neighbourliness and progress in the region? The answer to this surely lies in the EU's short- to medium-term interests and strategies in the region. Arguably, the EU has been much more focused on other issues such as Bosnia-Hercegovina, Kosovo and ICTY cooperation in Serbia and consequently it can be credibly argued that the EU has neglected this issue. However, this would be naive. An added and important dimension is that the EU's engagement in Serbia has not been able to transform the attitudes of consecutive governments in Serbia toward Bosnian Serbs. The limits of the EU's transformative capacity are firmly demonstrated on this matter and can be explained by the EU's political management of the process.

The primary method that the EU has used to influence the transformation of the political parties' perceptions of conflict in Serbia is through political conditionality, which, as previously described, is inbuilt into contractual relations between Serbia and the EU. This section argues that there has been a qualitative change in perceptions of political parties in Serbia regarding the relationships in Montenegro. However, the qualitative change

has occurred because of the adaptational pressures caused by EU conditionality rather than social learning.

A primary example for examining relationship transformation in Serbia is
its relationships with its former partner in the FRY and latterly State Union:
Montenegro. EU conditional diplomacy during the creation and dissolution of the State Union of Serbia and Montenegro played a significant
role in transforming the non-violent conflictual relationship between some
political parties in Montenegro and Serbia. The State Union of Serbia and
Montenegro came into being under the Belgrade Agreement, signed on 14
March 2002, which dissolved the former Republic of Yugoslavia (FRY). The
State Union lasted just over four years, until 21 May 2006. It represented a
temporary transformation of the relationship between Serbia and Montenegro. Mediated by the High Representative for the Common Foreign and
Security Policy (CFSP), Javier Solana, the Belgrade Agreement saw Serbia
and Montenegro commit to a loose federal structure with a common market
and a common objective of EU membership. The State Union was from the
outset a temporary remedy, as the Constitutional Charter adopted by the
State Union included a provision for re-examination of the Agreement after
a period of three years via member state support in a referendum.[24]

The EU enabled the Belgrade Agreement by directly influencing the
negotiating parties through a compulsory pathway. While it was important
for the EU to maintain the Union for reasons of regional stability and international credibility, the EU had an important role to play in Montenegro
and Serbia (Agence Europe 6 February, 15 March 2002). The EU's transformative capacity and reasoning behind the Belgrade Agreement focused
on maintaining stability in the region through dissipating separatist move-
ments in Bosnia and avoiding Kosovo status talks while being concerned
with the internal political discussion in Montenegro. In effect, the Belgrade
Agreement was the 'right policy at the right time'.[25] However, time passed
and demands for Montenegrin independence grew. The Serbian and Montenegrin relationships during this time are worth investigating further.

In addition to the compulsory influence, the EU had an enabling impact
on the Montenegrin and Serbian political parties. This was most evident
when the Montenegrin and Serbian elites returned from negotiating the
Agreement with the task of convincing their electorates of the benefits of
the Belgrade Agreement. The EU had proposed that closer integration with
the EU would be the reward should Montenegro and Serbia stay together.
According to Putnam (1988), the 'two-level game' in which the negotiator
must ensure domestic ratification of an internationally reached agreement is
central to the political survival of the negotiators as well as the Agreement

reached. Therefore, it was difficult for Montenegrin President Djukanović to return from negotiating the Belgrade Agreement and convince his electorate, whom he had been promising an independence referendum since 1999, that the Belgrade Agreement was good for Montenegro. According to a report in the *Guardian*, President Djukanović was on the 'verge of abandoning his dream of independence after heavy pressure from the European Union, including the threat of cuts in aid' (*Guardian* 2002). For his Serbian counterpart, Koštunica, the maintenance of the Union remained the central success of the Agreement, yet at home he was criticised for acquiescing to Djukanović at the expense of a substantial and functioning state union.

Given the wider context of the process of integration with the EU and the instrumental investment that the EU had made four years earlier, the shadow of the EU was present during the run-up to the referendum on 21 May 2006. Three EU decisions played an important role in the discourse surrounding the referendum debate in Montenegro. These decisions were the role played by the EU Special Envoy to Montenegro since December 2005; Solana's decision to raise the required majority for the vote to be successful to 55 per cent; and the stalling of Stabilisation and Association Agreement negotiations on 3 May 2006. Moreover, ahead of the referendum it was possible to see a rift emerging between the pro-Union and the pro-independence bloc (Table 5.1). Given that the pro-Union bloc was orientated toward Serbia and supported by Belgrade, there was a potential for a breakdown in relations between Serbian and Montenegrin political elites. However, working relationships between Serbia and Montenegro at an elite level did not disintegrate ahead of or after Montenegro's declaration of independence because of the technical linkages between institutions in the two countries.

The relationship between the two countries was impacted by EU engagement and by the prospect of closer integration with the EU. The transformation of the relationship between Montenegro and Serbia was undoubtedly influenced by the prospect of closer integration with the EU and the prospect of joining the EU. The elites in Serbia and in Montenegro responded to the potential rewards available following closer integration with the EU by acting in accordance with the EU's policies and agendas. Consequently, the relationship between Montenegro and Serbia was altered by the presence of the EU membership perspective. This section has found that the relationship between Montenegro and Serbia was transformed in the period under investigation and that the EU did play a role in this transformation. This is not to say that Montenegro and Serbia do not have open issues or issues that could arise that would create future conflict. In line with

Table 5.1 Polarised political parties in Montenegro ahead of the referendum on 21 May 2006

Pro-independence bloc	Pro-state union bloc
Party of Democratic Socialists (DPS)	Socialist People's Party (SNP)
Social Democratic Party (SDP)	People's Party (NS)
Democratic Union of Albanians (DUA)	Serbian People's Party (SNS)
Democratic League of Montenegro (DSCG)	Democratic Serbian Party (DSS)
Liberal Party (LP)	
Civic Party (GS)	
Bosniak Party (BP)	

conflict transformation theory, it should be expected that because of their shared past and many linkages, there will be conflicts in this relationship in the future. However, the way in which the difficult issue of Montenegrin independence was dealt with by both Montenegro and Serbia provides an indication that future conflicts in this relationship will be resolved peacefully.

One significant conflict relationship, which is a consequence of the wars of the 1990s, is the relationship between the Serbian government and the refugee returns process. Here, we investigate the ways in which the intensified EU engagement in Serbia since 2000 has affected how the Serbian government and conflict parties have responded to this conflictual relationship. The relationship between the Serbian government and refugees is a politicised and contentious one, mainly because of the implications the issue has for non-refugees within Serbia, who make up the majority of the Serbian electorate. Furthermore, the constant presence of this issue in EU Progress Reports and in the Feasibility Study has made it a matter of immediate importance for Serbia.

To set the scene, in Serbia there remain approximately 400,000 refugees from Croatia and Bosnia and over 200,000 displaced persons from Kosovo. The refugee issue in Serbia is therefore multi-faceted. Not only does the Serbian government have to deal with the refugees from neighbouring countries living in Serbia but it also has to deal with the returns to Serbia from third countries and assisting returns from Serbia to third countries. This complex refugee issue stemmed directly from the mass population exchanges, voluntary and forced, during the wars of dissolution. Consequently, the relationship has been complicated by deep and longstanding issues of mistrust and antagonism compounded by an inadequate institutional and legal framework for transforming the relationship.

In 2002, the strategy of dealing with the situation of refugees and displaced persons in Serbia was twofold: return and local integration. The EU, the Organization for Security and Co-operation in Europe (OSCE) and the UN Refugee Agency (UNHCR) made available funding for the implementation of this strategy. On the matter of local integration, significant issues arose which relate closely to the transformation of the conflict relationship. Local integration required improvement of access to education, employment, human rights protection and, on a legal level, the granting of citizenship. It is useful to consider the legal background in Serbia regarding refugees since 2000. The UNHCR was mandated to conduct the refugee status procedure in Serbia. Under the State Union, three legal regimes existed: the federal regime and those of the two member states (Serbia and Montenegro). In Serbia, the only refugee law was the 1992 Refugee Law of Serbia which referred to refugees from Croatia and Bosnia. However, at a federal level, a National Action Plan was drafted to deal with refugees, displaced persons and asylum laws. The Federal Ministry of Human and Minority Rights that dealt explicitly with refugee and asylum issues replaced the Federal Ministry of Interior. A major problem in Serbia is refugees and displaced persons from Kosovo, not in terms of their legal status but because of problems exercising their basic human rights. The main explanation for the continued problem of integration, human rights protection and assimilation of refugees lies in the existence of a multitude of institutions dealing with the issue but none bearing responsibility.[26]

In December 2004 the Minister of the Interior for Serbia agreed to establish a working group to draft new asylum legislation for the Republic of Serbia. The SCG Parliament passed the new Law on Asylum in draft form in March 2005. The law does not specify procedures for the reception and protection of asylum-seekers and only guarantees the right to seek asylum. A difficulty in assessing the transformation of this relationship of conflict lies in the limits of statistics available for analysis. In Serbia statistics are only kept of returnees who were officially deported and not those who returned 'voluntarily'. Therefore the data is incomplete. However, statistics show that the Roma represent the majority of returnees to Serbia. Roma in Serbia are returned with limited resources such as language skills and have difficulty in finding access to employment, education and welfare services. In 2005–6 the Serbian government, under the Ministry of Human and Minority Rights, sought to remedy this problem through a specific programme. Yet the impact of this programme was always limited, since it lacked the capacity to oversee and supervise fully the implementation of the programme. In response to the inadequate situation for the Roma in Serbia, the EU discontinued the pressure for returns in Serbia at the start of 2004.

In order to become a member of the EU, it is expected that Serbia harmonise its legislation and practices with the EU through processes of social learning and adoption of the acquis. Therefore, the Serbian government has been required to mind the concerns and issues of returns under pressure from the EU. As discussed in Chapter 4, a notable impact of the EU was discernible in 2005 when along with the OSCE and the UNHCR, the EU encouraged cooperation between Croatia, Serbia (and Montenegro) and Bosnia over the voluntary return and integration of refugees and displaced persons at a regional and national level. Responsibility for this initiative in 2005 lay with the recognition by the EU Commission Delegation, the OSCE and the UNHCR working in Belgrade, Sarajevo and Zagreb that the individual institutions were failing and more could be achieved by working together.[27] This was a significant development of previous cross-border cooperation between Serbia and Bosnia when in October 2003 they had signed a bilateral agreement on the return of refugees and the resolution of property issues. In 2005 the EU was focused on the 'precarious situation' of refugees as it had a 'significant impact upon the overall political situation and the current trend towards radicalisation in the country' (European Commission 2005b). In highlighting the shortcomings of Serbia's response to the problem of refugees and displaced persons the EU had pressed for, facilitated and supported an agreement between Croatia, Montenegro, Serbia and Bosnia-Hercegovina on the return of refugees. It was significant that these events occurred in 2005 when the EU was publishing a positive feasibility study. Arguably, the ambition to achieve a positive feasibility study featured heavily in the Serbian governments' cooperation with the various initiatives in 2005.

Serbia's new Constitution provided a concrete example of the country's attempts to deal with minority rights in Serbia, which relates to the status and rights of refugees also living in Serbia. While the new Constitution provides a guarantee of human and minority rights (Article 1 and Chapter 2), it also carries a clause in which the government can temporarily suspend these rights (Article 20). This signals a limitation of transformation of the relationship between Serbia and the minority groups in its territory. In fully assessing the implications of the post-2000 period for refugees and displaced persons in Serbia it is useful to examince the specific endeavours to enhance the returns process in Serbia and the EU's role in it.

Along with the UNHCR and the OSCE the European Commission launched a regional '3 × 3' initiative, which provided a roadmap via which a more sustainable returns process could be achieved. Emerging from this initiative was the Sarajevo Declaration on Refugee Returns, which was a joint endeavour, signed in January 2005, by Bosnia, Croatia and Serbia (and Montenegro). The purpose of the Sarajevo Declaration was to confirm the commitment of the signatories to resolve the refugee and displaced persons situation through returns or integration by the end of 2006. Combined with this initiative, various other activities on refugees occurred after 2000, such as the Serbian Law on Citizenship, which aimed at streamlining the procedure for acquiring Serbian citizenship for refugees choosing to settle permanently in Serbia. The legislative activities were complemented by grassroots programmes targeting refugee housing programmes. The impact and merit of these various legislative, regional and grassroots endeavours are ultimately limited by the continuing relevance of the Law on Refugees (1992). Under this law, which contradicts the United Nations Convention on the Status of Refugees, refugee status may only be granted to persons who fled from former Yugoslav republics.

Even with the various high-level and EU-sponsored initiatives, problems for returnees remain – suggesting that the EU's influence on this relationship of conflict has been far from pervasive. For instance, returnees face problems in Serbia over the lack of employment and insufficient frameworks and funding for successful re-integration, which has been compounded by discrimination and widespread intimidation.

The EU's influence should have targeted the Serbian government's attitudes and policies regarding the reconstruction of damaged properties, access to employment and the welfare state, as well as improvement of local community relations. Undoubtedly, the EU's attention to the refugee issue has been intermittent. Given the geo-strategic imperative of the refugee issues during the various wars, this is perhaps surprising. However, the changing context of other conflict structures and relationships in Serbia, the EU's attentions and therefore transformative capacity has shifted from the refugee relationship at various times.

Conflict transformed?

This discussion has shown that the central success of the EU's transformative capacity on conflict transformation in Montenegro and Serbia lies in the EU's role as a financial and political supporter and monitor of transition. During the transition period in Montenegro and Serbia external support for and monitoring of the reform process was important to reform efforts in Serbia. One interlocutor contended that transition and reform efforts 'slipped when there was no pressure and pressure was needed to maintain [reform]'.[28] As an actor in conflict transformation, the EU's record in Serbia has been mixed.

This then leads us to question in what areas has it been most and least successful and what determines the EU's success in transforming conflict in Serbia? The EU has been most successful in supporting and facilitating the transformation of political parties by rewarding parties for measures reached, as well as desecuritising certain political agenda issues. However, as this chapter has shown, the EU has been limited in its success at transforming the dominant political agenda issue, namely, the ICTY. Cooperation with the ICTY is a highly controversial agenda issue and one that has been framed by the international community as a measure of the degree to which Serbia has transformed from its past conflict. The logic of appropriateness (cost-benefit analysis) largely helps to explain why Serbia was willing to accept, deal with and comply with EU conditions in order to make progress towards integration with and accession to the EU. It is difficult for the transforming Serbian political parties to cooperate with the ICTY, given the limited public support for the ICTY, yet if they wish to achieve the end goal of EU membership it is a condition that must be met. Hence, the 'value of the benefit' in which the benefits outweigh the costs of compliance is significant here (Tocci 2007: 18)

The nature of relations between the EU and Serbia was manifested most recently when they were confronted with the immediacy of the independence of Kosovo. The EU's engagement in Serbia since 2000 should have better equipped the EU to deal with the Kosovo issue in a more proactive and credible way than it had done when faced with the chaotic and awkward situation of the 1990s. However, the reflexivity of the EU is questionable, because it appeared in 2008 to react in an equally confused way, despite its ongoing involvement in Serbia since 2000. The EU has adopted a bargaining style in managing the conflict transformation as well as the technical management of the Stabilisation and Association process. The added political bargaining dimension of the engagement jeopardised the conflict transformation process. As noted above, the EU did not pursue a strict conditionality, particularly when faced with Kosovan independence. For example, ICTY conditionality appeared to weaken when it did not obstruct the potential agreement with Serbia tabled ahead of the successive January and May elections. The implications of this ad hoc bargaining were that the pro-EU parties such as Tadić's DS became increasingly undermined and then when the EU lessened its conditionality over ICTY the SRS and Koštunica's SDS gained support. Therefore it is possible to conclude that for the EU's potential to transform relationships and structures of conflict, it is necessary for conditionality to be applied especially in light of variances within domestic political situations.

All of this discussion is premised on the assumption that for Serbia, EU accession is a commonly held ambition and that therefore the attractiveness of EU membership would be sufficient to encourage transformation among the political elites to adapt their interests, relationships and attitudes. However, this chapter has shown that this assumption does not accurately describe the situation in Serbia. While societal support for the EU has been consistently high since 2000, a rift has emerged and continued to deepen between parties involved in and affected by the wars in the 1990s. Additionally, at the centre of Serbian politics sits Koštunica and the Democratic Party of Serbia, which since 2000 has appeared for much of the time to be largely uninterested and immune to the attractiveness of EU membership. Therefore, this chapter casts significant doubt on the assumption that the EU, through the processes of integration with and the prospect of joining the EU, can transform conflict.

In its role as gatekeeper, the EU had a transformative impact on the structure of conflict in Serbia. This can be perceived more significantly as a negative transformation. When the EU halted Stabilisation and Association Agreement negotiations in May 2006, the EU raised the spectre of collective guilt in Serbia, something the ICTY purposely tries to avoid. This decision diminished the individualisation of guilt and transferred blame and punishment to the Serbian people. A further unintended impact of the EU's policy towards Serbia on ICTY cooperation lies in the failure of EU policy towards Serbia in April 2007 when the perceived weakening of EU conditionality on the ICTY issue undermined the previous policy that pushed for full Serbian cooperation with the ICTY. This chapter concurs with Smith's (2003: 120) assertion that when conditionality is applied inconsistently it can lose force.

As set out in the analytical framework, relationship transformation requires a change in the perceptions of conflict of the key political parties. This chapter demonstrated that relationship transformation in Serbia can be largely traced through the political parties' changing attitudes and behaviour towards the conflict. The political parties in Serbia are central in determining the future trajectory and projection of the conflict, as well as determining the pace and nature of integration with the EU. Therefore, the norms and accepted behaviour of the conflict are principally in the hands of the political elites.

6

EU INTERVENTION

Shortcomings and Successes

This chapter discusses in detail the policy shortcomings and successes of the EU and evaluates the reasons for these. It also evaluates the EU's approach in terms of the following five issues: the role of domestic factors; the pathways of EU influence; continuing reflexivity in the EU enlargement approach; timing and nature of socialisation and political conditionality; and the EU's management of the process. Finally, this chapter addresses the question: is integration into the EU a panacea for conflict in Croatia?

From the analysis in this study, we know that Croatia and Serbia have experienced the same set of EU institutions, policies, initiatives and personnel, yet the two cases are at different levels of contractual relations with the EU. Additionally, the analysis has demonstrated that Croatia and Serbia have qualitatively different experiences of conflict transformation. Therefore, it is necessary in this comparative chapter to assess critically and comparatively the reasons for the different outcomes of the EU's intensified strategy since 2000. The chapter draws together the empirical findings of this study first by comparing the EU's impact on the different dimensions of conflict in Croatia and Serbia. The chapter then evaluates the effectiveness of the processes of integration with and the prospect of joining the EU on conflict transformation. The chapter concludes with a discussion that addresses the research question of this study: did the EU's integration and enlargement approach bring about conflict transformation?

The role of domestic factors

Domestic factors were a key determinant of the EU's influence in the case studies. The two significant domestic factors relate to the administrative capacity of and the political will in the states under investigation. As described in Chapters 4 and 5, Croatia and Serbia each demonstrated the administrative capacity to integrate with and become members of the EU. Each case had the necessary institutions and potential for institutional flexibility, growth and adaptation – as was demonstrated by their preparedness to adapt institutions appropriately for EU integration. However, where the cases began to diverge was over political will. The word 'divergence' may overstate the case slightly, since Croatia's political will to cooperate with EU conditionality and pressures was hesitant only at times. Croatia demonstrated the political will to meet the conditions of integrating and preparing for membership of the EU on a variety of occasions. While Croatia was an eager signatory of various agreements the authenticity of reforms remained unclear and impartial. Overall, Croatia demonstrated a political orientation towards the EU among elites across the spectrum, which resulted in a more fluid process of integrating with the EU and of conflict transformation. Furthermore, the political elites in Croatia made the EU matter to their policies, attitudes and outlooks, which impacted the structural and relationship transformation processes in Croatia. Political will in part explains the different outcomes of EU engagement on structural and relationship transformation in Croatia and Serbia. Serbia does not have the same level of political will for EU membership and this partially dictated the pace of progress on contractual relations with the EU. Several issues arise from this conclusion: can the EU only have an impact on conflict transformation when it has willing and engaged conflict parties? In addition, can the EU do more to engage with all conflict parties? These are two crucial areas for the trajectory of conflict transformation and the EU's role in conflict transformation in Serbia. First, without cross-party support, the EU's role and the success of conditionality has been open to cross-party bargaining between the centrist/reform parties and the SRS. This has created a situation where conflict transformation has become inherently linked to interparty bartering, which ultimately chipped away at the electoral success and ability of the reformist parties to implement change. Second, the EU could do more to engage with the entire scope of conflict parties in Serbia. This would not necessarily contribute to a greater political will in Serbia to cooperate with EU conditionality but it would provide the EU with an enhanced role and understanding of conflict parties, their interests and strategies. Therefore, while the political will for conditionality may remain unchanged, opportunities for socialisation could increase. This is particularly salient in the post-2000 period when the EU did not liaise with the majority party in Serbia, the SRS.

The pathways of EU influence

Applying the model developed by Diez *et al.* (2003), this study has shown that in terms of structural and relationship transformation the EU's influence mainly occurred through the compulsory and enabling pathways, less so through the connective pathway and was not discernible through a constructive pathway. There was little evidence of a constructive impact on conflict transformation in Croatia and Serbia, perhaps because a constructive impact refers to a longer-term transformation process where identities are replaced and ethnicity is less significant. This study demonstrated that a constructive impact was not central to the EU's contractual relations in the cases which had implications for the EU's transformative capacity in post-war non-member states, suggesting that the pursuance of contractual relations shaped by carrot/stick instruments is ineffectual at transforming conflict.

The 'compulsory' power of the EU was most evident, mainly because both Croatia and Serbia are not yet member states and are explicitly exposed to EU conditionality through preparing for integration and membership. EU conditionality has been of different significance at different times. The EU's compulsory influence was most significant because the EU wielded effective compulsory instruments against Croatia and Serbia, namely through EU conditionality. An equally important impact of the EU on Croatia and Serbia has been through an enabling impact on the political elites. While the socialisation impact of the EU on the conflict parties was significant, an important finding of this study was that the political parties directly and indirectly involved in the Europeanisation processes of integration with and preparing for membership of joining the EU changed their relationship to each other, interests and representation, and this consequently affected conflict transformation in Croatia and to a lesser degree Serbia.

In terms of relationship transformation EU influence was also evident through the connective pathway. This was particularly notable in terms of relationship change at a regional level. Opportunities for the EU to have an influence on relationship transformation occurred because of a mixture of enabling, compulsory and, crucially, connective influences. The connective influence was crucial to relationship transformation because of the direct effect of the incentives of financial, technical and political assistance on the conflict parties across and within the region.

This study has demonstrated that a combination of pathways of EU influence were important to the structures and relationships of transformation in Croatia and Serbia, for two reasons. First, the variety of EU agencies means that the organisation's influence is diffused in a variety of ways. Second, the dynamic and multi-source conflict experienced in both Croatia and Serbia required that the conflict transformation process, and thus the EU's role, would necessitate an EU integration process that impacts at various levels across the scope of conflict.

The timing and nature of EU conditionality and socialisation

This study analysed the timing, nature and design of EU political conditionality in Croatia and Serbia, with a focus on the period since 2000. The analysis of political conditionality in Croatia and Serbia demonstrated that the EU's political conditionality toolbox has expanded, as relations with Croatia and Serbia consist of a mixture of stabilisation, democratisation and accession. In Croatia and Serbia, the EU expanded beyond the traditional scope of political conditionality demonstrated in Central and Eastern Europe. This study established that in the Balkans the EU employed a unique mix of stabilisation policies coupled with more traditional EU mechanisms of accession that have been manifested mainly through conditionality and socialisation instruments. The cases indicated that political conditionality functioned in several different ways, ranging from state building, democratisation and conflict transformation to the more traditional and technical matters of harmonisation with the acquis. The case studies, therefore, pointed to the unique role the EU is acquiring in these countries through the combination of an active player and a framework approach. Additionally, this study found that the timing of the use of political conditionality has an impact upon the incentive structures that operate both in the Union and in the candidate countries.

This study revealed several interesting conclusions about the impact of political conditionality as a mechanism of conflict transformation in Croatia and Serbia. First, the timing and nature of conditionality was crucial in both cases. As demonstrated in the analysis of Croatia, the timing and nature of EU conditionality was effective at advancing ICTY cooperation as well as facilitating the returns process. In Serbia, the timing and nature of conditionality was significant at promoting ICTY cooperation ahead of the positive Feasibility Study. Second, and related to the first point, is that the timing and nature of conditionality led the conflict parties to experience a greater sense of pressure as the rewards for compliance and costs of non-compliance became more tangible. A third point to be raised is that the various conditions inherent in the Stabilisation and Association process and enlargement process were made clear to both cases and this clarity was fundamental in fostering compliance. Non-compliance cannot be blamed on a lack of clarity over EU conditionality. A fourth dimension that affected the success of conditionality as an instrument of conflict transformation was the EU's preparedness to act as a gatekeeper in contractual negotiations with the two cases. As we noted previously, on two significant occasions the EU bluntly stalled progress with the two cases over failure to cooperate with the ICTY, with the result that cooperation increased in the aftermath. Related to this is the fifth crucial factor which impacted the effectiveness of conditionality in Croatia and Serbia: the evolving nature of conditionality. This study argues that conditionality employed in Croatia and Serbia builds on previous applications of conditionality. EU conditionality in the Western Balkans has been stricter, more extensive and intensive, and the EU has been seeking better prepared candidates. All of this has emerged as a result of lessons learned from previous engagement in the former Yugoslav countries in the 1990s and the lessons learned from the experiences of the fifth enlargement. While reforms and conflict transformation under the Stabilisation and Association process has been slow and at times fitful, conflict transformation is taking place largely thanks to EU conditionality pressures.

In turn, this study has highlighted the need for a change of the EU strategy in the Western Balkans. A problem emerged in that the EU, through the progress reports and the European Partnerships, adopted a uniform policy approach to a region with increasing intercountry differences. Moreover, while the progress reports and European Partnerships may have proven effective for promoting institutional and legislative change in the acquis areas, their value in the political sphere has been weaker, indicating the need for increasing EU involvement in the latter sphere.

This study demonstrates that a degree of social learning has already taken place since 2000. While previous studies of the EU in conflict resolution have suggested that social learning was a long-term process (Tocci 2007: 168), this study finds that in both cases, but more so in Croatia, social learning had a significant role to play in the conflict transformation process. An indication of social learning in both cases was the willingness shown by conflict parties to transform their interests, attitudes and policies in order to become closer to the EU. As this study establishes, the transformation of the HDZ and the attitude towards the returns process in both cases demonstrates the scope of social learning. However, the limitations of the social learning opportunities are significant and must be addressed here. While the social learning experienced thus far in both cases has been primarily elite-focused with little engagement at grassroots levels, social learning has nonetheless taken place. In Serbia, because of the EU's limited engagement with the SRS, for example, social learning opportunities have been inherently restricted and therefore the outcomes of social learning have been harmful for the conflict transformation process. In Croatia and in Serbia the social learning opportunities, perhaps anticipated as outcomes of integrating with and preparing for membership, have only been realised at an elite level. However, given the elite focus of these processes, this should have been expected.

Continuing reflexivity in the EU enlargement approach

Investigation into the ways in which the EU 'learned by doing' in Croatia demonstrated that engagement in Croatia has provided useful experience for the EU in terms of its capacity to transform conflict in aspiring member states. A series of EU actions, commitments and speech acts has shown that the EU has increased in confidence in its capacity to initiate and consolidate change in Croatia. This learning has been both incremental and innovative. From lessons learned the EU found solutions to existing and new problems that it faced in Croatia. This capacity to deal effectively with the challenges raised in Croatia demonstrated that the EU was able to handle areas that had changed fundamentally, as well as those that remained unchanged. The issue of ICTY cooperation represented a lesson-learning experience for the EU. Because of its previous failure to secure Croatia's full cooperation with the ICTY, the EU was able to recognise and operationalise the following lessons: it was beneficial to deal with painful issues earlier in the accession process; the consistent application of conditionality and monitoring matters; the EU's transformative capacity can be increased by using gatekeeping at significant moments in the accession process; and, ultimately, on some issues the prospect of joining the EU is insufficient to bring transformation.

The reflexivity and flexibility of the EU to adapt its policies and approaches specifically to what was happening in the countries of the former Yugoslavia was evident in the strategic policy planning and programme development to deal specifically with Montenegro and Kosovo. In the mid-1990s the EU developed policies and mechanisms which Montenegro and Kosovo could access without interference from the central political authority in Belgrade. In terms of the mechanisms and self-confidence the EU developed mechanisms in response to experiences and lessons learned from their engagement in Yugoslavia. Chapter 3 pointed out that EU policy was a mix of incremental and innovative learning; the Royaumont Process and the Regional Approach were based on an idea previously discussed by Greek Defence Minister Arsenis, which demonstrated that this was both incremental and innovative policy change in that it was the evolution of a new idea.[1]

Evidence existed in February 1997 that the EU was a reflexive actor, which had implications for its policy development and transformative capacity. The EU carried out a fact-finding mission to Belgrade in February 1997, and as result of lessons learned about the situation in Belgrade and the effects of its existing approach, decided to change its approach to Belgrade and 'apply conditionality gradually with the view to developing a coherent strategy for relations with the countries of the region' (Agence Europe 25 February 1997). However, in the academic discourse there are questions about whether this was actually a policy change; as Peterson points out, in times of crisis, 'almost instinctively, the EU becomes highly conservative and tends to fall back on some type of past policy, even if it is clearly no longer appropriate' (Peterson 1998: 130). Ultimately, the implementation of lessons learned was manifested after the war in Kosovo in the form of the Stabilisation and Association process and the offer of the membership perspective. The external shock of the war in Kosovo stimulated EU policy change, which had important consequences for the future transformative capacity of the EU – namely the change in enlargement strategy to include the countries of the former Yugoslavia and how EU leaders perceived the link between security and enlargement (Higashino 2004: 361). The external shock of the war in Kosovo provided a learning experience for the EU. During the war in Kosovo the EU was preparing for what would happen after the war and how it would stabilise the region. Therefore, the EU policymakers were making a conscious effort to improve their policies and approaches to the countries of the former Yugoslavia in 1999–2000.

Chapter 5 demonstrated that from its relationship with Croatia, combined with the experience from the 2004 and 2007 enlargements, the EU has learned a variety of lessons which it has implemented in the process of Croatia's integration with the EU. The EU has learned the lesson that in order to achieve desired results in aspirant countries reforms must be achieved earlier rather than later in the reform process. According to Grabbe, the experience of setting standards and creating monitoring mechanisms for the applicants was 'an important learning process for the European Commission – with potential feedback effects on the existing Union' (2006: 84).

The accumulation of engagements with external and internal pressures and the choices, commitments and reviews of choices made from these engagements has an impact on the internal development of the EU's mechanisms and self-confidence in conflict transformation. Arguably, innovations were made in the EU's conflict transformation capacity as a result of the external shocks of engagement in the countries of the former Yugoslavia during the 1990s, but it is evident that the EU has learned from this engagement and its policy which has led to adaptation of its policy and actorness in conflict transformation. The lessons learned have led to an innovative policy adaptation and incremental change such as the employment of benchmarks, the pressure to achieve progress in more difficult tasks earlier in the integration process, policy flexibility to adapt to changing context, balancing carrots and sticks, recognition that external perceptions of the enlargement project matter, and recognition, equally, that internal and external confining conditions impact the intended outcome of the engagement.

This analysis indicates clearly that the EU has refined and adapted its existing mechanisms, as well as developing new ones, as a result of the lessons it has 'learned by doing' in the countries of the former Yugoslavia. The lessons learned by the EU as result of engagement with the former Yugoslavia have led to a change of beliefs, skills and procedures and increased the institution's confidence in them. In the case of the policies in the countries of the former Yugoslavia this study has shown that the EU is learning lessons from itself rater than from other institutional actors such as NATO, the UN and the OSCE. Therefore, at the EU level, the lessons learned have been from policy evaluations and reappraisals of the enlargement policy. The indicators that this study has utilised for changes in enlargement policy are the enlargement strategy chapters by the Commission as well as policy decisions over a period of time. With the 2004 and 2007 enlargement completed, these lessons are also the consequence of capacity and experience of what can be achieved with enlargement based on the EU's experience with the Central and Eastern European countries. Nonetheless, the EU enlargement policy does not face the same scrutiny and monitoring that other CFSP policies and missions do. For example, the Policy Unit can produce reports on CFSP activities such as Mission Reports and Lessons Identified/Lessons Learned Reports. This is significant and made the task of identifying the reflexivity of the EU's enlargement policy much more difficult. Therefore, the measuring of the reflexivity of the EU's enlargement policy could be improved. This research and analysis has shown that it can be difficult for lessons to be learned, institutionalised and implemented. Evidence has suggested that it has been difficult for the EU to coordinate the lessons that the various EU agencies have learned.

The EU's management of the process

The history of the EU's enlargement process lacks a grand design; rather, enlargement happens because of a series of ad hoc decisions and bargaining processes. Arguably, the enlargement process is inherently uncertain. This uncertainty is compounded by the EU's capacity to stall the process and/ or refuse an aspirant further progress toward integration or accession at any given time. Paradoxically, the EU is able to encourage compliance with conditionality and social learning most effectively when the threat of removal or exclusion from the process is most clear. However, uncertainty about the future of the entire enlargement project is what is paramount for this discussion, not the inbuilt uncertainty of the approach. This study has demonstrated that since 2005 the EU's enlargement approach has continued to suffer from an affliction that has been striking it sporadically since the 1990s: the affliction of enlargement fatigue. Enlargement fatigue in the post-2000 period was a matter of concern for both cases in this study. Between 2005 and 2007 EU political elites and media focused attention on the challenges caused by EU enlargement. Particularly in the aftermath of the French and Dutch referenda (May 2005) and the accession of Bulgaria and Romania (January 2007), critics of the enlargement process gained credence and volume.

An appreciation of the ebb and flow of the enlargement project is important for understanding the EU's transformative capacity in Croatia and Serbia. The most important perceived challenge to the EU's transformative capacity was whether, if enlargement was further delayed in Croatia and Serbia, the pro-reform, pro-EU parties would be undermined so that conflict transformation would be impeded. In reality, the time frames for Croatian and Serbian accession were not significantly affected by the enlargement fatigue discourse. This was largely because of the nature of their respective contractual relations with the EU during the 2005–7 time frame: Croatia was already a candidate state about to commence accession negotiations, and Serbia was still attempting to sign a Stabilisation and Association Agreement. Hence, Croatia was close enough not to be adversely impacted by the negative discourse and Serbia was far enough from achieving candidacy for the political elites to be able to quieten fears by reaffirming the final destination of EU membership. Moreover, the reaction of the technocrats in Brussels had a significant impact, which arguably countered the negative impact of enlargement fatigue. The European Commission continued to meet with and conduct technical negotiations with Croatia and Serbia throughout this period. Arguably, then, enlargement fatigue did not impede the effectiveness of the mechanism of social learning because the relationships between the EU and the two cases were sustained and provided increased opportunities for socialisation of the Croatian and Serbian political elites. Furthermore, it became clear that the fears about the future of the enlargement project were neutralised by the Lisbon Treaty.

The uncertainty of the enlargement project did have an impact on Serbia, but in a less obvious way. That is, reforms did not stop instantly because the prospect of membership was increasingly doubtful. Rather, the discourses of enlargement fatigue occurred at a time when it was perceived in Serbia that the EU was acting irresponsibly regarding Serbia's integration with the EU. It was perceived that the EU opened SAA negotiations with Serbia reluctantly and then stopped them quickly over the Mladić/Karadžić ICTY cooperation issue. Particularly in Serbia, the doubt over the EU's sincerity to admit Serbia was fuelled by the various decisions taken by the EU which ultimately delayed Serbia's progress in integrating with the EU. For one interlocutor who recognised the 'tremendous perspective' that the EU has provided Serbia, it remained 'worrying that the EU is questioning the future of the enlargement project'.[2] Discourse on 'enlargement fatigue' provided a useful currency for anti-reform politicians in Serbia, who manipulated the uncertain climate over further EU enlargement to maximise their own electoral success. 'Enlargement fatigue' generated concern that EU conditionality was not working in Serbia because the commitment of membership was unclear and therefore the strategic bargaining that characterised the Europeanisation of previous EU membership candidates was undermined.[3]

The stronger EU framework and strategy has impacted the EU's transformative capacity since 2000. Largely, the confusion among member states over what the problems in Yugoslavia were, never mind the mayhem in attempting to create a united response to the events of the 1990s, left the EU very much marginalised as an actor in conflict transformation. As this study points out, after 2000 a qualitatively different nature of relationship and strategy emerged and was consolidated at Santa Maria de Feira, Zagreb and Thessaloniki. However, as this study argues, the assumption of the perpetual attractiveness of membership was very much an erroneous one. EU membership was not an answer, nor an appealing incentive for the conflict parties to transform the structures and relationships of conflict in the two cases. This is not to say that attractiveness is not a malleable or dynamic concept. To clarify, since 2000, the attractiveness of EU membership at societal and elite level has been inconsistent in both cases – mainly because of domestic circumstances but, importantly, because of the perceived EU response to internal changes. As this study points out, support for EU membership fell in Croatia as a result of the EU's perceived bargaining over ICTY cooperation and opening accession negotiations in March 2007. However, the fluidity of the attractiveness of EU membership has also impacted the conflict parties' willingness to respond to EU pressures and demands. Even in the case of Serbia, where support for EU membership has remained consistently high, EU membership was not a sufficiently attractive carrot to get political parties across the political spectrum to support the necessary conditions and reforms for preparing for EU membership.

The attractiveness of EU membership for the elites and societies in the case studies was clearly impacted by the costs of attraction. In other words, the lure of EU membership was insufficient for the political elites, most significantly in Serbia, to comply fully with all EU conditions, particularly political (rather than technical) conditions. This suggested that EU membership should no longer be perceived to be a cure-all strategy for post-war societies and that the current strategy of pursuing contractual relations with at times unwilling and uncooperative partners needs to be reconsidered. In the case of Serbia, the prospect of membership is perceived to be a long-term eventuality; the prospect of short-term transformation is limited. In Croatia, on the other hand, the attractiveness of EU membership did succeed in galvanising cross-party support for all EU conditions, indicating that conflict transformation and Europeanisation mattered.

The perceived value of the benefits of integrating with and the prospect of joining the EU has impacted the EU's capacity to transform conflict in Croatia and Serbia. 'Perceived' value refers to how Croatia, Serbia and, importantly, the EU view the benefits available in the EU's chosen strategies. This study discovered that the subjective value of EU membership is significant. The transformation of conflict in Croatia and Serbia is related to, and a reaction to, the overall context in the countries of the former Yugoslavia, a context that is changing. The attractiveness of the prospect of closer relations with the EU, or indeed EU membership, depends on the perceptions of the political elites and society in Croatia and Serbia. This has played a significant role throughout the evolution of relations between the EU and the aspirants since 2000. The level of trust and mistrust in the EU actions and the credibility of the membership perspective are important to the transformation of conflict in Croatia and Serbia. The long-term prospect of membership is not enough and should be sustained by intermediate rewards for the aspirants in order to keep reform-minded governments on track. Vachudova (2005: 251) advocates the implementation of intermediary rewards such as complete and unilateral access to the EU market, substantial economic aid and visa-free travel, which will help preserve the domestic political viability of moderate parties. Intermediate rewards are helpful because they help to lock the aspirants into a process of compliance by creating immediate and tangible benefits. The effectiveness of the prospect of membership has been impacted by the perceived value of the Stabilisation and Association Agreement, the credibility of the obligations, the timing and the targets of EU conditionality, rewards and punishments as well as the continued support for EU membership within the cases. This study found that political and economic reform is not embedded in the cases, as we would expect to find in countries with an EU membership perspective. This is evident in the lack of support for EU conditions in Serbia, and the degree of harmonisation and implementation in Montenegro and Croatia. An explanatory reason for this could be the fact that membership is such a distant prospect for the region (SEESOX 2007). The EU's impact on conflict transformation in Serbia has been less than that in Croatia and Montenegro. The experience in Serbia can be explained by the different historical context, the confining conditions of the situation in Kosovo and the issue of ICTY cooperation. Serbia may value EU membership, but must consider the perceived costs of EU-demanded obligations embedded in the contractual relations.

The Stabilisation and Association Agreements and the offer of membership included a provision that each country would progress toward the EU on its own merit at its own pace, demonstrating an appreciation of the unique situations in each of the countries of the Western Balkans. Additionally, this reflected in part a need to assure more advanced countries that their progress would not be impeded by less advanced countries. As demonstrated in this study, the creation of a symbolic label of 'potential' membership revealed both reflexivity and flexibility in the way that the EU dealt with the cases. It may have been expected that these characteristics would have continued in the EU's engagement with the cases. However, this has not transpired. As this study confirms, because of the nature of the EU's contractual relations through the Stabilisation and Association process and enlargement process, a high degree of flexibility is not possible. This study contends that, because the same conditions apply to each of the cases as well as the same rewards and the ever-present shadows of past and future, the EU's strategy for the Western Balkans is not flexible enough to cope with the different situations in Croatia and Serbia.

A further problem of the EU's present strategy, apart from its inflexibility, is the incompatibility of ambitions. The inbuilt ambitions of democratisation, conflict transformation, reform, stabilisation and member state building are not necessarily compatible. This emerged from the findings of the chapters 4 and 5. While on the surface, it would appear that the various conditions for EU membership that are inbuilt into the Stabilisation and Association process and enlargement process are complementary, as this study has shown, the various strategies of stabilising, democratising, reforming, and transforming conflict have been at times contradictory and have challenged the realisation of any of these objectives. There is a tension between and within each of these ambitions, and also a tension between the capacity of the EU to export EU norms and practices in Croatia and Serbia and the potential side effects of reaction, reproduction or causing conflicts. A possible solution to these limitations lies with the EU's strategy. The EU will have to work closely with the countries in devising policies relating to the political criteria, rather than only setting the conditions and benchmarks.

The EU's management of the integration and enlargement process impacted the EU's transformative capacity. This study demonstrates that the EU's interests have impacted the body's overall transformative capacity on conflict structures and relationships in the two cases. It also shows that increased salience of a particular conflict issue, such as ICTY cooperation, equals increased pressure on the domestic conflict parties, which determines the outcome of the conflict transformation process. Furthermore, investigation of the structures and relationships of conflict since 2000 has shown that the EU focused more on structures throughout this period than on relationships (perhaps with the exception of returns). For example, the ICTY issue was a constant focus for the EU in both cases throughout this period – although developments in Serbia since 2008 have suggested that ICTY cooperation has begun to assume a secondary role. During the same period, regional cooperation and attitudes to Bosnia were relationships that were qualitatively less focused on in comparison with ICTY conditionality. This can be explained by the EU's management of the process. While the EU's contractual relations require that aspiring member states meet various technical obligations, the EU's focus on various political conditions has been unpredictable and dictated by changing interests of EU agencies. The implication of the way that the EU has managed the processes of integration with and the prospect of joining the EU in both cases had an unintended impact of enhancing the role of bargaining in the process, which as highlighted above created difficulties for the conflict transformation process.

The EU's management of the process of integration with Croatia and Serbia leads us to question the EU's overall interests, ambitions and long-term strategies for the Western Balkans. These issues have a significant bearing on how the EU should be perceived as an actor in conflict transformation. In the case of Serbia, the EU's focus on Kosovo and Montenegro was in tension with other ambitions such as full cooperation with the ICTY. Did EU member states' interests and ambitions for the region therefore conflict with the technical and political conditions which the EU had been trying to achieve through negotiations and progress on closer contractual relations? While the EU's intensified strategy did change the context of conflict and party support, and facilitated new discursive frameworks among the conflict parties, the EU's strategy has revealed some serious limitations and unintended impacts. This leads us to question what is more important for the EU: conflict transformation, EU membership or member state interests. Are the three compatible?

Important and related determinants of the EU's transformative capacity are how the EU perceives its policies, what influences the effectiveness of its policies, and how thoroughly the policies are actually implemented on the ground. European Commission delegations played an instrumental role in highlighting potential pitfalls in the integration process, as well as communicating the feedback and outcomes of EU impacts on the ground in the two cases. In both cases, the delegations consisted of a sizeable number of experienced staff, which reflected the long-term importance of the two cases for the EU. (It also raises a question for future research to examine the role of delegations in other conflicts where the EU's interest was not so substantial.) Hence, the centrality of the Commission delegations has been influential in how the EU perceives its policies and their impacts, and on the accuracy of these perceptions. How the EU perceives the impacts of the chosen strategy is significant since it has implications for the way in which the EU shapes its future engagement. The accuracy of perceptions of the impacts of the EU's strategy dictated the nature and impact of the EU's policies in Croatia and Serbia. For instance, in both cases, the pursuit of EU conditionality over ICTY had tangible outcomes, for the EU, in terms of the number of indictees transferred to the ICTY; yet the impact on conflict transformation was much less clear as it was compounded by the unintended impact of fostering a sentiment of collective guilt. The EU's impact on conflict transformation in Croatia and Serbia through the chosen strategies of integration and enlargement was affected by the EU's perceptions about the outcomes of the policies, and the responses to these perceptions.

Is integration with and membership of the EU a panacea for conflict?
This study has explored the link between Europeanisation and conflict transformation in the cases of Croatia and Serbia. It has demonstrated that integration with and the prospect of joining the EU is significant for the two cases in terms of conflict transformation. Undoubtedly, the study has also shown that the integration carrot would not be as effective without the membership perspective, for it is the membership perspective that means

the most, not only to the elites, but to the people in Croatia and Serbia. According to one interlocutor, 'EU membership marks a move against the paradigm of Balkanisation; it represents a badge of progress and a code of conduct.'[4] It impacts on how the countries are perceived internationally, which ultimately influences their future success in terms of financial investment and political relationships. There are advocates and dissenters on both sides of this argument. In the case of Serbia, in regard to Kosovo, the pervasive emotion since Kosovo's declaration of independence is that an integral part of Serbia has been pilfered from them by the international community, including many of the EU member states. Advocates of the EU's transformative capacity would insist that, because of the impact on the border dispute in Northern Ireland, faith should prevail that the EU will provide a better context in which to resolve this dispute. The EU can help to accelerate how Serbia and Kosovo begin to deal with each other and given the domestic political will, the EU framework can facilitate and support change.

As a panacea for conflict, the EU relied upon its existing toolbox when it offered Croatia and Serbia the prospect of membership and a framework for closer integration into the EU. However, the suitability of this deployed strategy was questionable from the outset. Hence, it is debatable what the EU's intentions in the two cases are. Does the EU have a plan, or is the EU's strategy just wishful thinking pursued through an ad hoc series of responses? Is there a predetermined blueprint, or is its strategy simply to hope for domestic political situations that will be more conducive to realising its ambitions to stabilise and integrate the countries concerned?

Let us consider the EU's strategy in Serbia ahead of the 2008 elections. While the EU's role in Serbia was perceived by much of the Western media to have been instrumental in Tadić's success in the presidential election, this was perhaps not an accurate reflection of the political dynamics in Serbia. The 11 May 2008 elections failed to produce a visibly more nationalist government and the EU's 'wishful thinking' saw the emergence of a pro-EU integration coalition government. However, the persistence of a sizable return of nationalist and ultra-nationalist parties to seats in the assembly suggests that the EU faces a continued pressure to engage proactively across the entire political spectrum in Serbia.

The introduction to this book highlighted the contradictions inherent in the assumption that EU enlargement and integration could transform conflict in Croatia and Serbia. The study has revealed that, while the EU has had an impact on the conflict structures and relationships in both cases, these contradictions mean that the EU's actions have had both intended and unintended consequences. This means that the ultimate verdict on the EU's transformative capacity is much more nuanced than might at first have been imagined. Given the findings of this study, the EU could be criticised for not fostering an inclusive process involving all conflict parties, thus limiting its impact on structural and relationship transformation. Essentially, the EU seems to have realised that the main obstacles to the impacts of integration and enlargement dynamics lie with the conflict parties, yet the EU has not sought to engage proactively with all political parties, particularly in Serbia. Hence, the EU's transformative capacity could be improved by enhanced contact with the SRS combined with an increased field presence in both cases which would permit the EU to work with and be aware of the positions of all conflict actors rather than only the conflict parties at a government level. However, such reforms to the EU's transformative capacity in Croatia and Serbia will be determined by the internal dynamics within the EU, which have at times proven to be harmful to the EU's transformative capacity.

As shown above, this study demonstrates that the EU was most effective at transforming structures of conflict through compulsory and enabling pathways while relationships were primarily impacted by compulsory and connective pathways. This suggests that in Croatia and Serbia the EU can maximise its transformative capacity by focusing its efforts on enhancing the effects of the compulsory, enabling and connective pathways, which would require a stronger focus on EU conditionality and socialisation. Additionally, the potential for the EU to have a transformative impact on the structures and relationships of conflict in the two cases remains, but since the transformation of conflict is a dynamic process the balance between extemporised and prepared strategising must continue, which ultimately requires a more comprehensive engagement in the two cases.

CONCLUSION

Integrating Peace

This concluding chapter explores the policy implications of this book's examination of relationships between the EU and Croatia and Serbia, respectively. For example, it reflects on the question of when the EU can be more effective as a transformative power. It argues that the Croatian case demonstrates the importance of examining the relevant actors, issues and relationships and identifying their capacity to influence change, and points out that the specific political conditions in Croatia and Serbia have been instrumental in shaping the EU's policymaking and policy implementation. Taking the Croatian case as an illustrative example, this chapter recommends a series of policymaking lessons regarding the EU's effectiveness as an actor in conflict transformation. One lesson is that the EU can be most effective as a transformative power on conflict when dealing with conflict parties and issues when political conditionality is rigorously and consistently applied. The conclusion points out that while these lessons draw on the specificities of the Croatian case they have relevance for other post-conflict situations, an importance that will evolve as the EU positions itself as a major strategic and military power on the global stage. Furthermore, this chapter widens the application of this study to consider implications for the broader study of European enlargement, security, foreign policy, conflict transformation and regional studies.

The case studies investigated in this study demonstrated that political violence and war resulted from the use of ethnic mobilisation by political elites within some of the Republics of Yugoslavia to realise their varied ambitions. During the 1990s the EU's indecision and incapacity to formulate a strategic response to the escalating conflict sidelined EU agencies' and member states' capacity to stem the violence. After 2000, the EU developed a more intensified strategy for the Western Balkan countries in the form of the Stabilisation and Association process and membership perspective. As stated above, the EU's chosen and implemented strategy for the countries of the Western Balkans was similar in each case; in that case, why did such a similar set of instruments produce comparatively different results in Croatia and Serbia? This section draws on the empirical findings in the two case studies with specific focus on the structural and relationship transformation in Croatia and Serbia. It asks: why was the EU's intensified strategy more effective in Croatia than in Serbia? What other factors must be taken into consideration?

The main point to emerge from the empirical findings on structural transformation in the two cases regarding political parties is that the EU's strategy of offering contractual relations through integration and accession produced different outcomes on conflict transformation in Croatia and Serbia. A comparative analysis of the findings of the research must be carried out to establish the explanations for these disparate outcomes. To recap, structure transformation in Croatia and Serbia focused on the transformation of conflict parties and issues of conflict in the cases. In Croatia, evaluation of the transformation of conflict parties demonstrated that in terms of numbers, identities, interests and rhetoric the conflict parties were transformed by the changing context brought about by the processes of integration with and the prospect of joining the EU. On the other hand, in Serbia, evaluation of the transformation of conflict parties has been less clear. While all political parties in Serbia have demonstrated a transformation in their identities, interests and rhetoric, by relying less and less on ethnic mobilisation and war propaganda, the political parties remain detached from the European integration process and, therefore, have not responded to the pressures and challenges of integration with the EU as Croatia has.

In terms of the issue of ICTY cooperation, Croatia's and Serbia's experiences have not been too dissimilar. Both cases have experienced explicit EU political conditionality, with the added feature of the EU's handling of the progress of contractual relations through gatekeeping. Acting as a gatekeeper, the EU denied and stalled progress towards advancement on EU relations because of deficient cooperation with the ICTY. The EU's political management of this had a contradictory impact on the transformation of conflict issues in both cases. At a political elite level, ICTY cooperation represented a measure of conflict transformation for the EU and progress on advancement with EU relations would not take place without cooperation. Therefore, for political elites, particularly in Croatia, cooperation on this condition was a necessity. In both cases, the political parties pursued a strategy and rhetoric which asserted the obligation of achieving full cooperation while transferring blame to the EU and the conditionality associated with integration. The significance of EU conditionality was threefold. First, an unintended impact of EU conditionality was the fostering of a critique of collective guilt in both Croatia and Serbia, which undermined a core tenet of the ICTY – to individualise guilt. Second, it created cohesiveness among Croatian conflict parties, which all agreed that this conditionality must be met in order to achieve the bigger ambition. This established a solid and consistent approach by the political elites towards EU membership and the conditions which it entailed. Third, in Serbia, it was divisive for the conflict parties. The pro-EU parties led by Tadić's DS were the most conciliatory regarding ICTY cooperation. The SRS and the SDS, however, disagreed and disapproved of ICTY cooperation. Their stance on ICTY created opportunities for winning and losing in the conflict transformation process.

Having drawn together the key findings on the impact of the EU on structural transformation in Croatia and Serbia, it is worthwhile to conduct a detailed comparative evaluation which focuses on when and why the EU's transformative capacity is more or less effective at certain times and through certain pathways.

The EU's impact on conflict parties: radicalisation and moderation

In Croatia, all political and former conflict parties agreed on a government foreign policy ambition to become an EU member, which meant that there was less opportunity for credible opposition to government policies to meet EU membership conditions. Therefore, it was possible to see that the EU's perception of conflict transformation in Croatia was achieved because of the attractiveness of becoming a member of the EU. Serbia's situation was discernibly different. There was no cross-party support for EU membership in Serbia, and therefore the EU's ambitions in Serbia were much more constrained. There was a support base for an opposition to government policies and activities designed to enable Serbia to meet EU membership conditions. A clear indication of the comparative variance regarding Europeanisation between Croatia and Serbia came during the elections in Croatia in 2007 and in Serbia in 2008. The Croatian elections in November 2007 represented the first elections in 20 years in which voters could be sure that the winner would not impede Croatia's EU ambitions. This was not the case with the Serbian January 2008 elections, where the EU integration project very much relied on the re-election of Tadić. However, having cross-party support cannot explain the limits of Europeanisation on conflict transformation in Serbia; the explanation is much more nuanced.

In Croatia the political parties streamlined their agendas, interests and representation on many issues because of the prospect of becoming a member of the EU. Regardless of which party holds the parliamentary majority, the Croatian government's position on EU membership has not altered. This has had an implication for the wider policy areas. The perceived closeness of EU membership and the intensifying processes of integration with the EU had a transformative impact on the language, leadership style and policies of the HDZ. The HDZ were keen to prove their European credentials to the EU and to the population at home. The decision by the HDZ to transform the party was even more significant given the ambivalent feeling amongst the Croatian population about the prospect of EU membership. The transformation of the HDZ therefore reveals a degree of Europeanisation and socialisation. Ultimately, the processes of integration with and the prospect of joining the EU bought about a transformation of the political parties in Croatia.

An unintended impact of the EU enlargement and integration process on conflict parties in Serbia has been the alienation of anti-EU parties from the liberal peace-building project. This had the effect of undermining conflict transformation in Serbia. Since 2000 the SRS and the SPS have been absent from the EU integration process, so they do not have opportunities for social learning at an EU level. The reason for their absence from the EU integration and enlargement process is their own political agendas and because of the EU's refusal to negotiate with parties that do not cooperate, even partially, with the EU's concepts of conflict transformation. The support base for the SRS is largely found in the socio-economically deprived areas of Serbia. The wars in which Serbia was engaged during the 1990s had a tremendous impact on such communities at a grassroots level. Since 2000 the EU's top-down, elite-focused strategy has failed to engage sufficiently with the grassroots of Serbian society. The nascent liberal democracy in Serbia, and the EU as 'peace builders' or 'conflict transformers', have failed to deal with this situation as part of the problem of Serbia. The lack of any attempt to alleviate the serious political and socio-economic conditions at the grassroots level or to meet with the chosen elected representatives of these communities, coupled with the propensity for making liberal 'peace' at the political level with existing elites, has served to feed social discontent and encourage support for the SRS. Furthermore, when the EU is attempting to develop discourses of peace and conflict transformation in Serbia, this is a major obstacle. It will remain a major obstacle while the EU fails to engage more proactively with all political parties in Serbia and attempts to persuade previously excluded political parties such as the SRS that the EU integration project is legitimate. Should the EU engage proactively with the SRS and its electorate then there will be an opportunity for the EU to gain legitimacy as well as deal with the problems Serbia faces every day. This would create a more hybridised polity with increased prospects for a more holistic conflict transformation process.

This study has shown that the conflict transformation process in Serbia has been radicalised and politicised, partly as a result of the processes of integration with and the prospect of joining the EU. The SRS in particular, as a conflict party, has radicalised and politicised EU conditionality especially over ICTY, and augmented its electoral success by claiming to support those people negatively impacted by the processes of integration with the EU. Unlike the win–win outcomes of the conflict resolution approach, the transformation approach argues that there can be a win–lose outcome for all the parties involved in the transformation processes. Therefore, EU engagement in Serbia has produced a wide range of impacts on the various parties, with some winning at times and some losing at other times. For example, while the SRS has sustained its political support and significant profile, its capacity to affect legislative change has remained limited in its opposition role. The EU may have the ambition of achieving full cooperation on the ICTY issue, among other agendas, but the continued electoral successes of the SRS has meant that the EU integration process could not build a transformation process which represents merely the wishes of specific parties, Tadić's party in particular. The conflict transformation approach permits an understanding that various value systems, goals and perspectives can plausibly be accommodated within a transformation process – something that is at odds with the EU approach. The EU has favoured a pro-EU, pro-reform and pro-ICTY stance in Serbia, with rewards for parties that are working towards the EU's stated goals and ambitions for Serbia. The May 2008 election results suggested that political alignments among political parties in Serbia are very fluid. Both the SRS and the Socialists have changed, and the ideological and rhetorical distance between the conflict parties in Serbia has diminished. Since May 2008 the question of EU membership among the conflict parties has been less divisive; all parties have stated their ambition for EU membership, albeit with individual nuances, especially relating to ICTY cooperation.

The EU's consistent strategy of ad hoc bargaining with the Serbian political elites and electorate has proved to be perilous. The EU has consistently engaged in what can be described at best as 'wishful thinking', and at worst as 'blackmail', to provide political and financial support to the pro-EU elites such as Tadić's DS and (increasingly less so) Koštunica's SDS, particularly in the run-up to unpredictable elections. The claim of blackmailing emerged from the apparent 'sugar-coating' of the pill of Kosovo's independence with a relaxed visa regime and a Stabilisation and Association Agreement. The inefficiency of this tactic of offering rewards was compounded by a slow realisation of the rewards promised, if at all. Moreover, the policies of the SRS would decelerate Serbia's progress towards integration with and membership of the EU, particularly in light of its policy slogan: 'EU membership but only with Kosovo'. The EU's influence on the political parties in Serbia is further complicated by the perceived failure of the EU enlargement project among the political elites, which is compounded by the sentiment that the prospect is so distant its relevance is not immediately effective. In due course, the various attitudes among the conflict parties in Serbia towards the EU, and EU conditionality, have rendered the compulsory and enabling pathways less than effective. The varied outlook and interests of the conflict parties in Serbia added to a lack of cooperation with the ICTY.

Issue transformation: the utility of conditionality

The transformation of issues in Croatia and Serbia related primarily to the central political agenda and whether the prospect of EU membership could overwhelm the competing issues and transform their contentiousness. Cooperation with the ICTY was a highly controversial issue in the cases. More significantly, ICTY cooperation was an issue framed by the international community as a measure of how successfully Croatia and Serbia were moving beyond the mindsets of the past conflict. It can be concluded from the empirical findings of this study that Croatia and Serbia were influenced by EU conditionality over ICTY, particularly when the cost of non-compliance and the rewards of compliance were seen to be quickly achievable. Therefore, while ICTY cooperation was not explicitly in the hands of the political elites but rather in those of the security services, this study argues that without the political will to support it ICTY cooperation could not have bee achieved. So why did the political elites cooperate with this condition at different times, and what does this tell us about the EU's use of political conditionality? It was difficult for the conflict parties in the cases to cooperate with the ICTY given the limited support for the ICTY within their parties and among their electorate, and yet if they wished to achieve the end goal of EU membership such cooperation was a condition that had to be met. Hence, the 'value of the benefit' in which the benefits outweighed the costs of compliance was significant here (Tocci 2007: 18).

The decisions made by Croatia and Serbia to comply with ICTY conditionality reflect the logic of appropriateness (cost-benefit analysis) argument. Chapters 4 and 5 examined ICTY cooperation. In Croatia, since 2000 cooperation with the ICTY has been widely discussed and the issue of ethnic cleansing has featured on the political discourse agenda. Since Croatia became a candidate state in April 2004 the issue of cooperation with ICTY has dictated the pace of progress of integration with the EU. Before opening accession negotiations, the EU utilised its capacity as a gatekeeper and pushed Croatia to cooperate fully with the ICTY. This provides evidence of the 'blunt' way in which the EU can have a transformative influence on the issues of conflict. The EU postponed opening accession negotiations with Croatia which had been due to start on 16 March 2005. This decision was significant for two reasons: its implications for the wider region and future candidate states; and its implications for public support for the process of integration with the EU in Croatia. The 16 March decision had significant implications for Serbia, which struggled with ICTY cooperation from 2005 to 2007.

Closer integration with the EU had a transformative impact on issue transformation regarding ICTY cooperation in 2005 when, ahead of the feasibility study, Serbia increased its cooperation with the ICTY. Ultimately, the publication of a positive feasibility study was in response to wider pressure in the aftermath of the assassination of Prime Minister Đinđić. As Chapter 5 pointed out, after the publication of a positive feasibility study cooperation with the ICTY declined, which suggested that in the absence of overt EU pressure the EU's transformative capacity was limited. The EU then utilised this instrument of gatekeeping once more in May 2006 when it halted SAA negotiations with Montenegro and Serbia. The unintended impact of the two EU decisions that delayed the processes of integration with the EU in Croatia and Serbia was the effect that this had on the agendas of conflict in Croatia and Serbia. It raised the spectre of collective guilt in Croatia and Serbia. Collective guilt is an issue that the ICTY purposely set out to prohibit. Simeunović has argued against the EU's ICTY conditionality, which he describes as employing and propagating a notion of collective guilt in Serbia (2007). Chapter 4 of this book argues that the EU's decision to prevent and postpone Croatia's progress on integration with the EU because of the country's failure to transfer Gotovina to The Hague in March 2005 diminished the individualisation of guilt and transferred blame and punishment to the Croatian people. A further unintended impact of the EU's policy on Serbian ICTY cooperation lies in the perceived failure of EU policy towards Serbia in April 2007, when the perceived weakening of EU conditionality on ICTY undermined the previous policy that had pushed for full Serbian cooperation with the ICTY. This study concurs with Smith's (2003: 120) assertion that when conditionality is applied inconsistently, it can lose force.

The EU's impact on relationship transformation in Croatia and Serbia

In terms of relationship transformation, the EU has had an impact on the transformation of central relationships to the conflict in Croatia and Serbia mainly through compulsory, enabling and at times connective pathways. Chapter 4 dealt with the conflictual relationships in the Croatia case by examining the EU's impact on Croatia's relationship with the Bosnian Croats, and with refugees and displaced persons. Chapter 5 investigated conflict relationships in Serbia by investigating Serbia's relationship with Montenegrin political elites, with Bosnian Serbs and with refugees and displaced persons. The integration processes and membership perspective had an impact on relationship transformation in Croatia and Serbia, which was most evident in the relationship with Bosnia, in the case of Croatia on the returns process and, in Serbia, on the relationship with Montenegro.

Chapter 4 concluded that relationship transformation in Croatia was a matter of concern and an area of focus for the EU, as demonstrated by a continued emphasis in Commission annual progress reports. Given the constant focus by the EU, particularly on the issue of returns, the EU was actively attempting to increase its leverage on Croatia to make an impact on relationship transformation. However, in spite of this increased concentration on the returns issue, the gap between word and deed in Croatia remained. Subsequently, the EU's influence was realised through compulsory and enabling pathways, since the political elites in Croatia launched various initiatives, altered their rhetoric and actively encouraged the return of refugees. Ultimately, this provided crucial credibility for Croatia when it was negotiating with the EU. However, refugee return requires more than top-down processes. While the narratives regarding returns may have altered in Croatia, the re-assimilation of refugees was not painless or trouble-free. Although the more progressive governments of Račan and Sanader quickly aligned their policies with EU conditions, they were always reluctant to induce sustainable reforms as far as cornerstones of the national identity were concerned, such as the integration of the Serb minority. Therefore, while EU conditionality proved to be successful in transferring rules of minority protection and returns to Croatia, where an initial transition to democracy was taking place, the consolidation of minority protection and returns assimilation required a cultural adaptation of democratic norms and practices in the medium and long run. This involved substantial change of preferences which could not be achieved by strict conditionality. Therefore, the socialisation effect of integrating and becoming a member of the EU, which took place through the EU's connective pathway, provided a more effective means of relationship transformation.

Regarding the other conflict relationship in Croatia, its relationship with Bosnian Croats, the EU's influence was less salient but equally effective. The HDZ funded and assisted ethnic Croats in Bosnia. This is interesting, as the levels of support provided by the HDZ had to be balanced between its level of obligation towards the Bosnian Croats and the level it believed the EU would consider appropriate without being too intrusive or destabilising. The EU, through socialisation pressures rather than through a compulsory pathway of explicit conditionality, influenced the HDZ policies and attitudes towards Bosnia and Bosnian Croats. The issue for the EU on this conflict relationship was not whether it could limit the Croatian influence on Bosnian politics but whether it could harness Croatia to act as a pro-EU force or perceived stabilising force in Bosnia particularly over the Bosnian Croats. Croatia's response to Bosnia was particularly interesting as it represented a test for EU conditionality and socialisation. This was in contrast to the EU's influence in Serbia over Serbia's relationships with Republika Srpska and Bosnian Serbs.

Chapter 5 reached the conclusion that the wider political interests in Serbia diminished the EU's interest and focus on various relationships of conflict such as the relationship between Serbia and Bosnian Serbs. The chapter suggested that the EU's influence on conflict relationships in Serbia was undermined because of two interrelated factors: the EU's capacity to impact the conflict parties was limited, and the EU's interests lay elsewhere because of the divisions among EU agencies. Moreover, short-term interests were prioritised which conflicted with and contradicted ambitions for conflict resolution. The EU's influence on relationship transformation in Serbia was most notable when it came to the relationship between Serbia and Montenegro, mainly because of the appeal of membership for the Montenegrin political elites and the stability of the Serbian governments and presidency during the period under investigation. It is necessary to remember that Serbia and Montenegro continue to experience close relations, as would be expected, particularly in relation to technical aspects of integrating into the EU. At the same time, the dissolution of the Union between Montenegro and Serbia represented a transformation of conflict in a peaceful way.

It is clear that transformation of these conflictual relationships occurred in various ways and to varying degrees, which necessitates a comparative evaluation and an assessment of the EU's impact on conflict relationships.

The comparative evaluation of the research findings of this study has demon-strated that the EU was more effective at bringing about the transformation of structures than changing the relationship of conflict. This is explained because of the potency of the compulsory and enabling pathways of EU influence on the aspiring member states of Croatia and Serbia. In other words, the instruments for promoting change, conditionality and sociali-sation were most effectively targeted in the EU's integration/enlargement strategy at the conflict parties and conflict issues. This could be explained by two findings. First, the EU was primarily concerned with helping to foster a working and cooperative government in both cases in order to ensure the realisation of its stated ambitions. Second, the political management of the integration/enlargement process tended to target the conflict issue (ICTY cooperation), which represented an opportunity for a tangible and high-profile outcome.

Summarising the outcome of the EU integration/enlargement strat-egy on relationships of conflict is not straightforward, given the variety of relationships analysed in this study. First, regarding Croatia and Serbia's relationship with refugees and displaced persons, it is clear that the EU's use of conditionality and socialisation influenced the returns processes in both cases. However, the effect of this EU impact needs to be further critiqued as the debate about the returns process is far from clear. In the conflict transformation approach, as stated at the outset of this study, the outcome of the transformation process is open-ended, with winners and losers in various areas at various times. The results of the refugee process reflected the actual impact of the EU's attentiveness to the returns process where the EU linked advancement on integration or accession with the returns process. Aside from the explicit use of conditionality (a compulsory pathway), the EU, through an enabling pathway, impacted the political elites to encour-age a shift in their attitudes and policies towards a more conciliatory and hospitable environment for refugee returns. Furthermore, on this particular relationship the EU acted through a connective pathway by facilitating and actively encouraging cross-border cooperation on the returns process. The EU pressured diplomatically for a series of initiatives and agreements on the return of refugees between Croatia, Serbia and Bosnia.

Finally, having ascertained that the EU's influence was considerable, it is necessary to consider its actual impact on the conflict relationship. The outcome of the returns process has been contradictory. On the one hand, the returns process was portrayed by DG Enlargement as a partial success of the EU integration process because of the numbers returning, changes in legislation and elite-level cooperation facilitated by EU officials. On the other hand, the returns process was problematic for the conflict transformation process for two reasons: the EU was not the only actor involved in the returns process, which resulted in a lack of coordination between various agencies; and the limits of the EU's instruments of change, conditionality and socialisation quickly became apparent. On the second point, it is clear that, while the EU may have encouraged top-level responses to the returns process, this study found that discrimination against minority groups and returnees was entrenched in both Croatia and Serbia. Despite pressure from the EU, this situation still prevails in both cases. Therefore, it is possible to reach the evaluation that the various EU pathways at play on the relationships with returnees produced a mixed outcome that was at times contradictory and problematic.

Second, in terms of Croatia and Serbia's relationships with Bosnian Croats and Bosnian Serbs the EU's influence has been minimal. The findings of this study suggest that in terms of EU influence on how Croatia engaged with Bosnian Croats, the EU demanded little of Croatia so the compulsory pathway was not really utilised to exert influence. We can evaluate that the EU's influence may have been less evident but this may be explained because it was through the socialisation processes or rather through an enabling pathway that the EU's influence was being exerted. In Serbia's relationship with Bosnian Serbs, again the EU's political management of engagement in Serbia meant that after 2000 the focus was not on Serbia's attitude towards Bosnia or Bosnian Serbs; rather the EU was much more focused on Serbia's relationship with Montenegro and Kosovo. The EU's influence on this conflict relationship was therefore marginal, and because of this the EU was unable to prevent Serbia from influencing the Bosnian Serb communities. Therefore, it can be construed that the way in which the EU pursued contractual relations and the various focuses at different times largely resulted in other areas of conflict relationships being neglected. So, what did the EU focus on in Serbia?

Finally, regarding the case of Serbia, the third area of study in this book has been the relationship between Serbia and Montenegro and the impact that the EU has made on this relationship since 2000. As was demonstrated in Chapter 3, Montenegro was not a source of conflict during the 1990s. However, it was necessary to investigate the way in which the relationship evolved, partly after 1997 and more so after 2000, since it provided a micro-case study of how the processes of integration with and the prospect of joining the EU impacted a conflictual relationship that stemmed from the experience of the 1990s. The case study investigation demonstrated that after 2000 the elites in Montenegro and Serbia responded to the potential rewards available by closer integration with the EU and acted accordingly; the decision of Koštunica and Djukanović to sign up to the Belgrade Agreement signalled in part a willingness to respond to EU pressure. Furthermore, the critical assessment of the EU's role in the relationship between Serbia and Montenegro established that the EU played a key role in the development of the relationship during and at the end of the State Union, particularly through compulsory, enabling and connective pathways. The EU's impact on this conflict relationship revealed that the EU had the capacity to transform conflict relationships, something it had hitherto failed to do convincingly with regard to other conflict relationships, namely over Bosnia and over returns.

An evaluation of these findings led to the suggestion that the EU's strategy of offering closer integration and the prospect of membership means that, ultimately, the EU is more likely to have a transformative impact on the structures of conflict because of the technical and elite-level opportunities for conditionality and socialisation. This is not to diminish the impact of the EU on relationships of conflict. As highlighted above, the EU's impact on conflict relationships in the cases has been significant, particularly on Serbia's relationship with Montenegro, although arguably limited with wide-ranging unintended impacts on other conflict relationships. A number of reasons explain this anomaly regarding the EU's impact on conflict relationships. The EU's significant impact on the conflict relationship between Montenegro and Serbia was explained because of the instrumental role the EU agencies and figures played in creating, maintaining and dissolving the State Union. Therefore, the EU's enabling and compulsory pathways were more effective at transforming conflict under the conditions that were at the same time both part of and not part of the integration and enlargement strategy. To clarify, the EU's role in the State Union was predicated on bargaining the Stabilisation and Association process and membership perspective, yet at the same time the strategy did not employ strict political conditionality or socialisation instruments that would normally be associated with the EU's contractual relations. Hence, we can arrive at the conclusion that the EU was effective at transforming this conflict relationship but not through its expected, preferred or tried and tested methods of conditionality and socialisation.

The processes of integration and the prospect of joining the EU had a discernible and often contradictory impact on the structures and relationships of conflict in Croatia and Serbia, particularly after 2000. The post-2000 period was understood as the period when the EU was institutionalising and operationalising the various lessons it had learned from its engagement in the 1990s in the countries of the former Yugoslavia. This study has demonstrated that the main instruments used by the EU in Croatia and Serbia, political conditionality and socialisation, impacted the structures more than the relationships of conflict through compulsory and enabling pathways; the relationships of conflict were more likely to be impacted through a connective pathway by socialisation forces. The study demonstrates that the prospect of joining the EU, no matter how remote, was a motivating factor for the elites to transform the structures and relationships of conflict. Moreover, particularly in Croatia, the processes of integration not only prepared the country for EU membership but also helped to transform the structures of Croatia itself. Taken collectively and comparatively, the two case studies suggest that the EU has a potential to contribute to the transformation of conflict through the enlargement instrument, yet it is the enlargement instrument which often impairs the EU's actual results.

In Croatia, the EU has been increasingly well placed to transform conflict effectively, given the development and progress of relations between Croatia and the EU since Croatia has been a candidate state. In Serbia, the EU's impact on conflict transformation has been more limited, even though the EU has been both ubiquitous and salient. While the two cases have been exposed to the same instruments, rewards, sticks and personnel, the outcome in Croatia has been markedly different from that in Serbia. The EU's strategy pursued in the Stabilisation and Association process was not flexible enough to cope with the challenges and demands posed by Serbia's protracted integration into the EU. The EU's ad hoc and constant deployment of bargaining tactics suggests that the rewards, conditions and socialisation inbuilt in the Stabilisation and Association process were insufficient to transform conflict in Serbia and in fact created unintended and harmful results in Serbia. The faltering EU commitments to Serbia since 2005, compounded by inconsistent EU diplomatic initiatives, have soured relations between the EU and Serbia – creating rather than diminishing obstacles to Serbia's integration with the EU and conflict transformation.

A further conclusion highlighted in Chapter 5 was that the aims pursued in the Stabilisation and Association process were not necessarily complementary. The overarching aims of the Stabilisation and Association process were democratisation, stabilisation, member state building and conflict transformation. This study has shown that these aims are fundamentally at odds with one another. The inherent contradiction between these various aims was manifested by the EU's policy of attempting to prepare Croatia and Serbia for membership while at the same time pushing for full ICTY cooperation and completion of the returns process, which arguably did not have a positive impact on the structures and relationships of conflict. However, it is important to state that without the geo-strategic interest of the EU in Croatia and Serbia because of the membership perspective, the ultimate impact and interest of the EU in these cases would have been qualitatively less.

While the potential for an impact exists because Serbia and Croatia are engaged in a process of establishing contractual links with the EU which involves conditionality and social learning, there remains a gap between the slow process of social learning and the difficult, mistimed and inconsistent application of EU conditionality. In the case of structural transformation of conflict parties in Croatia and Serbia through a compulsory and enabling pathway, it could be expected that the EU would have a transformative influence on their interests, agendas, language and representation. Yet, as the case studies have shown, in Serbia – where a balance of power is absent and contested between pro- and anti-EU parties – the EU's impact has been diminished. Furthermore, even in Croatia, where cross-party support exists for the EU, the socialisation of the political elites is far from thorough, given the elitist nature of the EU integration/accession negotiations.

In the two cases, the EU's additional interests are not necessarily compatible with conflict transformation. Furthermore, wider political determinants influence the EU's conduct in contractual relations with the two cases. Therefore it is possible to conclude that while the EU has stated its ambition to promote stabilisation and democratisation these ambitions have not actually been realised. In fact, at times and under certain circumstances, the structures and relationships of conflict have been negatively impacted by the EU's political conditionality and socialisation process.

In both the conflict cases under investigation in the study, the political determinants which lay beyond the strict accession acquis shaped the nature of the impact that the EU could have on the structures and relationships of conflict. The EU's strategic and often clashing interests (short-, medium- and long-term) influenced its behaviour in pursuing relations with Croatia and Serbia and ultimately determined the impact that the EU could have. Associated with this is the EU's use of political conditionality, with a focus on certain established conditions – namely ICTY cooperation and refugee returns. This was significant in both cases as it politicised EU membership, resulting in EU membership being linked explicitly with the structures and relationships of conflict.

Implications for the study of conflict transformation and Europeanisation

This study enriches the two broad research areas that it covers: conflict transformation and Europeanisation, as well as providing a critical evaluation of the processes of transformation experienced in Croatia and Serbia. This section explores the implications that the study has for the combined study of conflict transformation and Europeanisation.

Chapter 1 outlined the conflict transformation approach, which indicated that conflict cannot be addressed sufficiently insofar as the conflict is deemed to be resolved (Richmond 2002; Tocci 2007; Miall 2001; Miall *et al.* 1999). This study has discovered that this description of the nature of conflict in post-war situations is accurately reflected in conflict transformation approaches. The processes of conflict transformation are ongoing in Croatia and Serbia. The conflict has not been resolved and outstanding issues continue to have implications for the post-war recovery in these two states. The conflict transformation approach was a valuable conceptual lens to understand the impact that the 'power of attraction' of EU membership is having on the legacies of conflict in Croatia and Serbia. Ultimately, this more holistic view of conflict accounts for the different outcomes of conflict in the case studies and also provides an insight into the transformative capacity of the EU. The case studies have shown that conflict transformation is an ongoing and complex process; this is reflected in the conflict transformation approach. Ultimately, according to Wallensteen (1991: 130), a transformed conflict 'is one where the parties, the issues and the expectations are changed so that there is no longer a fear of war arising from the relationship'. Surely this has been and is being realised in both Croatia and Serbia.

The wider significance of this study is that it clarifies the distinction between resolution and transformation theories and suggests that transformation theory is helpful when dealing with ethno-political conflicts. The study has found that conflict transformation is a useful approach for analysing, interpreting and understanding the changing dynamics of conflict by examining the transformation in terms of structures and relationships of conflict. This is more appropriate than conflict resolution for the chosen case studies, as resolution affirms that a conflict is resolvable. On the debate between resolution and transformation, Botes (2002: 22) contends that it is 'difficult to ascertain whether we are amidst a conceptual paradigm shift regarding these two terms'. In speaking to this wider theoretical debate the study finds that conflict transformation represents a challenge to the accepted paradigm that all conflicts are resolvable rather than able to be transformed into different representations of conflict that can be dealt with in ways other than violence. The study has shown that conflict transformation approaches remove the limitations of understanding a conflict as having a precise starting and finishing point, and help us to understand the dynamism of a conflict.

The study incorporated a study of the Europeanisation processes at play as well as considering their implications for the transformation of conflict in the two cases. This is a key implication for the study of Europeanisation and underscores the timeliness of this analysis of the transformative capacity of the EU on conflict. The analysis undertaken in the study enriched knowledge about the processes of integration with, and the attractiveness of the prospect of joining, the EU. In terms of the contribution made to Europeanisation, the study has shown that the enlargement approach has the capacity to make a significant impact on conflict transformation, particularly when socialisation and conditionality are employed consistently and when the membership perspective is a cohesive rather than divisive force among social and political elites. This research has also shown that Europeanisation is not simply a (pre-)accession mechanism. Rather, the impacts of EU engagement in Croatia and Serbia were increasingly evident when a framework for integration with the EU was established. This research has shown that the impact of Europeanisation on conflict transformation is intensified when the prospect of membership is close and tangible. Conflict transformation has been impacted most intensely during periods when the EU has published a positive feasibility study on opening Stabilisation and Association Agreement negotiations, opening Stabilisation and Association Agreement negotiations, providing a positive avis on membership application, and when opening accession negotiations. During these periods, EU conditionality and socialisation were heightened and much more salient, which must lead to the conclusion that the EU, in part, realised its ambitions to transform conflict in these cases.

This study established a theoretical framework for examining the EU's role in conflict situations by dovetailing the two approaches of conflict transformation and Europeanisation. The study has explained how the EU's transformative capacity on conflict transformation has been brought to bear, and in which circumstances it has been most and least effective. Significantly, the study discovered that in post-war societies such as Croatia and Serbia the instruments of Europeanisation and socialisation are insufficient to stabilise conflict. Rather, something else is needed to achieve conflict transformation. The EU has recognised this and has developed alternative ways of influencing the conflict transformation process in Croatia and Serbia.

The study of conflict transformation and Europeanisation requires the utilisation of a mixed methods approach including semi-structured elite interviewing alongside document analysis. This study has shown that semi-structured elite interviewing must be supported by document analysis for the purpose of triangulation, reliability and validity. The selection of interviewees was made on the basis of their experience and knowledge of the EU integration process, which potentially provided a biased and pro-EU opinion of the EU, its role in the conflict and the success of its approach. The study has discovered that such limitations are not unique to elite interviewing in societies recovering from conflict. However, the issues raised in the interviews were highly sensitive and called for rigorous triangulation.

Overall, the study has confirmed the value of using Europeanisation approaches to understand the conflict transformation process in Croatia and Serbia. Conflict transformation was used in the study to inform and provide an analytical framework to assess the EU's transformative capacity on conflict in the cases. Hence, it validates the claim to extend conflict transformation approaches to include analysis of the impacts of third parties such as the EU. In doing so, the study has facilitated an evaluation not only of the conflict parties but also of the impact of interveners. It is clear from the study that the processes of integration with and the prospect of joining the EU have impacted the structures and relationships of conflict for the most part through compulsory, enabling and connective pathways and at an elite level. Consequently, it is appropriate to use conflict transformation approaches to examine and analyse the EU's impact on conflict. Dovetailing the Europeanisation and conflict transformation approaches has shown how the processes of conditionality and social learning have affected the structures and relationships of conflict. Furthermore, the analytical framework used in the study revealed that often the conflict transformation is far from positive; it is not a win–win situation. The cases demonstrated that the EU's actions had both intended and unintended impacts, which in turn influenced the direction of transformation experienced. For this reason, the conflict transformation approach was particularly suited to the Europeanisation approach since it accommodated an understanding of mixed outcomes.

Areas for future research

While the above section studied the contribution made by the study to the theoretical discourses and empirical knowledge, it is useful to consider the implications of this contribution for the wider research area.

First, for future research, it would be useful to consider the application of this theoretical framework for analysing the EU's role in conflict transformation in other 'potential' and non-member states. The most logical step for the advancement of this research is to apply the same theoretical framework to post-war transition in other ex-Yugoslav states, namely the Former Yugoslav Republic of Macedonia and Bosnia-Hercegovina, as well as examining the situation in Kosovo. This would make an interesting study because, arguably, it would help provide more information and more evidence about the two hypotheses investigated in this study. Slovenia could be added to this study as an ex-Yugoslav state that has already achieved association and membership of the EU. Moreover, the conflict transformation and Europeanisation approach could be applied to other areas where conflict has existed and where the EU has been engaged, namely Cyprus and Turkey, Moldova and Georgia. It would be interesting and possible to adapt this framework to other cases where, although EU membership is not on offer, the EU engaged through offering alternative political and financial incentives, such as in European Neighbourhood Policy countries or African, Caribbean and Pacific countries, given the inbuilt focus on human rights promotion, democracy, rule of law and civil society in EU foreign policy (European Commission 2003).

Another area worthy of further investigation in future research is the reflexivity of the EU's enlargement approach, particularly in conflict situations. A focus on this in future research would provide policymaking conclusions on how the EU could institutionalise and operationalise lessons learned from experiences in conflict and apply them to engagement in conflict situations. This would involve an evaluation of the EU's reflexivity in conflict transformation in terms of who is learning what lessons from who and the role that other international agencies play in the transformation of conflict in Croatia and Serbia. Related to this, the conclusions of the study have raised a key question for further investigation: in what ways does the EU learn? This highlights a gap in the research completed thus far and raises two questions for further study: which learning agent is most effective at implementing lessons learned, and under which circumstances is lesson learning most effective? While it was possible to clarify the ways that DG Enlargement amended its policies, mechanisms and self-confidence in dealing with the conflicts in Croatia and Serbia it is much more challenging to understand how the various lessons learned feed back into decision-making. This is an area for further study and investigation.

Third, stemming from the previous point, the study has raised a question for further research about the role of other international agencies. The EU's transformative capacity in Croatia and Serbia was limited by additional or alternative sources of support or what have been referred to as 'black knights' by Hufbauer *et al.* (2004). These 'black knights' are other actors in the Balkans which provide a motivating influence, for example the USA or Russia. Appropriately and necessarily, the study examined the EU's role in order to test the suppositions of Europeanisation theories, which would indicate that given the wide-ranging scope of the EU on the political and economic transition in aspirant states it would have a substantial impact on the transition in Croatia and Serbia. Future research could engage more broadly to consider the implications of non-EU agencies on conflict transformation in Croatia and Serbia and focus on how this impacted the EU's transformative capacity.

In conclusion, this study has examined the role of integration with and the prospect of joining the EU on the transformation of conflict in Croatia and Serbia. The EU had enormous potential to influence the transformation of conflict, based on the speech acts and belief among EU policymakers and political elites, both in EU member states and the region. Much of this belief stemmed not from the EU's previous experience in conflicts such as Northern Ireland and Cyprus but from the EU's transformative capacity in Central and Eastern Europe. Beyond the attraction of the membership perspective the EU had the potential to influence cases by means of instruments of conditionality and socialisation through compulsory and enabling pathways which were ingrained in the Stabilisation and Association process. However, this study concludes that the EU's impact on conflict transformation has been weaker than may have been anticipated because of a variety of domestic circumstances in the case study countries combined with the contradictions, inflexibility and political management of the EU's integration enlargement processes.

NOTES

Introduction

1   The Annan Plan provided for the establishment of a United Cyprus Republic (UCR) constituted by a federal level and two constituent states (a Greek Cypriot and a Turkish Cypriot state). Competencies would be mainly focused at a state level; yet at a federal level competencies would focus on foreign relations, finance and monetary policies, immigration and citizenship. For further details see United Nations Secretary General (2004), *The Comprehensive Settlement of the Cyprus Problem*, at http://www.cyprus-un-plan.org

2   While, for much of the period under investigation, Serbia was in a union of various guises with Montenegro, Montenegro is not explicitly under investigation because it does not provide a comparative dimension to the types and nature of conflict under investigation. Therefore Montenegro will only be included in the discussion when appropriate.

3   Kosovo is the commonly used expression for the territory that has been under UN Security Council Resolution 1244 supervision since 1999, which declared independence from Serbia on 17 February 2008.

4   The 1974 Constitution consolidated the political power of the Republics in the Socialist Federal Republic of Yugoslavia away from the federal level.

5   See the following for further discussion: Uvalic (1997: 19–34); Schopflin (1997), 173; Dyker and Vejvoda (1997); Lendvai and Parcell (1991); Pavkovic (2000); Cohen (1995); Bookman (1994); Banac (1996); Ramet (1996); Silber and Little (1994); Woodward (1995); Gow (1997, 1994); Lewis (1993), 123; Weller (1992); Detervarent (1992).

Chapter 1

1   Following the 2004 enlargement, Kaliningrad became a Russia exclave, bordered by EU member states. For further reading see Aalto (2002).

2   Substantial critiques have emerged concerning the validity of Doyle (1983a); see Spiro (1994); Layne (1994); Kinsella (2005).

3   Featherstone and Radaelli (2003) provide a study of the 'EU-isation' of the southern periphery candidate states, including Malta and Cyprus.

4   Manners claims that 'The EU as a normative power has an ontological quality

to it – that the EU can be conceptualized as a changer of norms in the international system; a positivist quantity to it – that the EU acts to change norms in the international system; and a normative quality to it – that the EU should act to extend its norms into the international system' (2002: 252).

5   Alderson goes on to argue that at these deeper levels 'institutionalization not only alters incentives but also shapes the cognitive categories through which the world is perceived and strategies are crafted' (2001: 420). See also Finnemore and Sikkink (2001: 904–5).

6   Europeanisation can be defined as processes of (a) construction, (b) diffusion and (c) institutionalisation of formal and informal rules, procedures, policy paradigms, styles, 'ways of doing things' and shared beliefs; and as norms, which are first defined and consolidated in the making of EU decisions and then incorporated in the logic of domestic discourse, identities, political structures and public policies. See Radaelli (2000); Grabbe (2001b); Weiler (1991); Conant (2001); Majone (1996).

7   For further discussion about the effectiveness two-track conditionality-plus-dialogue approach see Checkel (2000).

8   To recap, in this book the process of integration with the EU involves both 'potential' candidate and candidate states, while the accession process refers to candidate states. Membership is the term used to describe becoming a member and/or joining the EU.

9   According to the EU, the 'Community *acquis* is the body of common rights and obligations which bind all the Member States together within the European Union' (Europa glossary).

10   In this book the roles of the various institutional actors are highlighted throughout. The book is not a comparative investigation of the institutional dynamics of the EU in conflict transformation.

11   For a discussion on the importance of studying conflict see Brown (1996).

12   The Croatian Democratic Union is translated as Hrvatska Demokratska Zajednica.

13   Crawford highlighted the democratic questionability of the Croatia and Serbian electoral system, stating that 'the representation of minority parties, opinions, cleavages, and ethnic groups was thus artificially diminished'. In the elections in Croatia and Serbia, the ethnic composition of the legislatures was maximised in the first-past-the-post voting system.

14   The Ustaše, founded in 1929, originally sought to secure an independent Croatia and Serbian state.

15   By 2001, the total Serb population in Croatia and Serbia had fallen to 4.5 per cent (from 12.2 per cent in 1991). See Bideleux and Jeffries (2007: 183).

16   Ethnic Kosovo Albanians in Kosovo boycotted Serbian elections.

17   European Council, 'Council Conclusions', Santa Maria de Feira, 19–20 June 2000, point 67 available online at http://www.consilium.europa.eu/ueDocs/cms_Data/docs/pressdata/en/ec/00200-r1.en0.htm.

18   Ibid., point 71.

19   'The declaration at the Zagreb Summit', 24 November 2000, available online at http://ec.europa.eu/enlargement/enlargement_process/accession_process/how_does_a_country_join_the_eu/sap/zagreb_summit_en.htm.

Chapter 2

1 Interview with official from Croatian Foreign Ministry in Ireland, 11 August 2006.
2 Lendvai (1991: 260) pointed out the paradox that 'though no one in Europe wishe[s] to see Yugoslavia collapse, no one knows how to control the destructive forces that are at work within it'.
3 While OBNOVA, later to become CARDS, was unconditional, recipients had to meet certain criteria. On the other hand, PHARE was a conditional programme.
4 For further discussion on British reluctance to intervene militarily in Yugoslavia see Hodge (2006: 2).
5 The Vance-Owen Plan is not discussed in detail in this book, as it relates specifically to the situation in Bosnia-Hercegovina. Nonetheless, it had implications for the regional situation, sanctions on Serbia and Montenegro, and Serbian–Croatian relationships.
6 Interview with official from Croatian diplomatic representation to Ireland, Dublin, 11 August 2006.
7 The implications of this decision are examined more fully in Chapter 5.
8 Interview with official from Croatian diplomatic representation to Ireland, Dublin, 11 August 2006.
9 Interview with official from European Commission, Brussels, 23 May 2006.
10 European Parliament, Document Number 93/081, 'Statement on Atrocities in Eastern Bosnia', 3 March 1993, Press Statement.

Chapter 3

1 General Affairs and External Relations Council, 19 July 1999.
2 General Affairs and External Relations Council, 14 February 2000.
3 General Affairs Council Conclusions, 22 May 2000.
4 General Affairs and External Relations Council Conclusions, 10 July 2000.
5 Council of the European Union, *Copenhagen European Council 21–23 June 1993*: Presidency Conclusions, revised version, Document SN 180/1/93 REV 1, Brussels, pt. 7Aiii.
6 Article 6(1) of the Treaty on European Union as amended by the Treaty of Amsterdam stated that 'The Union is founded on the principles of liberty, democracy, respect for human rights and fundamental freedoms, and the rule of law, principles which are common to the Member States'.
7 Interview with European Commission official, Brussels, 23 May 2006.
8 See Dayton Agreement, 1995, available online at http://www.ohr.int/dpa/default.asp?content_id=380, retrieved 29 November 2005.
9 UNSCR 1244, http://www.un.int/usa/sres1244.htm, see point 9, retrieved 28 November 2005. The aims of the Stability Pact are to: Bring about mature democratic processes, based on free and fair elections, grounded in the rule of law and full respect for human rights and fundamental freedoms, including the rights of persons belonging to national minorities, the right to free and independent media, legislative branches accountable to their constituents, independent judiciaries (and the) deepening and strengthening of civil society; Preserve the multinational and multiethnic diversity of all countries in the

region and protecting minorities; Ensure the safe and free return of all refugees and displaced persons. http://www.stabilitypact.org/about/default.asp, accessed 21 June 2007.

10   The European Council stated that the 'Stability Pact will give all Countries in the Balkans region a concrete perspective of stability and integration into Euro-Atlantic structures' (General Affairs and External Relations Council 26 April 1999).

11   Interview with official in Croatia Desk European Commission, 30 May 2006.

12   Interview with official in Croatia Desk European Commission, 30 May 2006.

13   Interview with official in Croatia Desk European Commission, 30 May 2006.

14   The Declaration of the Zagreb Summit, 24 November 2000, http://europa. eu.int/comm/enlargement/intro/sap/summit_zagreb.htm retrieved 29 November 2005.

15   Interview with official in Croatia Desk European Commission, 30 May 2006..

16   In 1999, the Europe Agreements were being negotiated with Cyprus, the Czech Republic, Estonia, Hungary, Poland and Slovenia with a view to opening Europe Agreement negotiations with Bulgaria, Latvia, Lithuania, Malta, Romania and Slovakia.

17   Council Regulation (EC) No 2666/2000 of 5 December 2000 on assistance for Albania, Bosnia and Herzegovina, Croatia, the Federal Republic of Yugoslavia and the Former Yugoslav Republic of Macedonia, repealing Regulation (EC) No 1628/96 and amending Regulations (EEC) No 3906/89 and (EEC) No 1360/90 and Decisions 97/256/EC and 1999/311/EC Official Journal L 306, 07/12/2000 P. 0001–0006.

18   Interview with official from European Commission Delegation in Croatia, 15 September 2006.

19   For a detailed discussion about the debates informing the Copenhagen decisions see Dahrendorf (2005), Mayhew (1998) and Vaduchova (2005: 161–78).

20   Copenhagen European Council 7–8 April 1978, Declaration on Democracy EC Bulletin no.3 (1978) at.6.

21   Lisbon European Council in 26/27 June 1992; 'Conclusions of the Presidency', Agence Europe, 28 June 1992.

22   General Affairs Council Conclusions, Luxembourg, April 2007 PRES/97/129.

23   Council Conclusions of 29 April 1997, Bulletin EU 4–1997, Pt. 2.2.1.

24   The EU monitors and assesses the transformation in aspirant states through annual Progress Reports, Stabilisation and Association reports and through its avis on their membership application. All of these are compiled by the Commission. The European Parliament also monitors the reform process in aspirant states in their annual Country Report. These various reports serve as a monitoring mechanism to scrutinise and appraise the reform processes in aspiring states. In the reports, the Commission examines the political, legal and economic transition in the aspirant states. In the case of a candidate state, such as Croatia, the Commission's annual Progress Report will also include an evaluation of the candidate's progress in the 35 chapters of the acquis. According to Barroso (2006), 'Candidate countries are sometimes surprised by the level of scrutiny during the negotiations. But this is only natural as you get closer to the EU and we get closer to you.' This means the Commission will continue to monitor and report on Croatia's progress towards meeting the requirements of membership.

This monitoring is part of the Commission's formal responsibilities under the EU's Treaties.

25 28 January 2005, Article 120

26 Commission of the European Communities, Communication from the Commission to the Council and the European Parliament: The Western Balkans and European Integration, 2003, p. 3. Available online at http://europa.eu.int/comm/external_relations/see/2003.pdf.

27 For further discussion of the effectiveness of the two-track conditionality-plus-dialogue approach see Checkel (2000).

28 Interview with official from Serbian European Integration Office, 30 September 2006.

29 Interview with Croatian academic, Zagreb, 15 September 2006.

30 Interview with Croatian academic, Zagreb, 15 September 2006.

31 Interview with Croatian desk office in European Commission, Brussels, 30 May 2006.

32 Interview with official from European Commission, 31 May 2006.

Chapter 4

1 Interviews with two officials from Croatian Ministry of Foreign Affairs and European Integration, Zagreb, 12 September 2006, and Croatian academic, Zagreb, 15 September 2006.

2 Interview with official from European Commission Delegation to Croatia, Zagreb, 12 September 2006.

3 During his electoral campaign Mesić was characterised as a 'jovial political maverick', suggesting that the contrast between Mesić's and Tudman's personalities had a significant bearing on Mesić's electoral success (*Financial Times* 18 February 2000).

4 Croatian Parliament, 'Resolution on the accession of the Republic of Croatia to the European Union', Zagreb, 18 December 2002.

5 Interview with official from European Commission delegation to Croatia, Zagreb, 12 September 2006.

6 General Antje Gotovina was Commander of the Split Military District of the Croatian Army (HV) from 9 October 1992 to March 1996 and overall operational commander of the southern portion of the Krajina region during the military offensive known as 'Operation Storm'. He was indicted by the ICTY in 2001. For further information on his indictment see Indictment of Gotovina *et al.*, 'Operation Storm' (IT-06-90), available online at http://www.icty.org/x/cases/gotovina/cis/en/cis_gotovina_al_en.pdf, accessed 14 June 2010.

7 Interview with official from European Commission delegation to Croatia, Zagreb, 15 September 2006.

8 Interview with official from European Commission delegation to Croatia, Zagreb, 12 September 2006.

9 Article 7 of the Statute of the International Criminal Tribunal for the Former Yugoslavia clarifies the position over individual criminal responsibility:

(1) A person who planned, instigated, ordered, committed or otherwise aided and abetted in the planning, preparation or execution of a crime referred to in articles 2 to 5 of the present Statute, shall be individually responsible for the crime;

(2) The official position of any accused person, whether as Head of State or Government or as a responsible Government official, shall not relieve such person of criminal responsibility nor mitigate punishment;

(3) The fact that any of the acts referred to in articles 2 to 5 of the present Statute was committed by a subordinate does not relieve his superior of criminal responsibility if he knew or had reason to know that the subordinate was about to commit such acts or had done so and the superior failed to take the necessary and reasonable measures to prevent such acts or to punish the perpetrators thereof;

(4) The fact that an accused person acted pursuant to an order of a Government or of a superior shall not relieve him of criminal responsibility, but may be considered in mitigation of punishment if the International Tribunal determines that justice so requires.

International Tribunal for the Prosecution of Persons Responsible for Serious Violations of International Humanitarian Law Committed in the Territory of the Former Yugoslavia since 1991 'Statute of the International Criminal Tribunal for the Former Yugoslavia', February 2006, available at http://www.un.org/icty/legaldoc-e/basic/statut/statute-feb06-e.pdf, accessed 28 June 2007.

10   Interview with DG Enlargement, Croatia Office, Brussels, 30 May 2006.
11   Interview with official from European Commission delegation to Croatia, Zagreb, 15 September 2006.
12   Interview with official from European Commission delegation to Croatia, Zagreb, 12 September 2006.
13   Interview with official from European Commission delegation to Croatia, Zagreb, 15 September 2006.
14   Interview with official from Croatian Ministry of Foreign Affairs and Ministry of European Integration (EU Institutions and Policies), Zagreb 12 September 2006.
15   Interview with Croatian Academic and policy advisor, Zagreb, 15 September 2006.

Chapter 5

1   The May 2008 results were as follows: Tadić's 'For a European Serbia' won 38.4 per cent of the vote, followed by Šešelj's 'Serbian Radical Party' who won 29.4 per cent of the vote and in third place was Koštunica's 'Democratic Party of Serbia- New Serbia' who won 11.62 per cent of the vote.

2   The European Council concluded that Tadić's election signalled that the Serbian electorate had made a choice in favour of a European future (European Council Conclusions 11 July 2004).

3   Interview with Serbian academic, 29 March 2008.

4   A confidential memo authored by the Finnish presidency encouraged high-level EU visits to Serbia in the run-up to the January 2007 elections to assure Serbians of their European future and downplay concerns over enlargement fatigue, as reported in *European Voice*: 'EU to launch Serbian charm offensive', 16 November 2006; for further evidence of the EU's 'charm offensive' see B92 News, 22 November 2006; B92 News, 'Sweden Pulls for Pro-European Government', 18 December 2006.

5   Serbian President Boris Tadić speaking after he called for elections on 10 November 2006 as reported by Transitions Online, 'Serbia's Elections: Patriots, Traitors, Reformers and Radicals', 21 December 2006.

6   Koštunica identified five key principles which the coalition government agreed to make their top priorities: 1) protect Serbia's sovereignty and territorial integrity; 2) European integration; 3) completion of cooperation with ICTY; 4) socio-economic issues; 5) the fight against organised crime and corruption. The full text of Koštunica's key note address on 15 May 2007 is available at http://www.srbija.sr.gov.yu/vlada/ (Accessed 31 May 2007).

7   Interview with representative of Independent Diplomat, 29 March 2008.

8   Ultimately, the fallout from Kosovan independence will need to be examined in future research.

9   The DG Enlargement Commissioner proposed that an agreement could be signed with Serbia with individual member states having a choice whether to ratify or not. Because the text of this agreement was substantively different from the Stabilisation and Association Agreement, the Dutch were able to agree to sign it.

10 Interview with official from European Commission delegation to Serbia, political section, 28 September 2006.

11 Interview with author from European Commission, politics, civil society and information section, 28 September 2006.

12 Interview with official from Serbia and Montenegro Mission to the EU, Brussels, 24 May 2006.

13 Interview with official from Serbian European Integration Office, 30 September 2006.

14 Gow continues: 'Without the peace constituted by the end of armed hostilities, there could be no scope for justice; but without a process to render justice once that version of peace had been established, there could be no guarantee that revenge would not motivate renewed hostilities in the future, and therefore that peace, in the deeper sense of removing the conditions for war and war crimes, had been created' (Gow 2003: 308).

15 Interview with an official Serbian and Montenegrin Mission to the EU official, Brussels, 24 May 2006.

16 SMMPI and Belgrade Centre for Human Rights, Public Attitudes towards ICTY, July 2003.

17 Interview with official from European Commission delegation to Croatia, Zagreb, 15 September 2006.

18 Koštunica added: 'This is something increasingly visible in the EU ... and perhaps those who believed at one time that things should be solved in a different manner, that is by suspending these negotiations, are now getting increasingly aware that a mistake has been made' (EU Observer 2006e).

19 Gowan pointed out that 'Serbian society is not monolithic. Many people disagree with the nationalism that prevails among the elites. However, the overall impression remains that Serbia's political classes find it a struggle to face up to the events of the 1990s. This prevents them from grasping current opportunities to promote political stability and EU integration' (Gowan 2007: 2).

20 This letter is available via Bosnian Institute, 'Maintaining ICTY co-operation as a condition for SAA talks with Serbia', http://www.bosnia.org.uk/news/news_body.cfm?newsid=2261 (Accessed 10 April 2007). The signatories of the letter were the Humanitarian Law Centre, Youth Initiative for Human Rights, Women in Black and Civic Initiative.

21 The Battle of Kosovo was fought on St Vitus Day 1939 and features heavily in the creation of Serbian nationalism. For further discussion see Judah (2002).

22 Republika Srpska was created in 1992 by General Karadžić and Serbian Democratic Party, and covers approximately 49 per cent of the territory of Bosnia-Hercegovina.

23 Interview with representative from Serbian Ministry of European Integration, Belgrade, 29 September 2006.

24 Constitutional Charter of the State Union of Serbia and Montenegro, Article 60.

25 Interview with official from European Commission, Brussels, 23 May 2006.

26 Interview with representative from Serbian Ministry of European Integration, Belgrade, 29 September 2006.

27 Interview with European Commission official, Brussels, 30 May 2006.

28 Interview with Croatian academic and policy advisor, Zagreb, 15 September 2006.

Chapter 6

1   The Royaumont Process was a programme stemming from the Stability Pact and the Dayton Agreement to promote Stability and Good Neighbourliness in the countries of the former Yugoslavia. It was initiated by the European Council and evolved in scope from implementing the Dayton Agreement to embedding civil society and democratisation in the region.

2   Interview with Serbia and Montenegro Mission to the EU official, Brussels, 24 May 2006.

3   Interview with European Commission official, Brussels, 31 May 2006.

4   Interview with official from Croatian Foreign Ministry in Ireland, 11 August 2006.

BIBLIOGRAPHY

Aalto, P. (2002) 'A European geopolitical subject in the making? EU, Russia and the Kaliningrad question', *Geopolitics*, 7(3), pp. 143–74.

Ágh, A. (1995) 'The paradoxes of transition: the external and internal overload of the transition process', in Cox, T., Furlong, A. (eds), *Hungary: The Politics of Transition*, London: Frank Cass, pp. 15–34.

—— (1999) 'Processes of democratisation in the East Central European and Balkan states: sovereignty-related conflicts in the context of Europeanisation', *Communist and Post-Communist Studies*, 32(3), pp. 263–79.

Albin, C. (2005) 'Explaining conflict transformation: Jerusalem', *Cambridge Review of International Affairs*, 18(3), pp. 339–55.

Alderson, K. (2001) 'Making sense of state socialisation', *Review of International Studies*, 27(1), pp. 415–33.

Anastasakis, O. (2002) 'EU democracy building in South-Eastern Europe: is there a contribution to the democratisation process?', in Phinnemore, D. and Siani-Davies, P. (eds), *South-Eastern Europe and European Union Enlargement – Conference Proceedings*, Cluj-Napoca, Romania: Cluj-Napoca University Press, pp. 201–27, available online at http://www.qub.ac.uk/ies/events/confenlarg/ana.pdf.

—— (2007) 'Power and interdependence: uncertainties of Greek–Turkish rapprochement', *Ethnic Conflict*, 28(4).

Anastasakis, O., Bechev, D. (2003) 'EU conditionality in South East Europe: bringing commitment to the process', *South East European Studies Programme*, Oxford: St Antony's College.

Axelrod, R. (1985) 'An evolutionary approach to norms', *American Political Science Review*, 80(1), pp. 1095–111.

Azar, E. (1990) *The Management of Protracted Social Conflict: Theory and Cases*, Aldershot: Elgar.

Bacarani, E. and Dellara, C. (2004) 'European Union democracy and rule of law promotion in South Eastern Europe', *European Analysis*, available online at http://www.europeananalysis.com/articles/0501-rps2.pdf (accessed 29 March 2007).

Balalvoska, A. (2004) 'Between "the Balkans" and "Europe": a study of the contemporary transformation of Macedonian identity', *Journal of Contemporary European Studies*, 12(2), pp. 193–215.

Banac, I. (1996) 'Introduction', in Ramet, S. P., *Balkan Babel: The Disintegration of Yugoslavia from the Death of Tito to Ethnic War*, 2nd edn, Boulder, CO: Westview Press, pp. 1–12.

Barnett, M. and Duvall, R. (2005) *Power in Global Governance*, Cambridge: Cambridge University Press.

Batt, J. (2003) 'The enlarged EU's external borders – the regional dimension', in Batt, J., Lynch, D., Missiroli, A. *et al.* (eds), *Partners and Neighbours: A CFSP for a Wider Europe, Chaillot Papers*, 64, Paris: Institute for Security Studies. Available online at http://www.iss.europa.eu/uploads/media/cp064e.pdf.

—— (2004) 'Serbia and Croatia: after the elections', *ISSEU Newsletter*, 10, April.

—— (2005) *The Question of Serbia, Chaillot Papers*, 81, Paris: Institute for Security Studies.

—— (2006) 'Making a success of Montenegrin independence – lessons from Slovakia', *EIC Bilten* (Podgorica), 9, and *DANAS* (Belgrade), weekend supplement 25–26 June 2006, available online at http://www.iss-eu.org/new/analysis/analy148.html.

Baun, M. J. (1995) 'The Maastricht Treaty as high politics: Germany, France, and European integration', *Political Science Quarterly*, 110(4), pp. 605–24.

Bechev, D. (2006) 'Carrots, sticks and norms: the EU and regional cooperation in Southeast Europe', *Journal of Southern Europe and the Balkans*, 8(1), April, pp. 27–43.

Belloni, R. (2007) 'The trouble with humanitarianism', *Review of International Studies*, 33(3), pp. 452–74.

Bendiek, A. (2004) 'Europe's conflict resolution: the Stability Pact for South Eastern Europe', Paper presented at ECPR conference, 2004.

Bennett, A. and Lepgold, J. (1993) 'Reinventing collective security after the Cold War and Gulf Conflict', *Political Science Quarterly*, 108(2), pp. 213–37.

Bercovitch, J. (1996) *Resolving International Conflicts: The Theory and Practice of Mediation*, Boulder, CO: Lynne Rienner.

Bercovitch, J. and Rubin, J. Z. (1992) *Mediation in International Relations: Multiple Approaches to Conflict Management*, New York: St Martin's Press, in association with the Society for the Psychological Study of Social Issues.

Bicchi, F. (2006) '"Our size fits all": normative power Europe and the Mediterranean', *Journal of European Public Policy*, 13(2), pp. 286–303.

Bideleux, R. and Jeffries, I. (2007) *The Balkans: A Post-Communist History*, London: Routledge.

Bieber, F. (2003) *Montenegro in Transition: Problems of Identity and Statehood*, Baden Baden: Nomos.

Bieber, F. and Wieland, C. (2005) *Facing the Past, Facing the Future: Confronting Ethnicity and Conflict in Bosnia and Former Yugoslavia*, Ravenna: Longo.

Bildt, C. (2005) 'Europe's third chance to get it right in the Balkans may be its last', *Europe's World*. Available online at http://www.europesworld.org/NewEnglish/Home_old/Article/tabid/191/ArticleType/ArticleView/ArticleID/20724/EuropesthirdchancetogetitrightintheBalkansmaybeitslast.aspx.

Bloomfield, D., Barnes, T., Huyse, L. and International Institute for Democracy and Electoral Assistance (2003) *Reconciliation after Violent Conflict: A Handbook*, Stockholm: International IDEA.

Bookman, M. Z. (1994) 'War and peace: the divergent break-up of Yugoslavia and

Czechoslovakia', *Journal of Peace Research*, 31(2), pp. 175–87.

Booth, K. (1990) 'Steps towards stable peace in Europe: a theory and practice of coexistence', *International Affairs*, 66(1), pp. 17–45.

Borzel, T. A. and Risse, T. (2000) 'When Europe hits home: Europeanization and domestic change', *European Integration online Papers (EIoP)*, 4(15), available online at http://http://eiop.or.at/eiop/pdf/2000-015.pdf.

Botes, J. (2003) 'Conflict transformation: a debate over semantics or a crucial shift in the theory and practice of peace and conflict studies', *International Journal of Peace Studies*, 8(2), pp. 1–27.

Bretherton., C. and Vogler, J. (2006) *The EU as a Global Actor*, London: Routledge.

Brewin, C. (2000) *The European Union and Cyprus*, Huntingdon: Eothen.

Brown, S. (1996) *New Forces, Old Forces and the Future of World Politics: Post Cold War Edition*, 2nd edn, New York: Harper Collins College Publishers.

Brusis, M. (2003) 'Instrumentalised conditionality: regionalisation in the Czech Republic and Slovakia', Paper presented at Workshop on the Europeanisation of Eastern Europe: Evaluating the Conditionality Model, The Robert Schuman Centre for Advanced Studies at the European University Institute, 4–5 July 2003.

—— (2005) 'The instrumental use of EU conditionality', *East European Politics and Societies*, 19(2), pp. 291–316.

Bryman, A. (1993) *Quantity and Quality in Social Research*, 3rd edn, London: Routledge.

—— (2004) *Social Research Methods*, 2nd edn, Oxford/New York: Oxford University Press.

Burton, J. (1996) *Conflict Resolution: Language and its Processes*, London: Scarecrow Press.

Buzan, B. (1991) 'New patterns of global security in the twenty-first century', *International Affairs*, 67(3), pp. 431–51.

Cameron, F. (2004) *The Future of Europe: Integration and Enlargement*, London: Routledge.

—— (2006) 'The European Union's role in the Balkans', in Blidtz, B. K., *War and Change in the Balkans: Nationalism, Conflict and Cooperation*, Cambridge: Cambridge University Press, pp. 99–109.

Carlsnaes, W., Sjursen, H. and White, B. (2004) *Contemporary European Foreign Policy*, London: Sage.

Centre for Democracy and Human Rights (CEDEM) (2002) *Public Opinion in Montenegro 2002*, April.

—— (2006) *Newsletter*, 17, May–June.

Centre for European Policy Studies (CEPS) (2002) 'Negotiating a viable State Union of Serbia and Montenegro', *Europa South-East Monitor*, 36, July.

Chandler, D. (2003) 'The European Union and governance in the Balkans: an unequal partnership', *European Balkan Observer*, Belgrade Centre for European Integration and the Vienna Institute for International Economic Studies, 1(2), pp. 5–9.

Chapman, J. (1994) 'Destruction of a common heritage: the archaeology of war in Croatia, Bosnia, and Hercegovina', *Antiquity*, 68, pp. 120–26.

Checkel, J. (2000) 'Compliance and conditionality', Paper prepared for delivery at the 2000 Annual Meeting of the American Political Science Association, Washington DC, August.

Checkel, J. (2001) 'Why comply? Social learning and European identity change', *International Organization*, 55(3) (Summer), pp. 553–88.

—— (2003) 'International institutions and socialisation in Europe: introduction and framework', *Arena*, Oslo, available online from www.arena.uio.no/Checkel.htm.

Choi, J. W. (1999) 'European Union's foreign and security policy integration: half full or half empty?', *Korean Journal of Defense Analysis*, 11(2), pp. 191–213.

Christou, G. (2002) 'The European Union and Cyprus: the power of attraction as a solution to the Cyprus issue', *Journal on Ethnopolitics and Minority Issues in Europe*, 2, pp. 1–24.

Cohen, L. J. (1995) *Broken Bonds: Yugoslavia's Disintegration and Balkan Politics in Transition*, 2nd edn, Boulder, CO: Westview Press.

—— (1997) 'Embattled democracy: postcommunist Croatia in transition', in Dawisha, K. and Parrott, B. (1997) *Politics, Power and the Struggle for Democracy in South-East Europe*, Cambridge: Cambridge University Press, pp. 69–121.

Conant, L. (2001) 'Europeanization and the courts: variable patterns of adaptation among national judiciaries', in Green Cowles, M., Caporaso, J. and Risse, T. (eds), *Transforming Europe. Europeanization and Domestic Change*, Ithaca, NY: Cornell University Press, pp. 97–115.

Coppieters, B., Emerson, M., Huysseune, M. *et al.* (2004) *Europeanisation and Conflict Resolution: Case Studies from the European Periphery*, Ghent: Academia Press.

Cornish, P. (1996) 'European security: the end of architecture and the new NATO', *International Affairs*, 72(4), pp. 751–69.

Cox, M., Booth, K. and Dunne, T. (1999) *The Interregnum: Controversies in World Politics 1989–1999*, Cambridge, New York: Cambridge University Press.

Crawford, B. (1998) 'Explaining cultural conflict in ex-Yugoslavia: institutional weakness, economic crisis and identity politics', in Crawford, B. and Lipschutz, R. D. (eds) *The Myth of 'Ethnic Conflict': Politics, Economics and Cultural Violence*, Berkeley: University of California, pp. 81–112.

Crawford, B. and Lipschutz, R. D. (eds) (1998) *The Myth of 'Ethnic Conflict': Politics, Economics and Cultural Violence*, Berkeley: University of California.

Creswell, J. W. (2003) *Research Design: Qualitative, Quantitative, and Mixed Method Approaches*, 2nd edn, Thousand Oaks, CA: Sage Publications.

Csergo, Z. and Goldgeier, J. M. (2001) 'Virtual nationalism', *Foreign Policy*, September, available online at http://www.globalpolicy.org/nations/sovereign/sover/flo12.htm (retrieved 30 August 2007).

Curle, A. (1971) *Making Peace*, London: Tavistock Publications.

Cviić, C. (1995) *Remaking the Balkans*, London: Pinter, Royal Institute of International Affairs.

Dahl, R. A. (1971) *Polyarchy: Participation and Opposition*, New Haven, CT: Yale University Press.

Dahrendorf, R. (2005) *Reflections on a Revolution in Europe*, Piscataway, NJ: Transaction Publishers.

d'Alançon, F. (1994) 'The EC looks to a new Middle East', *Journal of Palestine Studies*, 23(2), pp. 41–51.

Dannreuther, R. (2004) *European Union Foreign and Security Policy: Towards a Neighbourhood Strategy*, London, New York: Routledge.

Darmanovic, S. (2003) 'Montenegro: dilemmas of a small republic', *Journal of Democracy*, 14(1), pp. 145–53.

Davidson, I. and Gordon, P. H. (1998) 'Assessing European foreign policy', *International Security*, 23(2), pp. 183–88.

Dawisha, K. and Parrott, B. (1997) *Politics, Power and the Struggle for Democracy in South-East Europe*, Cambridge: Cambridge University Press.

Deighton, A. (2002) 'The European security and defence policy', *Journal of Common Market Studies*, 40(4), pp. 719–42.

Delanty, G. (1997) *Social Science: Beyond Constructivism and Realism*, Minneapolis: University of Minnesota Press.

Demetropoulou, L. (2002) 'The Europeanisation of the Balkans: EU membership aspiration and domestic transformation in SEE', in Phinnemore, D. and Siani-Davies, P. (eds), *South-Eastern Europe, the Stability Pact and EU Enlargement*, CLUJ, Romania: European Studies Foundation Publishing House, pp. 32–48.

Den Boer, M. and Monar, J. (2002) 'Keynote article: 11 September and the challenge of global terrorism to the EU as a security actor', *Journal of Common Market Studies*, 40(1), supplement, pp. 11–29.

Detervarent, P. D. (1992) 'The Treaty of Maastricht and its significance for third countries', *Osterreichische Zeitschrift Fur Politikwissenschaft*, 21(3), pp. 247–60.

Detrez, R. (2001) 'Colonialism in the Balkans: historic realities and contemporary perceptions', University of Ghent; available online at http://www.kakanien.ac.at/beitr/theorie/RDetrez1.pdf.

Deutsch, K. (1978) *The Analysis of International Relations*, 2nd edn, Englewood Cliffs, NJ: Prentice-Hall.

Diamandouros, N. P. and Larrabee, S. (2000) 'Democratisation in South-Eastern Europe: theoretical considerations and evolving trends', in Pridham G. and Gallagher, T. (eds), *Experimenting with Democracy: Regime Change in the Balkans*, London: Routledge, pp. 24–64.

Diamond, A. G. and Cobb, M. D. (1999) 'The candidate as catastrophe: latitude theory and the problems of political persuasion', in Mutz, D. C., Sniderman, P. M. and Brody, R. A., *Political Persuasion and Attitude Change*, Ann Arbor: University of Michigan Press.

Diez, T. (2002) *The European Union and the Cyprus Conflict: Modern Conflict, Postmodern Union*, Manchester: Manchester University Press.

Diez, T., Stetter, S. and Albert, M. (2004) 'The European Union and the transformation of border conflicts: theorising the impact of integration and association', *Working Papers in EU Border Conflicts Studies* 1, available online at http://www.polsis.bham.ac.uk/documents/research/euborderconf/wp01-eu-transformation-of-border-conflicts.pdf.

Dimitrova, A. (2002) 'Governance by enlargement? The case of the administrative capacity requirement in diversity', *Journal of European Public Policy*, 8, pp. 1013–31.

—— (2002) 'Governance by enlargement? The case of the administrative capacity requirement in the EU's Eastern enlargement', *West European Politics*, 25(4), October, pp. 171–90.

Dorman, A. M. and Treacher, A. (1995) *European Security: An Introduction to Security Issues in Post-Cold War Europe*, Aldershot, England; Brookfield, VT: Dartmouth.

Dosser, D., Gowland, D. and Hartley, K. (1982) *The Collaboration of Nation: A Study of European Economic Policy*, New York: St Martin's Press.

Doyle, M. W. (1983a) 'Kant, liberal legacies, and foreign affairs', *Philosophy and Public Affairs*, 12(3), Summer, pp. 205–35.

—— (1983b) 'Kant, liberal legacies, and foreign affairs, Part 2', *Philosophy and Public Affairs*, 12(4), Autumn, pp. 323–53.

Doyle, M. W. (2005) 'Montenegro's independence drive', *Europe Report*, 169, 7 December.

Duke, S. (2004) 'The European security strategy in a comparative framework: does it make for secure alliances in a better world?', *European Foreign Affairs Review*, 9, pp. 459–81.

Duric, D. (2004) 'Montenegro's prospects for European integration: on a twin track', *South-East Europe Review*, 4, pp. 79–106.

Dyker, D. A. and Vejvoda, I. (1997) *Yugoslavia and After: A Study in Fragmentation, Despair and Rebirth*, New York: Addison-Wesley Longman.

Eckart, A. (1991) 'German foreign policy and unification', *International Affairs*, 67(3), pp. 453–71.

Edwards, G. (1997) 'To act or not to act?', in Regelsberger, E., de Schoutheete, P. and Wessels, W. (eds), *Foreign Policy of the EU: From EPC to CFSP and Beyond*, Boulder, CO: Lynne Rienner, pp. 173–95.

Ehrhart, H. G. (2003) 'A good idea, but still a stony road ahead: the EU and the Stability Pact for South Eastern Europe,' in Schnabel, A. and Carment, D. (eds), *Conflict Prevention: Path to Peace or Grand Illusion?*, Tokyo, New York: United Nations University Press, pp. 112–31.

Ehrhart, H. G. and Schnabel, A. (eds) (1999) *The Southeast European Challenge. Ethnic Conflict and the International Response*, Baden-Baden: Nomos.

Eilstrup-Sangiovanni, M. and Verdier, D. (2005) 'European integration as a solution to war', *European Journal of International Relations*, 11(1), pp. 99–136.

Elbasani, A. (2008) 'The Stabilisation and Association process in the Balkans: overloaded agenda and weak incentives?', EUI Working Papers, 3.

Eralp, U. D. and Beriker, N. (2005) 'Assessing conflict resolution potential of the EU: the Cyprus conflict', Paper presented at the annual meeting of the International Studies Association, Hilton Hawaiian Village, Honolulu, Hawaii.

Emerson, M. and Noutcheva, G. (2005) 'The reluctant debutante: the EU as a promoter of democracy in its neighbourhood', *CEPS Working Document*, 223/July 2005, ESI, EU Balkan Salzburg meeting March 2006, available online at http://www.esiweb.org/index.php?lang=enandid=166.

Evenson, K., 'Becoming democratic: now for the real work', *Transitions Online*, 13, July 2006 , available online at http://www.freedomhouse.org/template.cfm?page=72andrelease=397.

Everts, S. (2005) 'An asset but not a model: Turkey, the EU and the wider Middle East', *Centre for European Reform*, available online at www.cer.org.uk/pdf/essay_turk_everts.pdf (accessed 30 June 2007).

Fatić, A. (2000) *Reconciliation via the War Crimes Tribunal?* London: Ashgate.

Featherstone, K. and Radaelli, C. (eds) (2003) *The Politics of Europeanisation*, Oxford: Oxford University Press.

Field, H. (2002) 'Awkward states: EU enlargement and Slovakia, Croatia and Serbia', in Ross, C. (ed.), *Perspectives on the Enlargement of the European Union,* Leiden: Brill, pp. 215–38.

Finnemore, M. and Sikkink, K. (2001) 'Taking stock: the constructivist research program in international relations and comparative politics', *Annual Review of Political Science*, 4, pp. 391–416.

Fisher, R. J. (1997) *Interactive Conflict Resolution*, Syracuse, NY: Syracuse University Press.

—— (2005) *Contributions of Interactive Conflict Resolution to Peacemaking*, Lanham, MD: Lexington Books.

Fisher, S. (2000) 'Croatia's EU Odyssey', *Central Eastern Review*, 2(19), available online at http://www.ce-review.org/00/19/fisher19.html (accessed 13 August 2007).

Flick, U. (2002) *An Introduction to Qualitative Research*, 2nd edn, London, Thousand Oaks, CA: SAGE Publications.

Franceschet, A. (2002) *Kant and Liberal Internationalism: Sovereignty, Justice and Global Reform*, New York, Basingstoke: Palgrave Macmillan.

Freed, A. O. (1998) 'Interviewing through an interpreter', *Social Work*, 33, pp. 315–19.

Freedman, L. (1993) 'The politics of military intervention within Europe', in Gnesetto, N. (ed.), *War and Peace: European Conflict Prevention,* Institute for Security Studies, October, pp. 29–39.

—— (ed.) (1994) *Military Intervention in European Conflicts*, London: Blackwell Publishers.

Friis, K. (2007) 'The referendum in Montenegro: the EU's postmodern diplomacy?', *European Foreign Affairs Review*, 12, pp. 67–88.

Friis, L. (1998) 'Approaching the "third half" of EU grand bargaining – the post-negotiation phase of the "Europe Agreement game"', *Journal of European Public Policy*, 5(2), pp. 322–39.

Friis, L. and Murphy, A. (2000a) 'Turbo-charged negotiations: the EU and the Stability Pact for South Eastern Europe', *Journal of European Public Policy*, 7(5), Special Issue, pp. 767–86.

—— (2000b) 'Negotiating in a time of crisis: the EU's response to the military conflict in Kosovo', *EU Working papers*, European University Institute, RSC No. 20.

Gadamer, H. G. (1979) *Truth and Method*, London: Sheed and Ward.

Gagnon, V. P. (2004) *The Myth of Ethnic War: Serbia and Croatia in the 1990s*, Ithaca, NY: Cornell University Press.

Gallagher, T. (2003a) *The Balkans after the Cold War: From Tyranny to Tragedy*, London: Routledge.

—— (2003b) 'The Balkans since 1989', in White, S., Batt, J. and Lewis, P. G. (eds), *Developments in Central and Eastern European Politics* 3, Basingstoke, New York: Palgrave Macmillan, pp. 28–42.

—— (2005) *The Balkans in the New Millennium: In the Shadow of War and Peace* Oxford: Routledge.

Gallagher, T. and Pridham, G. (2000) (eds), *Experimenting with Democracy: Regime Change in the Balkans*, London: Routledge.

Galtung, J. (1995) 'Conflict resolution as conflict transformation: the First Law of Thermodynamics Revisited', in Rupesinghe, K. (ed.), *Conflict Transformation*, London: Macmillan, pp. 48–61.

—— (1996) 'Visions of peace for the 21st century', in *Peace by Peaceful Means*, London: Sage Publications.

Giamouridis, A. (2007) 'Only through enlargement: the New European Myth?', *European Foreign Affairs Review*, 12, pp. 183–202.

Giddens, A. (1979) *Central Problems in Social Theory: Action, Structure and Contradiction in Social Analysis*, London: Macmillan.

Gilbert, G. N. (1993) *Researching Social Life*, London, Newbury Park, CA: Sage.

Ginsberg, R. H. (2001) *The European Union in International Politics: Baptism by Fire*, New York: Rowman & Littlefield.

Glarbo, K. (1999) 'Wide-awake diplomacy: reconstructing the common foreign and security policy of the European Union', *Journal of European Public Policy*, 6(4), pp. 634–51.

Glenny, M. (1999) *Balkans 1804–1999: Nationalism, War and the Great Powers*, London: Granta Publishers.

Gnesotto, N. (1992) 'European Union after Minsk and Maastricht', *International Affairs*, 68(2), pp. 223–31.

—— (1993) 'Introduction', in Gnesotto, N. (ed.), *War and Peace: European Conflict Prevention*, Institute for Security Studies, October, pp. 2–7.

—— (1994) 'Lessons of Yugoslavia', *Chaillot Papers*, 14(1), pp. 1–34.

Goertz, G. (2003) *International Norms and Decision Making: A Punctuated Equilibrium Model*, Lanham, MD: Rowman and Littlefield.

Gordon, P. H. (1997) 'Europe's uncommon foreign policy', *International Security*, 22(3), pp. 74–100.

Gordy, E. D. (1999) *The Culture of Power in Serbia: Nationalism and the Destruction of Alternatives*, University Park, PA: Pennsylvania State University Press.

—— (2005) 'What does it mean to break with the past?', in Beiber, F. and Wieland, C. (eds), *Facing the Past, Facing the Future: Confronting Ethnicity and Conflict in Bosnia and Former Yugoslavia*, Ravenna, Long, pp. 85–101.

Gow, I. (2003) *The Serbian Project and its Adversaries: A Strategy of War Crimes*, London: Hurst & Co.

Gow, J. (1994) 'New bunnies: the international community and the Yugoslav war of dissolution, the politics of military intervention in a time of change', in Freedman, L. (ed.), *Military Intervention in European Conflicts (Political Quarterly Special Issue)*, Oxford: Blackwell Publishers, pp. 14–33.

—— (1997) *Triumph of the Lack of Will: International Diplomacy and the Yugoslav War*, London: Hurst & Co.

Gowan, D. (2007) 'Serbia's European choice', Centre for European Reform, June.

Grabar-Kitarović, K. (2007) 'The Stabilisation and Association process: the EU's soft power at its best', *European Foreign Affairs Review*, 12, pp. 121–25.

Grabbe, H. (1999) 'A partnership for accession? The implications of EU conditionality for the Central and East European applicants', EUI Working Paper 99/12, San Domenico di Fiesole (FI): European University Institute.

—— (2001a) 'Profiting from EU enlargement', *Centre for European Reform*, London.

—— (2001b) 'How does Europeanization affect CEE governance? Conditionality, diffusion and diversity', *Journal of European Public Policy*, 8(6), pp. 1013–31.

—— (2002) 'European Union conditionality and the Acquis Communautaire', *International Political Science Review*, 23(3), pp. 249–68.

—— (2006) *The EU's Transformative Power: Europeanisation through Conditionality in Central and Eastern Europe*, London: Macmillan.

Grabbe, H. and Hughes, K. (1998) *Enlarging the EU Eastwards*, London: Pinter.

Greenwood, C. (1993) 'The International Tribunal for Former Yugoslavia', *International Affairs*, 69(4), pp. 641–55.

Greiçevci, L., Papadimitriou, D. and Petrov, P. (2007) 'To build a state: Europeanization, EU actorness and state-building in Kosovo', *European Foreign Affairs Review*, 12, pp. 219–38.

Haas, E. B. (1990) *When Knowledge is Power*, Berkeley, Los Angeles: University of California Press.

Hassner, P. (2007) 'La Serbie et les Balkans occidentaux après les elections serbs du 21 janiver et le rapport du groupe de contact de l'ONU sur le Kosovo', available online at http://www.robert-schuman.org/supplement/entretien15.htm (accessed 2 March 2007).

Helmer, R. and Anand Samy, J. (2006) 'Croatia at the crossroads', *European Journal*, November 2006, pp. 5–7.

Héritier, A., Knill, C. and Mingers, S. (1996) *Ringing the Changes in Europe: Regulatory Competition and the Redefinition of the State:Britain, France, Germany*, Berlin: De Gruyter.

Higashino, A. (2004) 'For the sake of "peace and security"? The role of security in the European Union enlargement eastwards', *Cooperation and Conflict*, 39(4), pp. 347–68.

Hill, C. (1993) 'The capability–expectations gap, or conceptualizing Europe's international role', *Journal of Common Market Studies*, 31(3), pp. 305–28.

—— (1998) 'Closing the capabilities–expectations gap?', in Peterson, J. and Sjursen, H., *A Common Foreign Policy for Europe: Competing Visions of the CFSP*, London, Routledge, pp. 18–38.

—— (2004) 'Renationalizing or regrouping? EU foreign policy since 11 September 2001', *Journal of Common Market Studies*, 42(1), pp. 143–63.

Hill, C. and Wallace, W. (1996) 'Introduction: actors and actions', in Hill, C. (ed.), *The Actors in Europe's Foreign Policy*, London: Routledge, pp. 1–16.

Hill, R. J. and Zielonka, J. (1990) *Restructuring Eastern Europe: Towards a New European Order*, Aldershot: Elgar.

Hillion. C. (2003) 'The Copenhagen criteria and their progeny', in Hillion, C. (ed.), *EU Enlargement. A Legal Approach*, Oxford: Hart Publishing.

Hodge, C. (2006) *Britain in the Balkans*, London: Routledge.

Hoffmann, S. (1996) 'Yugoslavia: implications for Europe and for European institutions', in Ullman, R. (ed.), *The World and Yugoslavia's Wars*, New York: The Council on Foreign Relations, pp. 97–121.

—— (2000) 'Towards a Common European Foreign and Security Policy?', *Journal of Common Market Studies*, 38(2), pp. 189–99.

Holbrooke, R. (1998) *To End a War*, New York: Random House.

Holland, M. (1988) *The European Community and South Africa: European Political Co-operation under Strain*, London, New York: Pinter.

—— (2004) *Common Foreign and Security Policy: The First Ten Years*, 2nd edn, London: Continuum.

Horowitz, D. (2000) *Ethnic Groups in Conflict*, California/London: University of California Press.

Hughes, J. and Sasse, G. (2003) 'Monitoring the monitors: EU enlargement conditionality and minority protection in the CEECs', *Journal on Ethnopolitics and Minority Issues in Europe*, 1.

Hurd, D. (1994) 'Developing the common foreign and security policy', *International Affairs*, 70(3), pp. 421–28.

İçener, E. and Phinnemore, D. (2006) 'Enlargement and the EU's absorption capacity: "oft-forgotten" condition or additional obstacle to membership?', *Insight Turkey*, Autumn, available online at http://www.insightturkey.com.

International Crisis Group (2002) 'A half-hearted welcome: refugee return to Croatia', *Balkans Report*, 138, 13 December, pp. 1–26.

—— (2002) 'Still buying time: Montenegro, Serbia and the European Union', *Europe Report*, 129, 7 May.

—— (2003) 'Serbian reform stalls again', *Europe Report*, 145, 17 July.

—— (2004) 'Serbia's U-turn', *Europe Report*, 154, 26 March.

—— (2005a) 'EU Visas and the Western Balkans', *Europe Report*, 168, 29 November.

—— (2005b) 'Montenegro's independence drive', *Europe Report*, 169, 7 December.

—— (2007) 'Ensuring Bosnia's future: a new international engagement strategy', *Europe Report*, 80(15), February.

Jelincic, J. (ed.) (2006) *Europeanisation of Serbia: Capacities of Local Authorities and Local (Self) Government Authorities*, Belgrade: Fund for an Open Society.

Jeong, H. (2005) *Peacebuilding in Postconflict Societies: Strategy and Process*, Boulder, CO: Lynne Rienner.

Jović, D., 'Croatia and the European Union: a long delayed journey', *Journal of Southern Europe and the Balkans*, 8(1), pp. 85–103.

Judah, T. (2002) *Kosovo: War and Revenge*, 2nd edn, New Haven, CT: Yale University Press.

Kaiser, W. and Elvert, J. (eds) (2005) *European Union Enlargement: A Comparative History*, London: Routledge.

Kant, I. (1795) *Perpetual Peace*.

Karadzole, B. (1990) 'Yugoslavia: tiptoeing into Europe', *European Affairs*, 4(3), pp. 93–97.

Katzenstein, P. (1996) *The Culture of National Security: Norms and Identity in World Politics*, New York: Columbia University Press.

Kavalski, E. (2003) 'The international socialization of the Balkans', *Review of International Affairs*, 2(4), pp. 71–88.

Keating, T. F. and Knight, W. A. (2004) *Building Sustainable Peace*, New York: United Nations University Press; Edmonton: University of Alberta Press.

Kelley J. (2004) *Ethnic Politics in Europe: The Power of Norms and Incentives*, Princeton, NJ: Princeton University Press.

Kempe, I. and van Meurs, W. (2003) 'Europe beyond EU enlargement', in van Meurs, W. (ed.), *Prospects and Risks Beyond the EU Enlargement: Southeastern Europe: Weak States and Strong International Supports*, Opladen: Leske & Budrich, pp. 11–75.

Kinsella, D. (2005) 'No rest for the democratic peace', *American Political Science Review*, 99, pp. 453–57.

Kintis, A. G. (1997) 'The EU and war in former Yugoslavia', in Holland, M. (ed.), *Common Foreign and Security Policy: The Record and Reforms*, London: Pinter, pp. 148–72.

Kirchheimer, O. (1965) 'Confining conditions and revolutionary breakthroughs', *American Political Science Review*, pp. 964–74.

Knaus, G. and Cox, M. (2005) 'Building democracy after conflict: the "Helsinki moment" in Southeastern Europe', *Journal of Democracy*, 16(1), pp. 39–53.

Knill, C. and Lehmkuhl, D. (1999) 'How Europe matters: different mechanisms of Europeanization', European Integration online Papers (EIoP), 3(7), 15 June 1999, available online at http://eiop.or.at/eiop/texte/1999-007.htm.

Koprivca, N. (2006) 'Consequences, tendencies and the role of the civil society in the accession process in Montenegro', CEDEM Newsletter July–October, pp. 3–14.

Kostovicova, D. and Basic, N. (2005) 'Conference report: transitionalism in the Balkans: the emergence, nature and impact of cross-national linkages on an enlarged and enlarging Europe 26–27 November 2004', *Contemporary European History*, 14(4), pp. 583–90.

Krastev, I. (2002) 'The Balkans: democracy without choices', *Journal of Democracy*, 13(3), pp. 39–53.

—— (2003) 'Bringing the state back up', Conference paper, September, available online at http://www.suedosteuropa-gesellschaft.com.

Kriesberg, L., Northrup, T. A. and Thorson, S. J. (eds) (1989) *Intractable Conflicts and Their Transformation*, Syracuse, NJ: Syracuse University Press.

Kubicek, P. (2003) 'International norms, the European Union, and democratization: tentative theory and evidence', in Kubicek, P. (ed.), *The European Union and Democratization*, London: Routledge, pp. 1–29.

Kuhne, B. (2006) 'Quietly, the Western Balkans is moving towards European integration', *Balkan Investigative Reporting Network*, 28 July.

Landman, T. (2003) *Issues and Methods in Comparative Politics: An Introduction*, 2nd edn, London: Routledge.

Landou, A. (1997) 'The European Union in a changing context', in Landou, A. and Whitman, R. G., *Rethinking the European Union*, London: Macmillan.

Layne, C. (1994) 'Kant or cant: the myth of the democratic peace', *International Security*, 19(2), Autumn 1994, pp. 5–49.

Lederach, J. P. (1995) *Preparing for Peace: Conflict Transformation across Cultures*, Syracuse, NJ: Syracuse University Press.

Lendvai, P., Parcell, L. (1991) 'Yugoslavia without Yugoslavs: The roots of the crisis', *International Affairs*, 67(2), pp. 251–61.

Levinthal, D. and March, J. (1993) 'The myopia of learning', *Strategic Management Journal*, 14, Special Issue, pp. 95–112.

Levitsky, S. and Way, L. A. (2005) 'International linkage and democratisation', *Journal of Democracy*, 16(3), pp. 20–34.

Levy, J. S. (1994) 'Learning and foreign policy: sweeping a conceptual minefield', *International Organization*, 48(2), pp. 279–312.

Lewis, D. W. P. (1993) *The Road to Europe: History, Institutions, and Prospects of European Integration, 1945–1993*, New York: P. Lang.

Lightfoot, S. and Burchell, J. (2005) 'The European Union and the World Summit on Sustainable Development: normative power Europe in action?', *Journal of Common Market Studies*, 43(1), pp. 75–96.

Lilleker, D. G. (2003) 'Interviewing the political elite: navigating a potential minefield', *Politics* 23(3), pp. 207–14.

Linden, R. H. (2002) *Norms and Nannies: The Impact of International Organizations on the Central and East European States*, Oxford: Rowman & Littlefield.

Linz, J. J. and Stepan, A. C. (1996) *Problems of Democratic Transition and Consolidation: Southern Europe, South America, and Post-Communist Europe*, Baltimore, MD: The Johns Hopkins University Press.

Lopandic, D. (1999) 'Multilateral cooperation in South Eastern Europe', in Minic, J. (ed.), *South Eastern Europe 2000: A View from Serbia*, Belgrade: Stubovikulture, pp. 67–84.

McCormack, T. (2006) 'Serbia; from pariah to EU member', 2 March, available online at http://www.spiked-online.com/index.php?/site/article/225.

McGarry, J. and O'Leary, B. (1993) *The Politics of Ethnic Conflict Regulation: Case Studies of Protracted Ethnic Conflicts*, London: Routledge. Majone, G. (1994) 'The rise of the regulatory state in Europe', *West European Politics*, 17(3), pp. 77–101.

Manners, I. (2002) 'Normative power Europe: a contradiction in terms?', *Journal of Common Market Studies*, pp. 235–58.

Manners, I. and Whitman, R. G. (2000) *The Foreign Policies of European Union Member States*, Manchester: Manchester University Press.

Mansfield, E. D. and Snyder, J. (2002) 'Democratic transitions, institutional strength, and war', *International Organization*, 56(2), pp. 297–337.

March, J. (1991) 'Exploration and exploitation in organizational learning', *Organization Science*, 2(1), pp. 71–87.

March, J. G. and Olsen, J. P. (1989) *Rediscovering Institutions*, London: Free Press.

Marshall, C. and Rossman, G. B. (1995) *Designing Qualitative Research*, 2nd edn, Thousand Oaks, CA: Sage Publications.

Maull, H. W. (2004) 'Europe and the new balance of global order', *International Affairs*, 81(4), pp. 775–99.

Mayhew, A. (1998) *Recreating Europe: The European Union's Policy towards Central and Eastern Europe*, Cambridge: Cambridge University Press.

Meurs, W. van (ed.) (2003) *Prospects and Risks Beyond EU Enlargement*, vol. 2, *Southeastern Europe: Weak States and Strong International Support*, Opladen: Leske & Budrich.

Miall, H. (2001) 'Conflict transformation: a multi-dimensional task', in Bloomfield, D., Fischer, M., Schmelzle, B., *et al.*, *Berghof Handbook for Conflict Transformation*, Berghof Centre, Berlin, pp. 1–18, available online at http://www.berghof-handbook.net/.

Miall, H., Ramsbotham, O. and Woodhouse, T. (1999) *Contemporary Conflict Resolution: The Prevention, Management and Transformation of Deadly Conflicts*, Cambridge: Polity Press.

Miller, B. (2005) 'When and how regions become peaceful: potential theoretical pathway to peace', *International Studies Review*, 7, pp. 229–67.

Miller, N. J. (1997) 'A failed transition: the case of Serbia', in Dawisha K. and Parrot, B. (eds), *Politics, Power, and the Struggle for Democracy in South-East Europe*, Cambridge: Cambridge University Press, pp. 146–89.

Missiroli, A. (2003) 'The EU and its changing neighbourhoods: stabilisation, integration and partnership, in Batt, J., Lynch, D., Missiroli, A. *et al.* (eds), *Partners and Neighbours: A CFSP for a Wider Europe, Chaillot Papers*, 64, Paris: Institute for Security Studies. Available online at http://www.iss.europa.eu/uploads/media/cp064e.pdf.

Mitchell, C. R. (1999) *Resolving Intractable Conflicts*, Fairfax, VA: ICAR Working Paper.

Monnet, J. (1978) *Memoirs*, London: Collins.

Moravcsik, A. and Vachudova, M. A. (2003) 'National interests, state power, and EU enlargement', *East European Politics and Societies*, 17(1), pp. 42–57.

Morris, H. M. (2003) 'EU enlargement and Latvian citizenship policy', *Journal on Ethnopolitics and Minority Issues in Europe*, 1, Brussels: Centre for European Policy Studies.

Muller, H. (2004) 'Arguing, bargaining and all that: communicative action, rationalist theory and the logic of appropriateness in international relations', *European Journal of International Relations*, 10(3), pp. 395–436.

Munuera, G. (1994) 'Preventing armed conflict in Europe: lessons from recent experience', *Chaillot Papers*, 15/16, Paris: Institute for Security Studies.

Niblett, R. and Wallace, W. (2001) *Rethinking European Order: West European Responses, 1989–97*, Basingstoke: Palgrave.

Nordstrom, C. (1995) 'Contested identities/essentially contested powers', in Rupesinghe, K. (ed.), *Conflict Transformation*, London: Macmillan, pp. 93–115.

Northrup, T., Kriesberg, L. and Thorson, S. J. (1989) *Intractable Conflicts and their transformations*, Syracuse: Syracuse University Press.

Noutcheva, G. (2004) 'The EU and the Western Balkans: a tale of mutual mistrust', *CEPS Europa South-East Monitor*, 58, September.

Nugent, N. (1994) (ed.), *The European Union 1993: Annual Review of Activities*, Oxford, Blackwell, pp. 11–26.

Nuttall, S. (1994) 'The EC and Yugoslavia: *deus ex machina* or *machina sine deo?*,' *Journal of Common Market Studies*, 32, August, pp. 11–25.

O'Donnell, R. (1999) 'Fixing the institutions', in Wilson, R. (ed.), *No Frontiers: North–South Integration in Ireland*, Belfast: Democratic Dialogue, p. 70.

Olsen, J. P. (2002) 'The many faces of Europeanization', *Journal of Common Market Studies*, 40(5), pp. 921–53.

Owen, D. (1996) *Balkan Odyssey*, London: Indigo.

Pahre, R. (2005) 'Formal theory and case-study methods in EU Studies', *European Union Politics*, 6(1), pp. 113–46.

Papadimitriou, D. (2002) *Negotiating the New Europe: The European Union and Eastern Europe*, Aldershot: Ashgate.

Pavkovic, A. (2000) *The Fragmentation of Yugoslavia: Nationalism and War in the Balkans*, 2nd edn, New York: St Martin's Press.

Pavlaković, V. (2005) 'Serbia transformed? Political dynamics in the Milošević era and after', in Ramet, S. and Pavlaković, V. (eds), *Serbia since 1989*, London: University of Washington Press, pp. 166–91.

Peters, B. G. (1998) *Comparative Politics: Theory and Methods*, New York: New York University Press.

Peterson, J. and Sjursen, H. (1998) *A Common Foreign Policy for Europe: Competing Visions of the CFSP*, London: Routledge.

Phinnemore, D. (2003) 'Stabilisation and Association Agreements: Europe agreements for the Western Balkans?', *European Foreign Affairs Review*, 8(1), pp. 77–103.

Phinnemore, D. and Siani-Davies, P. (eds) (2002), *South-Eastern Europe and European Union Enlargement: Conference Proceedings*, Cluj-Napoca: Cluj-Napoca University Press.

—— (2003) 'Beyond intervention? The Balkans, the Stability Pact and the European Union', in Siani-Davies, P. (ed.), *International Intervention in the Balkans since 1995*, London: Routledge, pp. 172–93.

Pippan, C. (2004) 'The rocky road to Europe: the EU's Stabilisation and Association Process for the Western Balkans and the principle of conditionality', *European Foreign Affairs Review*, 9(2), pp. 219–46.

Pop, A. (2003) 'Security: from powder keg to cooperation', in Wim van Meurs (ed.), *Prospects and Risks Beyond the EU Enlargement. Southeastern Europe: Weak States and Strong International Supports*, Opladen: Leske & Budrich, pp. 117–47.

Popper, K. (1959) *The Logic of Scientific Discovery*, 1st edn, New York: Harper & Row.

Pravda, A. and Zielonka, J. (2002) *Democratic Consolidation in Eastern Europe*, vol. 2, *International and Transnational Factors*, Oxford: Oxford University Press.

Pridham, G. and Agh, A. (2001) *Prospects for Democratic Consolidation in East-Central Europe*, Manchester: Manchester University Press.

Pridham, G. and Vanhanen, T. (eds) (1994), *Democratisation in Eastern Europe: Domestic and International Perspectives*, London: Routledge.

Pugh, M. (2002) 'Postwar political economy in Bosnia and Herzegovina: the spoils of peace', *Global Governance*, 8(4), Autumn, pp. 467–82.

Putnam, R. (1988) 'Diplomacy and domestic politics: The logic of two-level games', *International Organisation*, 42, Summer, pp. 427–60.

Radaelli, C. M. (2000) 'Whither Europeanisation? Concept stretching and substantive change', *European Integration online Papers (EIoP)*, 4(8), available online at http://eiop.or.at/eiop/texte/2000-008.htm.

Ram, M. H. (2001) *Built by Association: Legislating for the West in EU Candidate States*, Paper presented at the conference 'South-Eastern Europe and EU Enlargement', 16–18 September 2001, Cluj-Napoca, Romania, <http://www.qub.ac.uk/ies/events/confenlarg/ana.ram>.

Ramet, S. P. (1996) *Balkan Babel: The Disintegration of Yugoslavia from the Death of Tito to Ethnic War*, 2nd edn, Boulder, CO: Westview Press.

Ray, J. L. (1996) 'Does democracy cause peace?', *Annual Review of Political Science*, 1, pp. 27–46.

Richmond, O. (2002) *Maintaining Order, Making Peace*, Basingstoke: Palgrave.

Riedlmayer, A. (2002) 'From the ashes: the past and future of Bosnia's cultural heritage', in Shatzmiller, M. (ed.), *Islam and Bosnia: Conflict Resolution and Foreign Policy in Multi-Ethnic States*, Montreal: McGill-Queen's University Press, pp. 98–135.

Rothman, J. (1992) *From Confrontation to Cooperation: Resolving Ethnic and Regional Conflict*, Newbury Park, CA: Sage Publications.

—— (1997) *Resolving Identity-Based Conflict in Nations, Organizations, and Communities*, 1st edn, San Francisco: Jossey-Bass.

Rumelili, B. (2007) 'Transforming conflicts on EU borders: the case of Greek–Turkish relations', *Journal of Common Market Studies*, 45(1), pp. 105–26.

Rupesinghe, K. (1995a) 'Introduction', in Rupesinghe, K. (ed.), *Conflict Transformation*, London: Macmillan, pp. 1–18.

—— (1995b) 'Conflict transformation', in Rupesinghe, K. (ed.), *Conflict Transformation*, London: Macmillan, pp. 19–32.

Rupnik, J. (2005) 'Europe's challenges in the Balkans', *Europa South-East Monitor, Centre for European Policy Studies*, 61, January.

Sadurski, W. (2004) 'Accession's democracy dividend: the impact of the EU enlargement upon democracy in the new member states of Central and Eastern Europe', *European Law Journal*, 10(4), pp. 317–401.

Salmon, T. C. (1992) 'Testing times for European political cooperation: the Gulf and Yugoslavia, 1990–1992', *International Affairs*, 68(2), pp. 233–53.

—— (2002) 'The EU's role in conflict resolution: lessons from Northern Ireland', *European Foreign Affairs Review*, 7, pp. 337–58, Kluwer Law International.

Samardžija, V. (2003) *Croatia's Preparation for EU Accession*, Global Development Network Southeast Europe, November.

Sandole, D. J. (1993) *Conflict Resolution Theory and Practice: Integration and Application*, Manchester: Manchester University Press.

Sarantakos, S. (1993) *Social Research*, Melbourne: Macmillan Education Australia.

Schimmelfennig, F. (2002) 'Introduction: the impact of international organisations on the Central and Eastern European States – conceptual and theoretical issues', in Linden, R. H. (ed.), *Norms and Nannies: The Impact of International Organisation on the Central and East European States*, Lanham, MD: Rowman & Littlefield, pp. 1–29.

—— (2003) *The EU, NATO and the Integration of Europe. Rules and Rhetoric*, Cambridge: Cambridge University Press.

Schimmelfennig, F., Engert, S. and Knobel, H. (2003) 'Costs, commitment and compliance: the impact of EU democratic conditionality on Latvia, Slovakia and Turkey', *Journal of Common Market Studies*, 41(3), pp. 495–518.

Schimmelfennig, F. and Sedelmeier, U. (2004) 'Governance by conditionality: EU rule transfer to the candidate countries of Central and Eastern Europe', *Journal of European Public Policy*, 11(4), pp. 669–87.

—— (2005a) 'Conceptualising the Europeanization of Central and Eastern Europe', in Schimmelfennig, F. and Sedelmeier, U. (eds), *The Europeanization of Central and Eastern Europe*, Ithaca, NY: Cornell University Press, 2005, pp. 1–28.

—— (2005b) 'Conclusions: the impact of the EU on the accession countries', in Schimmelfennig, F. and Sedelmeier, U. (eds), *The Europeanization of Central and Eastern Europe*, Ithaca, NY: Cornell University Press, 2005, pp. 210–28.

Schivelbusch, W. (2003) *The Culture of Defeat*, London: Granta Books.

Schmitter, P. C. (1995). 'More liberal, preliberal, or postliberal?', *Journal of Democracy*, 6(1), pp. 15–22.

Schmitter, P. C. (2003) 'Making sense of the EU: democracy in Europe and Europe's democratisation', *Journal of Democracy*, 14(4), pp. 71–85.

Schnabel, A. and Carment, D. (2003) *Conflict Prevention: Path to Peace or Grand Illusion?*, Tokyo, New York: United Nations University Press.

Schopflin, G. (1997) 'The rise and fall of Yugoslavia', in McGarry, J. and O'Leary, B. (eds), *The Politics of Ethnic Conflict Regulation: Case Studies of Protracted Ethnic Conflicts*, London: Routledge.

Sedelmeier, U. (2005) *Constructing the Path to Eastern Enlargement: The Uneven Policy Impact of EU Identity*, Manchester: Manchester University Press.

Silber, L. and Little, A. (1996) *The Death of Yugoslavia*, London: Penguin.

Simeunovic, D. (2006) *The Collectivisation of Guilt*, Belgrade: Nolit.

Sjursen, H. (1999) 'Enlargement and the CFSP: transforming the EU's external identity?', in Henderson, K. (ed.), *Back to Europe: Central and Eastern Europe and the EU*, London: UCL Press, pp. 37–51.

Smith, A. and Wallace, H. (1994) 'The European Union: towards a policy for Europe', *International Affairs*, 70(3), pp. 429–44.

Smith, J. (2000) 'Enlarging Europe', *Journal of Common Market Studies*, 38(1), pp. 122–5.

Smith, K. E. (2001) 'Western actors and the promotion of democracy,' in Zielonka, J. and Pravda, A. (eds), *Democratic Consolidation in Eastern Europe: International and Transnational Factors*, Oxford: Oxford University Press, pp. 31–57.

—— (2003a) 'The evolution and application of EU membership conditionality', in Cremona, M. (ed.), *The Enlargement of the European Union*, Oxford: Oxford University Press, pp. 105–40.

—— (2003b) *European Union Foreign Policy in a Changing World*, Cambridge: Polity Press.

Smith, M. E. (2000) 'Conforming to Europe: the domestic impact of EU foreign policy co-operation', *Journal of European Public Policy*, 7(4), pp. 613–31.

—— (2004a) 'Institutionalization, policy adaptation and European foreign policy cooperation', *European Journal of International Relations*, 10(1), pp. 95–137.

—— (2004b) 'Toward a theory of EU foreign policymaking: multi-level governance, domestic politics, and national adaptation to Europe's common foreign and security policy', *Journal of European Public Policy*, 11(4), pp. 740–58.

Snyder, J. (1989) 'International leverage on Soviet domestic change', *World Politics*, 42(1), pp. 1–30.

Soberg, M. (2007) 'Croatia since 1989: the HDZ and the politics of transition', in Ramet, S. P. and Matic, D. (eds), *Democratic Transition in Croatia: Value Transformation, Education and Media*, College Station, TX: Texas A and M University Press.

Solana, J. (2004) 'From Dayton implementation to European integration', *NATO Review, Historic Change in the Balkans*, Winter.

Soveroski, M. (1999) 'European Union enlargement: prospects and potential pitfalls along the way', *Eipascope*, 2, pp. 16–20, available online at http://www.eipa.eu/files/repository/eipascope/scop99_2_col.pdf.

Spiro, D. E. (1994) 'Give democratic peace a chance? The insignificance of the liberal peace', *International Security*, 9(2), pp. 50–86.

Steil, B. and Woodward, S. L. (1998) 'A European "New Deal" for the Balkans', *Foreign Affairs*, 78(6), Nov/Dec, pp. 95–105.

Steunenberg, B. and Dimitrova, A., 'Compliance in the EU enlargement process: the limits of conditionality', *European Integration Online Papers*, 11(5), available online at http://eiop.or.at/eiop/texte/2007-005a.htm.

Tannam, E. (2006) 'Cross-border co-operation between Northern Ireland and the Republic of Ireland: neo-functionalism revisited', *British Journal of Politics and International Relations*, 8(2), pp. 256–76.

Tanner, M. (2001) *Croatia: A Nation Forged in War*, New Haven, CT: Yale University Press.

Taylor, S. J. and Bogdan, R. (1984) *Introduction to Qualitative Research Methods: The Search for Meanings*, 2nd edn, New York: Wiley.

Thisse, J. (2004) 'An unhappy marriage between Serbia and Montenegro', *CaféBabel. com*, 11 October 2004, available online at http://www.cafebabel.com/en/article. asp?T+TandId+2501.

Thomas, R. (1999) *Serbia under Milosevic: Politics in the 1990s*, London: C. Hurst and Co. Ltd.

Tidwell, A. (1998) *Conflict Resolved? A Critical Assessment of Conflict Resolution*, London: Pinter.

Tocci, N. (2004) *EU Accession Dynamics and Conflict Resolution: Catalysing Peace or Consolidating Partition in Cyprus?*, Aldershot: Ashgate.

—— (2007) *The EU and Conflict Resolution: Promoting Peace in the Backyard*, London: Routledge.

Toje, A. (2005) 'The 2003 European Union security strategy: a critical appraisal', *European Foreign Affairs Review*, 10, p. 118.

Triantaphyllou, D. (2003) 'The Balkans between stabilisation and membership', in Batt, J., Lynch, D., Missiroli, A. *et al.* (eds), *Partners and Neighbours: A CFSP for a Wider Europe, Chaillot Papers*, 64, Paris: Institute for Security Studies. Available online at http://www.iss.europa.eu/uploads/media/cp064e.pdf.

Türkes, M., Gökgöz, G. (2006) 'The European Union's strategy towards the Western Balkans: Exclusion or integration?', *East European Politics and Societies*, 20(4), pp. 659–90.

Uvalic, M. (1997) 'European economic integration: What role for the Balkans?', in Bianchini, S. and Uvalic, M. (eds), *The Balkans and the Challenge of Economic Integration Regional and European Perspectives*, 1st edn, Ravenna: Longo Editore, pp. 19–34.

Vachudova, M. A. (2001). 'The leverage of international institutions on democratizing states: Eastern Europe and the European Union', European University Institute, Working Paper No. 2001/33.

—— (2003) 'Strategies for democratization and European integration in the Balkans', in Cremona, M. (ed.), *The Enlargement of the European Union*, Oxford: Oxford University Press, pp. 141–60.

—— (2005) *Europe Undivided: Democracy, Leverage, and Integration after Communism*, Oxford: Oxford University Press.

Vaknin, S. (1998) 'Balkan encounter: the new colonies', *Central Europe Review*, 12, December.

Vayrynen, R. (1999) 'From conflict resolution to conflict transformation: a critical review', in Jeong, H. W., *The New Agenda for Peace Research*, Aldershot: Ashgate.

Vayrynen, R., and International Social Science Council (1991) *New Directions in Conflict Theory: Conflict Resolution and Conflict Transformation*, London: Sage Publications.

Vermeersch, P. (2003), 'EU enlargement and minority rights policies in Central Europe: explaining policy shifts in the Czech Republic, Hungary and Poland', *Journal on Ethnopolitics and Minority Issues in Europe*, 1, pp. 1–32.

Vuckovic, G. (1997) *Ethnic Cleavages and Conflict: The Sources of National Cohesion and Disintegration: The Case of Yugoslavia*, Aldershot: Ashgate.

Vukadinovic, R. (2001) 'Former Yugoslavia: international efforts to link peace, stability and democracy', in Pravda, A. and Zielonka, J. (eds), *Democratic Consolidation in Eastern Europe*, vol. 2, *International and Transnational Factors*, Oxford: Oxford University Press, pp. 437–54.

Wallace, H. (1991) 'The Europe that came in from the cold', *International Affairs*, 67(4), pp. 647–63.

Wallensteen, P., Vayrynen, R. and International Social Science Council (1991) *New Directions in Conflict Theory: Conflict Resolution and Conflict Transformation*, London: Sage Publications.

Wallensteen, P. and Bercovitch, J. (1998) *Preventing Violent Conflicts: Past Record and Future Challenges*, Uppsala, Sweden: Dept. of Peace and Conflict Research, Uppsala University.

Watkins, I. (2005) 'Croatia at the crossroads: the EU–ICTY debate', *Balkan Series*, 5(15), March, Camberley: Defence Academy of the UK, pp. 1–5.

Weiler, Joseph H. H. (1991) 'The transformation of Europe', *Yale Law Journal*, 108(8), pp. 2403–83.

Weller, M. (1992) 'The international response to the dissolution of the Socialist Federal Republic of Yugoslavia', *American Journal of International Law*, 86(3), pp. 569–607.

Whitman, R. (1998) *From Civilian Power to Superpower? The International Identity of the European Union*, Basingstoke: Macmillan Press; New York: St Martin's Press.

Wolf, M. (1995) 'Cooperation or conflict? The European Union in a liberal global economy', *International Affairs*, 71(2), pp. 325–37.

Woodward, S. L. (1995) *Balkan Tragedy: Chaos and Dissolution and the Cold War*, Washington, DC: Brookings Institute.

Yannis, A. (2005) 'EU foreign policy in the Balkans: a credibility test', *CFSP Forum*, 3(2), March.

Youngs, R. (2004) 'Normative dynamics and strategic interests in the EU's external identity', *Journal of Common Market Studies*, 42(2), pp. 415–36.

Yusufi, I. (2001) 'Stability Pact and its role in the development of regional cooperation in South East Europe', in Phinnemore, D. and Siani-Davies, P. (eds), *South-Eastern Europe, the Stability Pact and EU Enlargement*, CLUJ, Romania: European Studies Foundation Publishing House

Zielonka, J. (1998) *Explaining Euro-Paralysis: Why Europe is Unable to Act in International Politics*, Basingstoke: Macmillan Press in association with St Antony's College, Oxford.

—— (ed.) (2002) *Europe Unbound: Enlarging and Shaping the Boundaries of the European Union*, 1st edn, London: Routledge.

Zimbardo, P. G., Ebbesen, E. B. and Maslach, C. (1977) *Influencing Attitudes and Changing Behaviour*, London: Addison Wesley Publishing Company.

Zucconi, M. (1996) 'The EU in the former Yugoslavia', in Chayes, A. and Chayes, A. (eds), *Managing Conflict in the Post-Communist World: Mobilizing International and Regional Organizations*, Washington, DC: Brookings Institute, pp. 237–78.

Zurn, M. (2000) 'Democratic governance beyond the nation-state: the EU and other international institutions', *European Journal of International Relations*, 6(2), pp. 183–222.

Documents

Council of Ministers (1999) General Affairs and External Relations Council, Brussels, 19 July 1999, Brussels General Affairs and External Relations Council.

—— (1998) General Affairs and External Relations Council, Brussels, 26 October, Brussels General Affairs and External Relations Council.

—— (2000) General Affairs and External Relations Council, Brussels, 22 May, Brussels General Affairs and External Relations Council.

European Council Conclusions, 9 November 1998.

European Commission (1988) 'The European Community and Yugoslavia', *External Relations*, 280/x/88-EN, July.

—— (2002a) CARDS Assistance Programme to the Western Balkans, Regional Strategy Paper 2002–2006.

—— (2002b) The Stabilisation and Association Process for South East Europe, *First Annual Report* (SEC 2002 339).

—— (2003) *Communication From the Commission to the Council and the European*

Parliament: The Western Balkans and European Integration.

—— (2004) *Communication from the Commission: Opinion on Croatia's Application for Membership of the EU*, 20 April, COM (2004) 257 Final.

—— (2004b) *Communication from the Commission to the Council and to the European Parliament: Strategy Paper of the European Commission on progress in the enlargement process*, Brussels, 6 October, COM (2004) 657 Final.

—— (2005a) 'Report on the preparedness of Serbia and Montenegro to negotiate a Stabilisation and Association Agreement with the EU', Brussels, 12 April, SEC 478 Final.

—— (2005b) *Communication from the Commission: 2005 Enlargement Strategy paper*, Brussels, 9 November, COM (2005) 561.

—— (2006a) Croatia 2006 *Progress Report.*

—— (2006b) Serbia 2006 *Progress Report.*

—— (2006c) Montenegro 2006 *Progress Report.*

—— (2006d) *Enlargement Strategy and Main Challenges 2006–2007*, COM (2006) 649 Final.

—— (2006e) *Communication from the Commission, 'The Western Balkans on the road to the EU: consolidating stability and raising prosperity'*, available online at http://ec.europa.eu/enlargement/pdf/com_2006_27_en_acte.pdf.

—— (2006f) 'Annex 1: *Special Report on the EU's capacity to integrate new members*, *Enlargement Strategy and Main Challenges 2006–2007*, COM (2006) 649 Final.

—— (2006g) *Western Balkans: Prospect of EU membership incites peace in the Western Balkans*, available online at http://ec.europa.eu/world/peace/geographical_themes/west_balk/index_en.htm (retrieved 19 August 2006).

—— (2007a) *Enlargement Newsletter*, 7 March.

—— (2007b) 'Frequently asked questions on Instrument for Pre-Accession Assistance', available online at http://europa.eu/rapid/pressReleasesAction.do?reference=MEMO/06/410&format=HTML&aged=0&language=EN&guiLanguage=en.

—— (2007c) 'Serbia gets a government – concludes negotiations on EU Serbia visa facilitation and readmission agreements', *Enlargement Newsletter*, 30 May.

—— (2007d) 'Commission Staff Working document, Croatia 2007, Progress Report', Brussels, SEC (2007) 1431.

—— (2007e) 'Commission Staff Working document, Serbia 2007, Progress Report, Brussels, Brussels, 6.11.2007 SEC(2007) 1435.

—— (2008) 'Western Balkans: Enhancing the European perspective', Brussels, COM (2008) 127 Final {SEC(2008) 288}.

European Council Conclusions (2005a) Brussels, 16 2005.

—— (2005b) Brussels, 16–17 December, pt.16.

—— (2006a) Brussels, 30–31 January.

European Council Regulation (EC) No 2666/2000 of 5 December 2000 on assistance for Albania, Bosnia and Herzegovina, Croatia, the Federal Republic of Yugoslavia and the Former Yugoslav Republic of Macedonia, repealing Regulation (EC) No 1628/96 and amending Regulations (EEC) No 3906/89 and (EEC) No 1360/90 and Decisions 97/256/EC and 1999/311/EC Official Journal L 306, 07/12/2000 P. 0001 – 0006.

European Council Regulation (2000) (EC) No. 2666/2000, 5 December 2000.

European Council, 'Declaration at the EU-Western Balkans Summit', Thessaloniki, 21 June 2003, 10229/03 point 2.

European Council, Presidency Conclusions, Thessaloniki European Council, 19 and 20 June 2003, point 41, available online at http://ue.eu.int/ueDocs/cms_Data/docs/pressData/en/ec/76279.pdf (retrieved 29 November 2005).

European Parliament (2005) Report on The Commission's 2005 enlargement strategy paper (2005/2206(INI)), FINAL A6–0025/2006, 3 February 2006 RR/364920EN.doc.

—— (2007) Report on Croatia's 2006 progress report, Committee on Foreign Affairs, A6–0092/2007, 29 March 2007.

European Parliament and Parliament of Serbia and Montenegro (2005) 'Statement' Belgrade, 5 December 2005, available online at http://ue.eu.int/ueDocs/cms_Data/docs/pressdata/EN/reports/85228.pdf.

The Declaration of the Zagreb Summit, 24 November 2000, available online at http://europa.eu.int/comm/enlargement/intro/sap/summit_zagreb.htm (retrieved 29 July 2006).

Treaty on Europe, available online at http://www.europa.eu.int/eurlex/en/treaties/dat/C_2002325EN.000501.html#anArt11Presidency Conclusions of the Santa Maria de Feira European Council, No. 200/1/00, 19–20 June 2000.

Media

Ashdown, P. (2006) 'EU must speed up Balkans accession', United Press International, 8 March.

Balkan Insight (2006) 'Croatian Serbs question deal with government: the minority community increasingly believes that a landmark agreement was only a gesture', 19 October.

—— (2008a) 'Serbia's radicals change image', 16 January.

—— (2008b) 'Serb socialist leader admits government dilemma', 20 May.

Balkan Investigative Reporting Network (2007) 'Serbia may "trade" Mladic for concessions in Kosovo', 21 June.

BBC News (2006) 'Serbia nationalists claim victory', 22 January.

Djukanovic, M. (2002) 'Balkan betrayal', *The Washington Post*, 20 August.

—— (2006) 'Montenegro is no one's junior partner', *Financial Times*, 2 May.

EU Observer (2004) 'EU prepares for Bosnia mission', 30 November.

—— (2005a) 'Croatia warned on starting EU talks', 31 January.

—— (2005b) 'Serbia hoping for EU membership' 17 January.

—— (2005c) 'Serbian enlargement to carry on', 16 June.

—— (2006a) 'Montenegro slams EU referendum threshold', 21 February.

—— (2006b) 'EU awaits Montenegro Independence vote', 19 May.

—— (2006c) 'EU states divided on Serbia strategy', 18 July.

—— (2006d) 'Serb radicalism threat puzzles EU', 11 December.

—— (2006e) 'EU deeply wrong on Serbia' 19 May.

—— (2007a) 'Europe needs a stable Serbia' 12 February.

—— (2007b) 'Serbia receives EU membership horizon', 7 March.

Financial Times (2000) 'Nurturing the spoils of peace: Croatian democracy's rebirth is a benign influence on its neighbours – but without economic help it could yet be short-lived', 12 June.

—— (2005a) 'Freedom is gateway to the future. The republic is looking beyond uneasy union with Serbia to the European Union', 12 July.

—— (2005b) 'Austrian leader claims 'double standards' over Croatia talks', 29 September.

—— (2006a) 'Dividing loyalties Montenegro votes this weekend on severing ties with Serbia. Is it strong enough to stand alone – and might a split reignite hard-line Serbian nationalist ambitions?', 20 May.

—— (2006b) 'Brussels suspends talks with Belgrade', 4 May.

Guardian (1995) 'EU report accuses Croatia of atrocities against rebel Serbs', 30 September.

—— (2002) 'Montenegro to drop aim of independence', 18 February.

—— (2005) 'Suddenly, bigger is no longer better: European enlargement is afflicted with growing pains', 1 July.

—— (2006) 'Europe: Montenegro fights to change rules for independence vote: EU says referendum needs 55% majority to be valid: Serbian nationalists warn of war if split approved', 27 February.

—— (2008) 'EU offers Serbs trade and travel deal before poll', 29 January.

International Herald Tribune (2003) 'Yugoslavia's new name is awful (but it shouldn't last)', 10 March.

—— (2004) 'Montenegro quits Hague panel in protest', 24 September.

—— (2005a) 'Deadlock in Croatia over EU's conditions: official criticises demand for arrest', 28 February.

—— (2005b) 'EU warns Croatia to help in arrest', 10 March.

—— (2005c) 'Croatian president trusts judiciary; he calls it impartial on war crimes', 22 November.

—— (2006a) 'In Montenegro resort, a rift over independence; opponents fear Serbian retaliation', 18 April.

—— (2006b) 'Montenegro has its favourite son; Djukanovic, leader for 15 years, expects to be re-elected', 9 September.

New York Times (1991a) 'Europe to press a Yugoslav pact', 30 June.

—— (1991b) 'Conflict in Yugoslavia: a toothless Europe?', 4 July.

—— (1992) 'Yugoslav strife: challenge for Europe', 26 May.

—— (2002) 'Serbia and Montenegro sign a plan for Yugoslavia's demise', 15 March.

—— (2006a) 'Dispute festers in Slovenia, or is it Croatia?', 18 July.

—— (2006b) 'Tiny Montenegro booms and eyes the Russian hand that's feeding it', 24 December.

RFE/RL Newsline 9 March 2007.

Serbianna.com (2006) 'Montenegro hopes on pre-entry deal with EU by end of year', 7 July, available online at http://www.serbianna.com/news/2006/02070. shtml.

Southeast European Times (2006) 'Croatia, Slovenia spar over unresolved issues'.

The Economist (2006a) 'Aftermath of a dictator: the Balkans after Milošević', 18 March.

—— (2006b) 'Serbia out in the cold', 3 May.

—— (2006c) "A symbolic change in Belgrade" 8 June.

—— (2006d) 'The absorption puzzle', 1 July.

Transitions (2005) 'EU enlargement: sliding doors', 6 June.

—— (2006a) 'Serbia: hanging on Mladic', 9 May.

—— (2006b) 'Serbia: the silent treatment', 5 May.

—— (2007) 'Nationalists: weakness in numbers', 31 January.

Vreme News Digest Agency (1997a) 'Revenge comes from Dedinje', 286, 29 March.

—— (1997b) 'No sadder music, no sadder company', 312, 27 September.

Speeches

Barroso, J.M. (2006) 'Leading by example: Croatia's road to EU membership', speech at Parliament of Croatia, 16 February.

Glenny, M. (2005) 'Crunch time: Kosovo, Serbia, Montenegro and Macedonia', 19 September, Institute of European Affairs, Dublin.

Patten, C. (2004a) 'The Western Balkans: the road to Europe', Speech to German Bundestag, European Affairs Committee, Berlin, 28 April.

—— (2002) 'Serbia and Montenegro sign a plan for Yugoslavia's demise', 15 March.

(2004b) 'Commissioner Patten announces launch of Feasibility Report on Serbia and Montenegro', IP/04/1202, Brussels 11 October.

Prodi, R. (1999) Speech at the European Parliament, Brussels, SPEECH/99/130. 13 October, retrieved from http://www.europa.eu.int.

Rehn, O. (2005a) 'Bringing the Balkans into mainstream Europe', Friends of Europe, 8 December.

Rehn, O. (2005b) 'Exchange at European Parliament plenary session', November 15, *Enlargement newsletter,* available online at http://europa.eu.int/comm/enlargement/docs/newsletter/latest_weekly_281105.htm.

Solana J. (2000) 'Intervention to public debate on Western Balkans', General Affairs Council, Brussels, 10 July.

—— (2007) Speech at Charlemagne Award, Aachen, 17 May.

INDEX

LIBRARY OF EUROPEAN STUDIES

Series ISBN: 978 1 84885 239 6

See www.ibtauris.com/LES for a full list of titles